A House Divided

'Superb and Poignant! This is public interest writing at its best. Authored by South Africa's foremost public intellectual on local government, *A House Divided* lays bare the political machinations that prevailed in Cape Town's municipal government, and within the DA, at the height of the City's water crisis. Sparing none of the political actors, it demonstrates how ordinary citizens and the poorest among us are the real victims when politicians get detracted by intra-party battles and business interests. A must read for all those interested in the future of both the city and local government.'

– Adam Habib

A House Divided

The feud that took Cape Town to the brink

Crispian Olver

Jonathan Ball Publishers

JOHANNESBURG AND CAPE TOWN

© Text 2019 Crispian Olver
© Published edition 2019 Jonathan Ball Publishers

Originally published in South Africa in 2019 by
JONATHAN BALL PUBLISHERS
A division of Media24 (Pty) Ltd
PO Box 33977
Jeppestown 2043

ISBN 978-1-86842-968-4
ebook 978-1-86842-969-1

Lyrics of 'Weeping', produced by Ian Cohen, Peter Cohen, Tom Fox and Dan Heymann
from Bright Blue, used with permission from Pay Music and Muffled Music.

Every effort has been made to trace the copyright holders and to obtain their
permission for the use of copyright material. The publishers apologise for any errors or
omissions and would be grateful to be notified of any corrections that should
be incorporated in future editions of this book.

Twitter: www.twitter.com/JonathanBallPub
Facebook: www.facebook.com/JonathanBallPublishers
Blog: http://jonathanball.bookslive.co.za/

Cover by publicide
Design and typesetting by Triple M Design
Printed and bound by CTP Printers, Cape Town
Set in 11.25/16pt Ehrhardt MT Std

For Gammie,
the friend I left behind.

Contents

Abbreviations

ANC	African National Congress
Bokag	Bo-Kaap Action Group
BKYM	Bo-Kaap Youth Movement
Bokcra	Bo-Kaap Civic and Ratepayers' Association
CBD	central business district
CFO	chief financial officer
Cope	Congress of the People
CTICC	Cape Town International Convention Centre
CTSDF	Cape Town Spatial Development Framework
DA	Democratic Alliance
DP	Democratic Party
ECC	End Conscription Campaign
EFF	Economic Freedom Fighters
FSB	Financial Services Board
FSCA	Financial Sector Conduct Authority
ID	Independent Democrats
IDP	integrated development plan
MDA	Mitchell Du Plessis Associates

MEC	member of the executive council (of a province)
MFMA	Municipal Finance Management Act
MP	member of Parliament
MSP	Multi Spectrum Property
NGO	non-governmental organisation
NNP	New National Party
NP	National Party
OCA	Observatory Civic Association
ODTP	Organisational Development and Transformation Plan
PAC	Pan Africanist Congress
PHA	Philippi Horticultural Area
RDP	Reconstruction and Development Programme
SFB	Sea Point, Fresnaye and Bantry Bay Ratepayers' and Residents' Association
SPU	Strategic Policy Unit
TDA	Transport and Urban Development Authority
UCT	University of Cape Town
UDF	United Democratic Front
US, USA	United States, United States of America
VOC	Vereenigde Oostindische Compagnie (Dutch East India Company)
WCPDF	Western Cape Property Developers Forum

*'Every kingdom divided against itself is brought
to desolation, and every city or
house divided against itself shall not stand.'*

Matthew 12:25

Map of Cape Town and surrounds

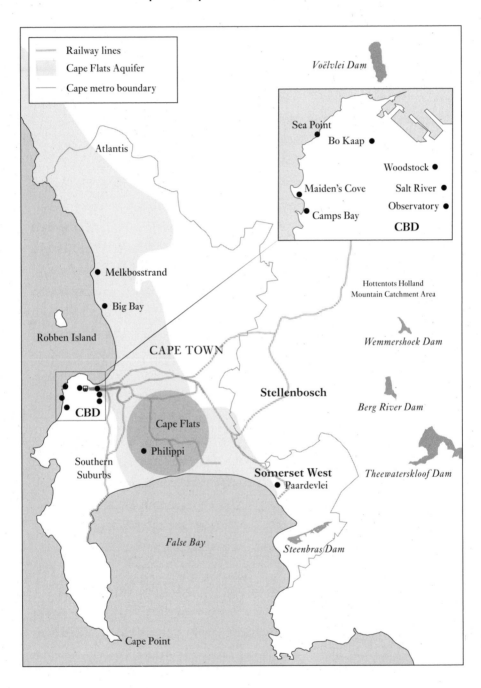

Railway lines
Cape Flats Aquifer
Cape metro boundary

Voëlvlei Dam

Sea Point
Bo Kaap
Woodstock
Maiden's Cove
Salt River
Observatory
Camps Bay
CBD

Atlantis

Melkbosstrand

Hottentots Holland
Mountain Catchment Area

Big Bay

Wemmershoek Dam

Robben Island

CAPE TOWN

Stellenbosch

Berg River Dam

CBD

Cape Flats

Philippi

Southern
Suburbs

Somerset West
Paardevlei

Theewaterskloof Dam

False Bay

Steenbras Dam

Cape Point

Prologue

'This city has gone mad,' my friend Miriam said over the phone in January 2018. 'I never thought it would get to this.'

She had just returned from dropping off her three kids at school, and driving through the suburb of Newlands in Cape Town had encountered a chaotic jam of cars and people trying to get to a natural spring that flows in the area.

My heart sank when the call came in; Miriam always chooses to phone in the middle of a working day when I'm juggling work pressures. But I knew this was important: Cape Town was in the grip of the most severe drought in its history, and the municipality had just told people that the city was going to run out of water in four months' time. Panic was infesting the residents, who were desperately stockpiling bottles of water and flocking to the few natural springs in the city where fresh water still flowed.

The beautiful Mother City and its iconic Table Mountain sit on top of a deep and ancient aquifer that nourishes some 36 artesian springs that run off the mountain. The original name for Cape Town, given to it by its indigenous olive-skinned Khoi people, was Camissa, meaning 'place of sweet waters', and it couldn't have been more appropriate. The Khoi venerated the springs as mystical sites connecting them to another world, and now Capetonians were venerating them for their life-sustaining resource.

During the drought, the Newlands spring had become a point of congregation. People from across the desolate stretch of sand dunes and wetlands known as the Cape Flats mingled with the well-heeled residents of the affluent, still predominantly white Southern Suburbs as they gathered crystal-clear spring water in plastic bottles. Traffic and throngs of people congested the narrow Newlands roads. On the day of Miriam's phonecall there had been a punch-up as people jostled to get to the spring, and traffic police had been deployed to patrol the area to control the situation.

Miriam is a remarkable woman. She exemplifies the best of the Cape liberal tradition – she wears her heart on her sleeve, always stands up for the underdog in any situation, and isn't afraid to speak her mind. At the time, she'd recently sorted out the archives at the Legal Resources Centre, instructed George Bizos at the Marikana Commission of Inquiry, and co-written Bizos's memoir about his 65 years of friendship with Nelson Mandela (which was longlisted for the Alan Paton non-fiction award), at the same time as moving her household from Johannesburg to Cape Town. Her relentless energy combined with a very human and fun-loving streak made for a great friend. But she also felt that I was some sort of expert on the workings of government, so chose to bend my ear every time she was aggrieved by the municipality.

'I'm so angry I could cry,' she said. 'These complacent Newlands residents are objecting to the traffic and the people, and the City just does what they ask. It's a colour thing: what they really mean is that they don't want black families from the Cape Flats coming in to their nice clean suburb to collect water. Next thing they're going to call in the army and we'll have a water war. Who do you think is going to lose out then?'

This wasn't the first time Miriam had phoned to offload about the water issue. The previous weekend she'd been wound up by her visit to some well-off friends on their Tokai wine estate. When she arrived at their house with exquisite views across the valley, she'd seen their lush green lawns being watered by sprinklers, which she thought was an obscene display of insensitivity in the middle of the drought. 'There are water restrictions across Cape Town. They apply to everyone. You can't just opt out because you're willing to pay high water tariffs,' she railed to me. 'When I objected, they said the water was from their borehole, but isn't that also bad? What if they pump all the groundwater out from the aquifer? If everyone in Cape Town is expected to cut down on the water they use, why do the rich get to opt out just because they can afford to drill a borehole?'

A few days later, the city closed the Newlands spring and announced that its precious water would be rechannelled to a new location nearby, from where people would still be able to queue and draw water. The new water-collection point opened in May 2018, with a limit of 25 litres per person.

Miriam's phonecall was interlaced with other anxieties. As Cape Town's water crisis reached it height, the most bizarre drama played out in City Hall. The feisty mayor, Patricia de Lille, who had recently won an over-whelming mandate for a second term in office, was stripped of her powers, and a bitter factional dispute broke out in the corridors of the Cape Town civic centre. The very foundations of the City had seemed to come adrift, and Capetonians were left wondering what was going on.

1

The dead sea

〜〜〜

In March 2015 I got a graphic sense of the drought in the Western Cape when I travelled from Johannesburg to Cape Town to ride the world-famous annual Cape Town Cycle Tour, the largest timed bicycle race in the world attracting some 50 000 participants. The summers in the Cape had been getting steadily hotter and drier – 'It's climate change,' my friend Miriam said glumly – and in the midst of a heatwave, with a furious south-easterly wind blowing, fires had broken out on Table Mountain and quickly engulfed the whole peninsula, burning perilously close to people's houses.

Friends whose homes were perched on the mountainside in Kalk Bay posted alarming pictures of themselves fleeing down to the safety of the main road as a wall of fire approached. In horrendous temperatures, an army of firefighters worked round the clock for four days trying to control the flames, while helicopters buzzed overhead dropping buckets of water on the fire. As fire engines raced along the hazy smoke-filled highways, sirens blaring, there was an impending sense of crisis and doom – a dry and tortured city punished by the gods with blazing infernos.

That year, the cycle-race route was dramatically shortened, and I'd gone back home to Johannesburg with a sense of alarm, a feeling that some subterranean force had shifted. I worried about what sins might have been committed for a city to be punished like this.

Over time, Cape Town's City Hall had been growing increasingly strident and berating about water. The City of Cape Town had begun communicating with its citizens about the crisis in November 2016, when they'd launched a rather lacklustre 'Think Water' campaign, with the limp slogan 'Care a little. Save a lot'. Even though the administration knew there were only about 135 days of usable water left, no plan was in place for what would happen when it was finished.

(At that stage, the City administration hadn't yet invented the concept of 'Day Zero' – popularly regarded as the day when the taps would run dry. When and if it was announced, Day Zero would in fact entail water rationing through an alternative municipal supply system, reducing consumption to 25 litres of water per person to eke out the supply through the rest of the summer season.)

At the press conference to launch 'Think Water', Mayor Patricia de Lille presented a worst-case scenario that would kick in if dam levels fell below 10%, a cut-off point at which most water remaining in the dams wasn't usable: the City would then provide a 'lifeline' water supply, with minimal supply pressures, intermittent supply, and very stringent restriction measures. At that stage, switching off the taps and queuing for water wasn't mentioned. Eighteen months later, a journalist covering the crisis crisply referred to this period of City communications as the 'ineffectual' phase of the campaign.[1]

It wasn't until late 2016 that real action started to happen. In November 2016, as the Western Cape entered the hottest, driest summer months on record, and with dam storage levels at a disturbingly low 36%, Cape Town introduced Level 3 water restrictions. These banned the use of hosepipes or automatic sprinklers, permitting watering of gardens only using a bucket or watering can; watering times weren't restricted but residents were 'urged' to limit their watering to the mornings and evenings. Washing or hosing-down of hard-surfaced or paved areas with drinking water wasn't allowed, while washing of vehicles and boats with potable water had to be done using a bucket. Swimming pools could still be topped up as long as they were fitted with a cover.

The situation was so severe that Helen Zille, the premier of the Western Cape province and former mayor of Cape Town, announced a project called 'Avoiding Day Zero' with measures to restrict water flow. 'It is very important that everyone saves water. I shower with a bucket and I hope everybody is doing that too,' she said.[2]

The notion of the premier bathing in a bucket every few days caught on, but township residents caustically pointed out that they'd been washing in buckets all along, so the new restrictions made little difference to them.

In March, the metro was declared a local disaster area, which unlocked R20 million of disaster-fund monies, but little more in terms of infrastructure solutions. In May 2017 a water indaba (conference) was convened, at which the national Water and Sanitation Department announced that the situation had deteriorated significantly, and that the capacity of dams in the Western Cape was the lowest recorded in 30 years. The Western Cape disaster-management centre and its interdepartmental team (a permanent structure that pulls together officials from various departments in response to any crisis) pleaded for interventions such as procuring desalination plants, digging boreholes at hospitals and tapping into the aquifer under the city. That same month, Zille finally declared the whole province, including the Cape Town metro, a disaster area.[3] But besides cajoling residents of Cape Town to use less water, the City administration introduced no new infrastructure solutions.

Then the winter rains forecast for 2017 didn't arrive.

According to Zille, the South African Weather Service had bluntly acknowledged that they couldn't predict whether or when rain would come, as previous forecasting models had proven useless in the era of climate change. 'The [South African] Weather Service informed us that as far as forecasting goes, we are flying blind,' she said[4] – a terrifying prospect for a city that relied for the replenishment of its potable-water resources mostly on the runoff from winter rainfall.

The City formally requested information for water-augmentation proposals in June 2017, and followed up with requests for tenders for various water-augmentation schemes from August, starting with land-based reverse-osmosis desalination plants. But by November it was clear that Capetonians weren't cutting back enough on water use, and that the limited water-augmentation efforts hurriedly undertaken would be insufficient to avert the impending crisis.

The tone of communications soon became more punitive. On 15 November 2017 De Lille graphically outlined what hitting Day Zero would entail – extreme rationing, a partial shutdown of the water system, and water provision through designated water points. She also gave an exact date for when this was expected to take place: 13 May 2018.

As the media noted, this new tack in communications coincided with the involvement of a prominent former leader of the Democratic Alliance (DA), Tony Leon, and his communications agency. Resolve Communications had been contracted by the City to manage publicity around the crisis, and they were the architects of the more assertive strategy that used Day Zero to frighten Capetonians into using less water.[5]

Xolani Sotashe, the leader of the African National Congress (ANC) in the city council, subsequently accused the DA, which ran the municipality, of cronyism in hiring Leon as communications adviser. 'Tony Leon is now all of a sudden the spokesperson for Capetonians,' he scoffed.[6]

The tone of the City's communications shifted from cajoling to stern, with references to 'stubborn' residents 'behaving badly'.[7]

On 17 January 2018 De Lille made an announcement that massively stoked Capetonians' anxiety. The city had reached the point of no return, and Day Zero was now inevitable, she said. The mayor argued that 60% of Capetonians weren't complying with the water restrictions, and that the city now had to compel them to. 'It is quite unbelievable that a majority of people do not seem to care and are sending all of us headlong towards Day Zero. We can no longer ask people to stop wasting water. We must force them.'[8]

De Lille announced further water restrictions – the hitherto unknown Level 6, which restricted water consumption to 87 litres of water per person per day, regardless of where they were (at home or at work) or what they were doing; by the following month, with dam levels at around 25%, Level 6B kicked in, bringing daily permitted water consumption down to 50 litres per person, with limits on irrigation from boreholes and wellpoints, and fines and the mandatory installation of 'water-management devices' for those who didn't comply. It wasn't clear how these restrictions would be implemented, however, since the City had no mechanisms to monitor or enforce them.

These measures rubbed against the interests of large property owners in the city, while the mood among the citizens of Cape Town was verging on panic – public anxiety was amplified by the fact that the mayor didn't have a credible disaster-management plan in place when she made the announcement.

The media were scathing. 'Don't let the City of Cape Town gaslight you – the water crisis is not your fault,' wrote one journalist, pointing out that attacking your clients isn't usually the best tactic in disaster communications. 'We paid our taxes,' he pointed out. 'We relied on government to build infrastructure and make plans and do its job. We did save water when we were asked. You'd be hard-pressed to find this 60% of callous

Capetonians in a city obsessed with saving water. The 60% number is never justified or clarified, and its source is never revealed.'[9]

The mood of panic was now accompanied by a growing sense of distrust, a feeling among Capetonians that they weren't being told the truth.

On 24 January 2018 the DA's national leader Mmusi Maimane, accompanied by (among others) Helen Zille and Deputy Mayor Ian Neilson – but not Patricia de Lille – announced that dam levels had dropped even further and that Day Zero was being moved up to 12 April. 'The crash the City has been trying to avoid now seems inevitable. We are bracing for impact,' Zille told a provincial official. 'Sticking to the Province's constitutional mandate of support and oversight is not enough in these circumstances. When Day Zero arrives, how do we make water accessible and prevent anarchy?'[10]

Capetonians were then presented with an apocalyptic vision of their immediate future. According to the City's plan, municipal water would be made available at 200 distribution points across the metro. As Zille pointed out, if every family sent one person to fetch their water allocation, about 5 000 people would congregate at each point every day.[11] Given that families would need some form of transport to carry their allocation of water, it was going to be a logistical and traffic nightmare. Zille said she was awaiting a full operations plan, including personnel requirements, security, infrastructure and budgets, but this did little to quench people's anxiety. The sense of doom and crisis was palpable.

While City Hall was increasingly pointing a finger at residents, government agencies had also been engaged in a petty blame game. The City and province, both controlled by the DA, said the ANC national government had penalised them by not allocating infrastructure funds. Maimane said that the City of Cape Town was hamstrung by national government's refusal to cooperate. Questions were raised about why Cape Town wasn't getting the same level of support extended to ANC-run councils – there had been national support for a desalination plant at Richard's Bay in KwaZulu-Natal, for example, and the Johannesburg metro had been supported to set up 'restriction committees' with tougher enforcement for water-saving measures.[12] Maimane also hinted at corruption in the national Water Department with 'price-rigging from water-related service providers'.[13]

His concern was well founded. The minister for Water and Sanitation, Nomvula Mokonyane, an ardent supporter of then-President Jacob Zuma and known as 'Mama Action' within ANC circles for her ability to mobilise the ruling party's constituencies and to channel resources into its campaigns, presided over wide-scale fraud and corruption in her department. Mokonyane had, for example, caused favoured companies such as LTE Consulting to be given massive infrastructure projects (it had R5-billion worth of projects in 2016), while LTE had made generous donations to the ANC.[14] Mokonyane had also notoriously interfered in the Lesotho Highlands Water Project to get LTE appointed,[15] and the company had been awarded a project in Giyani in the northern province of Limpopo, where costs ballooned from R502 million to R2,7 billion before the project ran out of funds and collapsed.[16] Irregular expenditures of R4 billion in her department had been picked up by the auditor-general in the 2016/17 financial year.[17]

When reviewing her department's financial statements for 2016/17, the auditor-general commented sarcastically that 'the only consistency is consistently missed targets'. The auditor-general's office also castigated the minister and her department for attempts to bully them into not giving a negative opinion, referring to 'the contestation and pressure placed on the audit teams'.[18] Such intimidation of the auditor-general has become commonplace in departments and municipalities where widespread corruption has taken place.

National incapacity aside, however, there's no escaping the constitutional reality that City Hall was supposed to be primarily responsible for managing Cape Town's water infrastructure and services, and controlling the way people used them.

When one looks back at the water crisis that engulfed Cape Town between 2016 and 2018, the lack of government planning at all levels is striking.

None of the government agencies – national, the Western Cape province or the City of Cape Town – can credibly argue that they didn't know about the impending disaster. As far back as 2009, the then Department of Water Affairs and Forestry had issued some dire predictions about Cape Town running out of water. In that same year, the massive Berg River Dam[19] had been built to supply more water to the city, but at the time the department had predicted that, even with a water-conservation strategy, the city would need further 'supply interventions' by 2019 or the taps would run dry.[20] Back then, the deal had been that the national department would take charge of surface-water augmentation, such as transfers from the Berg and Breede rivers, while the City of Cape Town would be responsible for other water-augmentation measures, such as water reuse and desalination, and tapping water from the Cape Flats Aquifer.[21]

Nonetheless, when in 2014 city officials took a proposal to council for a desalination plant, council rejected it: there had been very good rains that winter, dams were overflowing, and the cost of desalination was deemed too high.

At the peak of the crisis, in January 2018, former Deputy Mayor Grant Haskin mentioned two reports from 2002 that predicted 'dangerous water scarcity'. In a statement to the city council, Haskin ridiculed the City and senior politicians who said the drought had caught them by surprise. 'That is utter nonsense,' he said.[22]

'So, government knew the problem was coming,' the *Daily Maverick* concluded in January 2018. 'They even had a pretty good idea of when it would happen. And they had all the plans in place to mitigate the disaster. Somewhere between planning in 2009 and today, the wheels fell off, nothing was done.'[23]

Nic Spaull, an economist from Stellenbosch University, summed it up

11

when he asked, 'How the hell did we get this close to what will be the biggest natural disaster of the post-apartheid period, and the majority of Capetonians are carrying on business as usual?' He pointed out that the scale of the crisis was such that, if unresolved, it could cripple the city. 'It is clear that there has been an outright failure of leadership in the City of Cape Town ... Patricia de Lille has been the mayor of Cape Town for more than six years, and the DA has run the Western Cape for more than seven years. It's been years in the making. It is beyond clear that the blame for this crisis lies ultimately with the City of Cape Town and their too-little-too-late responses to an imminent catastrophe.'[24]

How could this modern city have been so ill served by the custodians elected to look after it? How had it come to this? What was really going on?

2

The black swan[1]

〰〰〰

As Cape Town's water crisis was coming to a head, I was still strug-gling to make sense of what I'd come across in Nelson Mandela Bay. In 2015, as a local-government-turnaround expert working under Pravin Gordhan, I'd been sent to Port Elizabeth to lead a clean-up of corrupt syndicates, which came horribly unstuck when those syndicates and their political allies staged a fightback.[2] Apart from the stress of the assignment, I was disturbed by how effortlessly I'd crossed the dividing line between politics and the administration, and found myself privy to the same kind of dubious transactions I was investigating.

Writing a book about this experience had been cathartic, but I'd been left with many unanswered questions about corruption, the way municipal governments navigate the often-conflicting demands of politics and public administration, and the influence of economic interests in that equation. I was struggling to get back into work, and instead set out to take a deeper look into these questions. So I registered to do a PhD in the Department of Political Studies at the University of the Witwatersrand.

These academic endeavours were only the latest manifestation of my longstanding interest in local government. After a decade of civic campaigning and underground activism against the apartheid system, I'd joined President Mandela's office in the 1990s. I was part of the team in charge of the Reconstruction and Development Programme (RDP),[3] where I got involved in local government and development planning issues.

My early days in the new ANC government were heady – the new local-government system had to be set up, a major redemarcation of municipalities was required, and a raft of new legislation about structures, powers and functions had to be passed. I was centrally involved in crafting and implementing the legislation for local government, and some of my colleagues still joke with me about what a mess local government is in today, and how all of us early idealists are complicit in its systemic failures. Maybe this is why I keep coming back to the morbid illness that seems to beset local government – although I left government in 2005, much of my subsequent work as a consultant has remained focused on distressed and broken municipalities.

I've seen first hand how in dysfunctional municipalities business and even criminal interests control local politics and manipulate municipal decisions to extract maximum financial advantage. Apart from what this forensic interest might reveal about the darker sides of my character, I find dysfunctional municipalities interesting because they highlight so much about the inner workings and skeletal topography of local government, and in so doing reveal the systemic faultlines within the system.

The 2018 plunge into academia, late in my career, was a shock. Not only did I find myself woefully ill prepared for the rarefied theoretical debates about the nature of the state and power, but I found it distressing to have to objectively observe without rolling up my sleeves and trying to fix what was broken. Yet after the Nelson Mandela Bay crucible, I wondered whether some of the catastrophic dysfunction racking the Port Elizabeth city administration was the manifestation of systemic faultlines and tensions inherent in local government that also existed in better-run cities under different political coalitions.

I've always been interested in the nature of power and how it's exercised. Both as a politician and as a senior civil servant, I've had the opportunity to use it and discovered its intoxicating effects as large schemes come alive with resources and administrative fiat. But power is by nature Janus-faced – I quickly learnt the pragmatic compromises I needed to make to get things done, compromises that could undercut the principles I'd started out with.

I have no doubt that power is a messy business, not for the faint-hearted – but is it possible to stay on the right side of your principles and still get things done? For political parties, in particular, is it possible to reconcile the twin imperatives of serving the public interest and keeping yourself in power, especially when it comes to political fundraising and organising to win the next election?

To illuminate that central question, I decided to examine three cities in some detail. The first was Nelson Mandela Bay, where I'd seen how public interest had been thrown under the bus as the City administration became a mechanism to siphon off public funds, not only for competing factions within the ruling ANC but also for personal gain. The second was Johannesburg, the City of Gold and heart of the South African economy, where economic interests have reconfigured themselves under a new DA-led coalition which ended a long period of ANC rule.

And, finally, Cape Town seemed an obvious choice to include in the research, for several reasons. First, the municipality, as well as the Western Cape province, were controlled by the DA, and thus its local politics would offer an interesting contrast to that of Nelson Mandela Bay and the Eastern Cape, which had historically been ANC strongholds. At the same time, the City administration had garnered a string of clean audits over the years, another glaring difference from the rampant looting and corruption I'd observed in some other municipalities. Yet, while the local government was ostensibly well managed and relatively clean, there were clearly problems behind that facade. Drowned out by the noise and panic surrounding the water crisis were concerns and uncomfortable questions raised over a series of property deals involving the mayor. And besides highlighting what appeared to be a mind-boggling leadership failure, the water crisis was also revealing a level of infighting within the DA that seemed to go far beyond garden-variety political competition.

Political control in the City of Cape Town has always been fiercely contested, partly because of the city's unusual demographics. The largest part (42%) of its population is designated as 'mixed race' or 'coloured', while black Africans make up 39%, and European descendants ('whites') account for 16% of the city's residents. This means that no population group completely dominates.

While whites have mostly voted for the DA and its forerunners, and Africans have mostly stuck to the ANC, the shifting allegiance of coloured voters has been the key to controlling the city. Since the coloured vote swung away from the ANC in the 2000 elections, the party has steadily lost its hold on the City and the province, even though it has so far maintained its control over the national government. Nevertheless, in each election, the DA has had to fend off attempts by the ANC and other parties to make inroads into its base, and to erode the ANC's hold on the African vote.

After a hotly contested campaign, the local election in August 2016 solidified the DA's position, however. Patricia de Lille, a well-known and highly respected figure in South African politics, was the party's secret weapon. A former trade unionist, De Lille was a feisty and street-smart politician with a solid track record in liberation politics. In 2003 she had branched out of the Pan Africanist Congress (PAC) to form her own party. While in national Parliament, she had famously campaigned for a robust investigation into the arms deal.

In 2010, she merged her Independent Democrats (ID) party with the

DA, which positioned her to be appointed as Cape Town's mayor the following year. At the time of the merger, Helen Zille, who was then the national leader of the DA, had already moved on from City Hall to become premier of the Western Cape.

De Lille's first term as mayor appeared successful – she brought a more racially and socially inclusive politics to the city, which combined well with the DA's track record of efficiently running municipal affairs. Even though standards of living in Cape Town were still largely determined by race, De Lille was popular among coloured and African constituents.

De Lille and a close team of loyalists worked tirelessly in the 2016 local-government elections, leading the DA to another victory with a resounding 66% of the vote – the strongest mandate that any City leader obtained that year.

Former DA leader Tony Leon put out a congratulatory opinion piece in which he claimed that the election's biggest winner was Patricia de Lille. 'By winning more than 66% of the votes last week, she posted the biggest win of any party in any city,' he wrote. 'Just consider this: 10 years ago, the DA barely edged into power [in the City] with just over 41% of the vote – a plurality win which required mayor Helen Zille to build a ramshackle coalition with seven other minor parties.'

Leon pointed out that there were many ironies in that story. 'At that stage, De Lille aligned unsuccessfully with the ANC to stop the DA. She later folded her tent into Zille's coalition and stands today as the top woman in the party, heading the province which provided the blue team [the DA, whose party colour and branding is blue] with the most gold medals.'[4]

The DA seemed poised to break through the glass ceiling of racial stereotyping and build a strong constituency among black voters. It was an exhilarating moment for the party's leaders, with major national implications.

Yet within 18 months of that resounding electoral victory, De Lille had been drawn into an increasingly public battle within the party. Squabbles between city councillors are fairly commonplace, and initially the public didn't pay too much attention. But the factional battle between DA councillors started to look like a herculean contest for political control within the party itself. Worse still, that battle unfolded while the city was in the midst of its devastating water crisis.

Towards the end of 2017 De Lille announced a punitive drought charge that was to be based on property prices. It was a drastic measure, designed to radically cut water consumption, especially by high-volume water consumers. The tariff would fund new water schemes that would assist in meeting water needs.

The DA councillors in the City initially approved the charge, but property owners were furious about the financial burden this would create. The DA received a substantial number of complaints from some of their wealthiest funders; 60 000 public comments were submitted to the council, almost all objecting to the charge. This seemed to be the last straw,[5] and in the middle of December, when the focus of the country was on the ANC's 58th national conference and the election of a successor to Jacob Zuma, the DA released a press statement saying that the party's federal executive had been aware of 'a number of issues' in the DA's City of Cape Town caucus, including troubling allegations of maladministration, and that the party's national leadership had therefore decided to suspend Mayor De Lille.[6]

Despite the announcement, nothing happened. Instead, in early January 2018, as the nation was still trying to digest the opaque outcome of the ANC's national leadership contest – Cyril Ramaphosa had narrowly been elected president of the ANC, but with many Zuma loyalists in the national executive committee and in the so-called 'top six' – De Lille went on a charm offensive, saying that even though she faced suspension, she remained committed to making sure that the 'well-run city' did not run

18

out of water. 'We can all avoid Day Zero,' she said, 'but we must do it together.'[7]

In the middle of January 2018, Mmusi Maimane announced that De Lille would be relieved of her water-related responsibilities 'immediately', although he then clarified that the DA would 'bring a resolution to Council that removes the Mayor from any role in managing and directing the City's response to the prolonged drought'. This was despite his assurances a mere three months earlier that he fully agreed with De Lille's approach and had regular updates with her. The reason for the action was, according to Maimane, that the party required 'unity of purpose and cohesion' in the City of Cape Town to effectively tackle the water crisis. He said that the DA wanted the deputy mayor, Ian Neilson, and the mayoral committee member in charge of water, Xanthea Limberg, to take over the management of the water crisis.[8]

I found the announcement extremely confusing – the intervention was bound to deepen the factional split in the council, not lessen it. And if the DA didn't trust De Lille to manage the water crisis, surely she should no longer be mayor?

I also wondered what had happened to the earlier announcement about her immediate removal as mayor – Maimane told a media briefing following a DA federal-council meeting on 14 January 2018 that they had decided not to suspend De Lille as mayor after all 'in adherence of due process', which seemed to be an admission that due process hadn't been followed before.

The media started asking questions, wondering whether more was going on behind the scenes.[9]

The day after Maimane's announcement, De Lille arrived at City Hall wearing her mayoral chain, and told the waiting media that she was going straight in to chair a drought-relief meeting. 'I am carrying on with all my work as usual and focusing on the water crisis,' she said.[10] When questioned about whether she'd been distracted by the internal battles from performing her role in managing the crisis, as the DA alleged, De Lille said, 'I spend 80% of my day on the water crisis. I start with [the water crisis] first thing in the morning. I'm out in the field with it, because I believe we need to show Capetonians what we are doing. I work 16 hours a day.'[11]

On Friday 19 January 2018 De Lille called a special council meeting at the Cape Town civic centre, supposedly to approve the drought charges and water restrictions. In a closed session, the councillors took the decision to suspend one of De Lille's main allies in the administration, the city's head of transport, Melissa Whitehead, while a formal investigation into her was undertaken. There were apparently three ongoing investigations into Whitehead, each of which could result in criminal action. Then De Lille's drought levy was voted down, although the councillors did approve substantial tariff increases for high-volume water users.

The opposition was scathing in the debate on the matter in the council, with the Economic Freedom Fighters (EFF) calling the DA the 'Drought Alliance' and later the 'Deurmekaar [Muddled] Alliance'. At the end of the fractious meeting, Ian Neilson read out a list of proposed changes to De Lille's powers as mayor, stripping her of all management of water issues.[12]

The bizarre nature of the decision was summed up by the ANC's Xolani Sotashe, who asked, 'Who is a mayor but doesn't have powers? Does the mayor go to the caucus, drink coffee, eat biscuits and go home?'[13]

De Lille was furious, telling the council that the amendments to her delegated powers hadn't followed due process, and that she hadn't been consulted about them.[14]

The abiding impression was that the water crisis had become a political device for rival sides within the DA to pursue other agendas, while the citizens of Cape Town bore the cost.[15]

What also became clear as the furore gathered pace was that the battle between parts of the DA and De Lille was doing enormous reputational damage to the party, and even to De Lille herself. The DA's internal polling data showed a precipitous drop in its support in Cape Town as a result of the fallout.[16] Capetonians were growing tired of the ongoing brittle drama while they stared at a bone-dry future.

It seemed incomprehensible that a party that had just 18 months earlier won the 2016 local-government elections in Cape Town with two-thirds of the vote could commit political suicide in the face of a crisis that demanded clear-headed vision and leadership.

There were two entirely different narratives in circulation, and public opinion veered from one to the other. In the one version, Patricia de Lille was the victim of a conservative racist pushback within the DA, as the old guard and their conservative funders were alarmed at the pace of transformation and level of social integration that De Lille was championing. According to this version, De Lille's popular appeal and power base posed a threat to right-wing forces within the DA, who felt that she had to be dealt with.

The alternative narrative was that De Lille was a narcissistic bully who overestimated her role and importance, had massively centralised power, and was now engaged in dispensing patronage and doing backroom deals that seemed more reminiscent of an ANC-run municipality. According to this version, the DA had to get rid of her if it was to retain any claim to its clean-governance agenda, regardless of the political cost.

Discussions around dinner tables in the Cape swung between these polarities. Which version were we to believe? Could both versions be true? And, more importantly, what was really at the root of this conflict? What were we *not* being told by either side?

While both sides were willing to throw wild allegations of impropriety at each other, there were some areas that they both avoided talking about. For instance, many rumours were floating around about links between business and local politicians. The DA and even Patricia de Lille herself had been championing some big property deals that seemed at odds with her socially inclusive agenda. In light of the city's history, did property and land ownership offer a vector of investigation into how party, economic and public interests were being handled in Cape Town?

I was convinced that neither side was telling the whole truth, and that there was some subterranean drama to which we, the public, weren't privy.

Attempting to unpack that very drama aligned perfectly with my study of local government and might reveal broader lessons that reverberated beyond the City itself.

3

A tale of two cities

'Not approved.'

There it was, next to a nonchalant tick in a box. At first, I thought it was a mistake. It had to be. How could the City of Cape Town have turned me down? Surely someone had ticked the wrong box.

Then I saw it. The perfunctory one-pager carrying the City seal rejected my request to research the municipal government 'due to the high risk and significant impact on the CCT [City of Cape Town]'.

High risk? What risk could a researcher pose – unless the city administration didn't want something revealed?

I kept reading and re-reading the document, flabbergasted. What was the municipality afraid of? This was supposed to be the best-managed metro in South Africa, with a long string of clean audits. This was the administration that claimed to be 'Making progress possible. Together', according to the slogan at the bottom of the very letter slamming the door in my face. The contrast couldn't have been more jarring. Clearly, 'progress' didn't involve scrutiny, and 'together' didn't include the likes of me.

Six weeks earlier, I'd gone through the motions of formally applying to do research in the City of Cape Town. Topical and symptomatic as the water crisis was, I didn't set out to look at it directly: I'm not a water expert, and I felt drawn more to the deeper institutional and social issues behind the crisis. I wanted to focus on how the city was governed, and in particular the way that financial interests intersected with politics and the City administration. The emergence of red flags around several property deals had piqued my interest, suggesting that, in Cape Town at least, battles over land, social policy and housing may offer broader lessons about how the often-conflicting demands of money, politics and public interest were being navigated. I framed the research as a study into how different interest groups leveraged their position to extract benefits from the municipal government – what I grandly worded as 'the political economy of rent-seeking' – and I blithely requested access to records and officials without thinking about how threatening this might appear.

My research request had followed a chance meeting in April 2018 with Craig Kesson, one the DA's key political appointees in the City, who used to run Patricia de Lille's office and now headed the powerful Strategic Policy Unit (SPU) in the mayor's office, which coordinated all City policy and its implementation. Kesson was part of a delegation of Cape Town councillors and officials attending an executive-leadership programme in Johannesburg organised by National Treasury. It was a high-powered initiative, with national ministers and mayors from South Africa's main cities engaging international experts on city governance.

As an invited expert I participated in the teaching programme, but was also able to network freely with the delegates. Because of my research project, I was keen to get to know the Cape Town delegation better and see if I could make some contacts. It turned out to be not so straightforward. The tension within the delegation was palpable, with members of Cape Town's mayoral committee not speaking to each other.

The programme included a gala dinner, which I dreaded – even the term 'gala dinner' hints at the prickly vanity typically on display at these events. But I mustered just enough motivation to attend and plonked myself down at the Cape Town table. Kesson, his dark eyes flashing behind thick glasses, oozed confidence and dominated the conversation. While coming across as somewhat brash, he struck me as intelligent and concerned about social issues. He claimed to be acutely aware of injustice, having himself been bullied when growing up in what is now KwaZulu-Natal.

The conversation rekindled memories of my own feelings of rejection and sense of alienation, tied up in my case with being gay and trying to find my own identity in a cloistered and suffocating world cut off from the country's social life and politics during the struggle against apartheid – I'd attended an English colonial boarding school in what was then Natal that was deeply homophobic.

On returning to my native Cape Town to attend medical school, I had enthusiastically got involved in the anti-apartheid movement as part of the End Conscription Campaign (ECC), which opposed the conscription of all white South African men into military service in the South African Defence Force. After the ECC was banned in 1986 along with the United Democratic Front (UDF) – a countrywide coalition against apartheid created when civic and church organisations eventually joined hands in 1983 – and a whole raft of mass democratic organisations, the ECC leaders were rounded up and put in prison for a few weeks, giving us white activists a small taste of what black anti-apartheid leaders went through all the time.

I had then traded the city of my childhood for the rolling green hills of the Eastern Cape, where as a young doctor I'd joined the ranks of the mass democratic movement and the ANC, before making Johannesburg my home.

In response to my confession about having been away from Cape Town for so long, Kesson was surprisingly enthusiastic. 'When you come to Cape Town, I'll show you around all the places,' he said. I left the dinner with his email address and an undertaking to meet on my next trip.

I wasted no time emailing Kesson with a request to meet, explaining what I was planning to research and investigate. The next day I received an email from the City's head of organisational research, along with a long list of documents I'd have to submit for my research request to be considered. This seemed unduly bureaucratic, but I heaved a sigh and got on with compiling the documents.

Naively, I'd thought the DA-controlled city would cooperate, and maybe even support my research. I certainly didn't think that it would perceive me as a threat. The party had been widely quoting my last book, dealing with my experience in the municipal clean-up in Nelson Mandela Bay. Helen Zille, the former national DA leader and then still premier of the Western Cape, had been one of the book's best promoters, tweeting about it over a number of months and quoting sections in support of her argument that the ANC was irredeemably rotten. I felt ambivalent about this marketing, worrying that the book would be interpreted as a DA propaganda piece and relegated to the 'moaning whites' section of the bookshelf. Nevertheless, I thought it would stand my credentials in good stead if I ever wanted to research a DA-run city.

I was therefore utterly stunned when, two weeks later, I received the rejection email. Was it even legal? After all, South Africa's constitution gives every citizen the right to have access to any information held by the state, unless that information has been classified as secret.

The rejection was signed by one Hugh Cole, Director: Organisational Policy and Planning. I knew that name. I'd met the young man a year earlier when he was finishing up his doctoral thesis at Oxford. I'd been awarded an Oppenheimer Fund grant for an academic exchange with Oxford, and Cole and I had both attended a reading group at the African Studies Centre. After I'd shared my understanding of the state of South African local politics over coffee one day, he'd told me he was taking up a job in the mayor's office in Cape Town.

Oxford seemed to be a favourite recruiting ground for the DA: Craig Kesson himself had studied there some years earlier, and Cole also seemed to fit the mould of the young technocrats whom the DA likes to bring into its fold and deploy to government. When we'd met, he'd struck me as deeply thoughtful but somewhat earnest, perhaps taking himself a bit too seriously. Even back then, he appeared ideally suited to a career in politics or the diplomatic service.

The rejection mail from the City of Cape Town came with an offer to discuss the decision and the reasons behind it, so I immediately phoned Cole. I told him that I felt that the refusal fundamentally undermined the DA's claims to good governance, and he fumbled around for reasons to justify the decision – it wasn't a good time for the metro, and research probing into sensitive political and governance issues could jeopardise political stability.

Quite frankly, this didn't hold water. Most municipalities hardly ever feel it's a 'good time' to unearth lapses in governance, I argued, and while painful, full access to records and officials is the only way to properly address problems. Cole didn't relent, though, and I ended the conversation by telling him bluntly that I'd go ahead with the research, regardless of whether the City chose to participate or not.

I shared the rejection on social media, and it attracted a fair amount of support and interest. Not long afterwards, I was contacted by a journalist from the *Sunday Times*, who asked whether I thought the City was hiding something. 'It is difficult to understand why, despite their public commitment to transparency and good governance, the City would not want to investigate an area in which malpractices have been so evidently deleterious to the functioning of the city,' I replied.

The article appeared two days later, also quoting the City's communications director, Priya Reddy. The refusal, she said, was 'about the timing of the research, given the administrative and legal processes currently underway'. She further advanced that 'the city does not rely on academic research to reveal corruption ... which is dealt with in a decisive manner according to strict procedures'.[1]

In spite of what I'd defiantly told Hugh Cole, I had to decide whether to go ahead with my plans. My insights into Nelson Mandela Bay's municipal government and ANC local politics had been tied largely to my being an insider, as I'd been dispatched to the metro by both the party and the central government to be part of the clean-up operation. In Cape Town, without formal access to any of the officials and politicians, I would have to rely mainly on off-the-record conversations. Given my reputation and my outsider status, would I be able to get sufficient access to penetrate the veil of municipal politics? Maybe I should choose a simpler target for my case study?

I shared my dilemma with a close friend, Pam Yako. She grew up in the Eastern Cape under apartheid, and became a highly respected manager in local government and then the national public service.

'Hah!' she said. 'Now you've experienced a little bit of what African people in Cape Town experience every day.'

As irritating as it was to be shut out of City Hall, I thought that comparing the denial of a research request to the serious offence of racism was a giant stretch. But Pam went on to make her point about exclusion and discrimination in Cape Town: she explained that her experience of the city as an African woman was of a subtle form of exclusion, of being shut out in ways that were hard to detect. For example, she had run a leadership-development project with a large organisation in the Cape that at face value seemed progressive, but had been amazed at the preponderance of white staff in charge of the institution, while a sprinkling of black staff subserviently played more junior roles. She felt there was an unstated expectation of the black staff to express views that reinforced the white managers' place in the world, while at the same time her own views were discounted. 'It was as if my own views were being ignored, as if I didn't exist,' she remarked. 'And it's not just the [seemingly progressive institution],' she went on. 'I feel that I have to fight for every little piece of respect due to me in Cape Town.'[2]

Pam felt that Capetonians' outward shows of friendliness were forced. 'Everyone is so effusive about the laidback lifestyle of Cape Town, but when Capetonians smile at you, it feels cold; there's no emotion behind it.' Unlike the hard boundaries of apartheid, Pam experienced this as a new kind of segregation, a more insidious form of exclusion, which was infinitely subtle and hard to pin down.

I was disturbed by Pam's views of Cape Town, which echoed the words of Xolani Sotashe, the leader of the opposition ANC in the Cape Town City Council. 'There are still racial undertones,' he had observed. 'There is still the view that people of colour should not be integrated into where rich people are living.' He'd compared Cape Town to Johannesburg, which he felt was 'a totally different world', with people interacting freely.[3] As a resident of Johannesburg's still very white Northern Suburbs, I wasn't so sure he was right.

Patricia de Lille rubbished claims that Cape Town was a racist city. 'It is labelled a racist city by the ANC because it is the only metro in the country they don't control,' she said.[4] But she did acknowledge the challenge of overcoming 'the spatial development of apartheid', which the City was trying hard to change.

According to Priya Reddy, 'Cape Town, as with every other major city in South Africa, is still dealing with the spatial and socioeconomic legacy of apartheid.' However, she added, there had been an 'undeniable level of integration in areas across the city'.[5]

Pam Yako's comments prodded me to dig into the history of racial exclusion in Cape Town and how it related to land, displacement and spatial control. Although the entire country is still wrestling with the devastating legacy of apartheid's institutional racism, were Cape Town's demons even more entrenched? And if so, why? Were the city's own ghosts still haunting its administration today, like an invisible hand silently weaving the same patterns over and over?

The first thing that struck me is not only how much older but also how multilayered the legacy of exclusion and displacement happened to be in Cape Town.

In 1652 the Dutch East India Company (Vereenigde Oostindische Compagnie, or VOC) had set up a small resupply post at the Cape of Storms (now Cape Town) and proceeded to build the early colony on the backs of slaves captured in Africa and the Dutch colonies in the East, who were uprooted and forcibly displaced to the southern tip of the continent. Slaves were denied any recognition of rights and even humanity, and instead treated as property that could be disposed of or sold on their owners' whim.

This was graphically brought home to me by a moving exhibition about women slaves in the Cape, called 'Under Cover of Darkness', in September 2018. As I walked around the exhibition, fittingly housed in the old Slave Lodge at the top of Adderley Street, I was chilled to the bone reading about the lives of the women whose humanity had been stripped from them. There was China, renamed Rosa, who from early childhood was sold five times to different owners; Dina van Rio de la Goa, who'd escaped from the appalling conditions in which she worked only to be recaptured and tortured; Rosa van Bengalen, who was sold for refusing to obey; and Zara van der Caab, who committed suicide and was posthumously tried and whose body was mutilated. There were also moments of hope, for instance, when Magdalena van Batavia bought the freedom of her daughters, or when Armosyn Claasz became a Slave Lodge matron, founding a dynasty.

The weight of this history is still very present in the city, whose walls and landscape are infused with the vestiges of this painful past. The curator of the exhibition, Carine Zaayman, pointed to the story of Susanna van Bengal, who was sentenced to death for infanticide – a grave crime to the Dutch, because her child would have been considered property of the company. At her trial, she spoke about how, exhausted after a day's back-breaking labour in the VOC's gardens, she had walked back to the slave lodge where her sick child, who would die that night, lay. This was the very same Slave Lodge where Zaayman and I both now stood. 'I walked her walk, through the Company Gardens, and I ended up at the place that she would have ended up,' Zaayman said. For her crime, Susanna was sewn into a bag and thrown into Table Bay to drown.

For Zaayman, who was raised on the South African Highveld as a white South African, this history is deeply personal. Ten years ago, her cousin compiled a genealogy of their family, tracing their ancestry back to a Khoi woman, Eva, who worked in Jan van Riebeeck's household. Eva's Khoi name was Krotoa, and her history is closely tied to that of the early Dutch settlement at the Cape.

Krotoa was high born, the niece of the chief of the Goringhaicona, the first of the Khoi tribes to make contact with the Dutch; Krotoa's tribe initially viewed the Dutch arrival as an opportunity to advance trade. The chief sent the 12-year-old Krotoa to work in Van Riebeeck's household, doubling up as a translator and intermediary. Van Riebeeck's journals mention her frequently and fondly, and she might even have been a consort. Eventually she was baptised, married a Dutch surgeon, and for some time lived inside the Castle.

However, Zaayman's ancestor seems to have straddled an increasingly fraught relationship between her people and the Dutch, and in the end, neither side completely trusted her. After Krotoa's husband died, she developed a fondness for the rough spirits that were distilled in the Cape, and when a new VOC commander arrived, she was sent to live in the

Khoi kraals outside the Castle. On a number of occasions she was unjustly imprisoned and banished to Robben Island.

Relations with the Khoi were deteriorating as the VOC began taking their traditional grazing lands and cattle, and Krotoa's story illustrates how the Khoi themselves, in spite of their initial hopes that they could benefit from the European settlement, ended up displaced and relegated to the lower margins of the Dutch outpost's social and economic order.

Krotoa was survived by three children, one of whom married a VOC vegetable farmer called Daniel Zaaijman. These were Carine Zaayman's ancestors.

Zaayman told me that when she moved to Cape Town as young adult, she was struck by a feeling she struggled to name. 'I felt the weight of history as very powerful, and, having not grown up here, it was quite striking. I felt deep undercurrents, about how exclusionary Cape Town can be. You know, the unique feature of Cape Town was that it had slavery, long before apartheid, and it was a particular form of dehumanising other people, of not recognising their humanity.'

Zaayman told me about the stories of women slaves that hadn't been documented in the archives, and what we could learn from the absences and silences in the historical record. Walking with me back through the Company Gardens after touring the exhibition, she pointed to the slave bell that hangs next to the aviary. There's a sign next to it that tells all about how and where the bell was made, but nothing of the lives of the people whose work in the gardens was governed by the bell.

'What kind of oppression does that talk to?' Zaayman said. 'There's so much missing from the record, and if we just concern ourselves with what we know, we only get glimpses and slivers, a highly distorted picture. I know it's trite, but if we can't learn from history, we're condemned to repeat it.'

The path from slavery to modern-day racial exclusion, although convoluted, is clearly paved with displacement and spatial control.

After the collapse of Dutch rule through the VOC, the British occupied the Cape in the early 19th century, imposing an imperial distaste for racial mixing. Despite its liberal promise, the emancipation of the slaves under British rule in 1834 led to much greater levels of tension between Europeans and darker-skinned race groups. The spatial manifestation of racial exclusion was embedded in the British obsession with epidemics, public health and slum clearances, and a smallpox outbreak in the early 20th century led to Africans being cleared out of parts of the city and pushed into the first separate township for Africans in Ndabeni near modern-day Pinelands.

Exclusion and spatial control were further entrenched with the accession to power in 1948 of the National Party (NP). The foundation of its apartheid policy was a bizarre process of racial categorisation in terms of the Population Registration Act, 1950, according to which people were designated as white, African, Indian or coloured. The last category lumped together everyone who didn't fall neatly within any of the first three groups, but most of those rejected the imposed 'coloured' identity, insisting that it was an artificial racial identification imposed by the government to divide and rule black people.[6]

As a sop to people who shared their Dutch parentage, the NP decided that the Western Cape would become a 'coloured labour preference area', where coloured workers got preferential employment over Africans, in a ploy designed to promote a stronger sense of 'colouredness' by privileging coloureds economically relative to Africans.[7]

At the same time, the Cape has a long legacy of integration and oppressed people fighting back. Despite its history of slavery, in the 18th and 19th centuries the Cape became increasingly racially mixed, as soldiers and sailors settled down and intermarried with freed slaves and local Khoi women. Three centuries of living together meant that, before the implementation

33

of the Group Areas Act, Cape Town was arguably the most racially integrated city in South Africa.[8]

When my parents moved from Natal to Cape Town in the early 1960s, they were struck by how much more racially integrated the Cape was compared to colonial Natal, where Zulu and Indian servants didn't socialise with white settlers. Even though petty apartheid manifested in other ways, buses in Cape Town weren't segregated, for instance. But, more importantly, my parents were able to build enduring friendships across racial lines.

Yet my parents were also struck by the climate of fear that permeated the city. The year before they arrived, a large crowd of Africans (variously estimated at between 30 000 and 50 000) from the Langa and Nyanga townships, situated about 15 kilometres from the city centre, had marched on Cape Town to protest against the humiliating legislation that required every African to carry a pass. The march, organised by the PAC, was peacefully dispersed, but it was followed over the ensuing months by a violent security crackdown in which many of the black intellectual elite whom my parents were to befriend were rounded up and jailed.

My mother also remarked about the endemic social elitism that seemed to permeate the Cape, which created invisible barriers far more pronounced than those in other parts of the country where the colonial influence was more recent. The old Cape families were reluctant to mingle with people who were from out of town and considered of inferior social standing. 'I was certainly aware that if you weren't born in Cape Town, you were much lower down the ladder and should be grateful for their recognition,' my mom told me. 'We all laughed about it – all our friends were from out of town!' The running joke about old Cape families was that the Van Bredas talked only to the Cloetes, and the Cloetes talked only to God.[9]

In the context of apartheid, this social elitism was to take a very horrible form.

I grew up in the 1960s in Constantia, at the foot of the Constantiaberg. Now it's an upmarket residential area forming part of Cape Town's Southern Suburbs, but back then, Constantia was a rather laidback and racially diverse farming community, even though the large wine estates were all owned by white English and Afrikaans families. My mother was chair of the newly formed Progressive Party in Constantia (a role she combined with raising three children, running a farm and managing my wild and fun-loving father). At the time, Helen Suzman was the sole representative of the 'Progs' (members of the Progressive Party) in the white Parliament, fighting a lonely battle against a raft of apartheid legislation and a violent security clampdown.

My closest friend, Gammie, whose family was Cape Malay,[10] lived nearby, and my mom used to drop me off there to play whenever she went to do volunteer work with Kupugani, a non-governmental organisation (NGO) that assisted with nutritional programmes for poor and needy communities. Gammie and I roamed the neighbourhood freely, fighting imaginary battles among the gnarled oaks and rows of grapevines, losing ourselves in each other.

Then, one day, my mother told me that I wouldn't be able to play there any more: Gammie's family had to move. 'Because the government told them to,' she answered when I asked why.

My liberal parents tried to explain that the Group Areas Act of 1950 – against which they had campaigned – had given the authorities the power to decide where each racial group could live and own property, but obviously this made no sense to me.

When the trucks arrived to collect Gammie and his family, there were no protests or placards, and I stood silently watching as everything in their house was piled onto the vehicle. I couldn't understand why my boyhood friend was being sent to a ghetto on the desolate Cape Flats, despite having done nothing wrong. It was a horrendous act of injustice, uprooting a family who'd lived and worked in the area for over a century.

The apartheid planners had used the railway as dividing lines, and worked to remove all black families who lived north of the Bellville line and west of the Southern Suburbs' Simonstown line. Once an area had been proclaimed a white group area, only whites could reside and own property there; black families were forced to sell at discounted prices and move to designated townships on the Cape Flats.

The fate of our suburb was decided by the Group Areas Board, who said that they would determine the racial character of our area after public consultation. A public hearing was duly convened in Constantia, at which many of our neighbours, black and white, stood up and said that they opposed the removals; Constantia should stay just as it was, they argued. The Cape Town city council added its opposition to the proclamation, but it made no difference. In 1961, a whole raft of suburbs were proclaimed white areas, including Constantia, Newlands, Claremont, Wynberg and Mowbray. A vast and inhuman social-engineering project got underway – by 1961 more than 100 000 coloured and African people had been moved, and many thousands more were to follow.

My parents felt powerless as successive proclamations of white group areas gathered pace. My mom felt that she couldn't do anything on the ground to stop apartheid but she thought she could get people elected who could do something once in power, even if it was through an illegitimate whites-only Parliament. Throughout the 1960s and early 1970s, my mother and her fellow Progs worked to build enough of a support base to get more Progs into Parliament. She would rope us children into putting up posters for city council and national elections. On the evening of polling day, my dad would wash and feed us, and we would go down to the polling station in our pyjamas to stand with mom until the polling booths closed at 9 pm.

Eventually, the Progs managed to get an additional six members of Parliament (MPs) into Parliament in 1974, ending Helen Suzman's lone marathon. Yet they remained a minority party with a limited impact on the grinding machinery of apartheid.

During this time I lost many of my childhood friends, who were forcibly relocated with their families; it disoriented and confused me. It was difficult to keep contact with them, as they had been exiled to faraway places such as Grassy Park, Lotus River, Belhar, Hanover Park and Manenberg.

Visiting Gammie was painful: the area where he lived in Manenberg looked more like a concentration camp than a community. All the hurt and longing of the move seemed concentrated in his sad little face. We could no longer roam around freely, as Gammie's mom told us that we had to watch out for the gangs and criminals in their new suburb. There was a general feeling of devastation among people who'd been ripped out of neighbourhoods where they had deep roots; they'd lost their social networks and economic livelihoods. People found themselves thrown together with strangers from other communities, and they had to recreate their sense of self and their social lives.[11]

Eventually, I stopped going to Gammie's house, but he would still come and play on the farm on weekends. A few years later, Gammie's dad committed suicide, depressed by the way their lives had fallen apart after the move. Gammie seemed determined to be brave, walking around stiffly, but looking like he was about to burst into tears.

Gammie's dad was by no means the only case. My mother told me that two other coloured men, in Sea Point and Rondebosch, had committed suicide rather than move to the new ghettos.

No one could escape the sadness that pervaded communities when they were ordered to go. Every family faced the removals with great bitterness and resentment, some with a sense of hopelessness and resignation, others with impotent rage. The forced relocations were particularly hard on old people, many of whom died just before or after moving.[12]

When I started junior school in Claremont in 1965, there wasn't a single coloured or black child in the school.

Soon afterwards, the coloured families living in neighbouring Claremont, Harfield Village and Newlands were relocated as well. Police cordoned off the streets around our school during some of the protests, and even though we weren't told what was happening, I knew something terrible was taking place.

I overheard my parents talking about what to do about the relocation of District Six, a large multi-ethnic community close to the city centre. For the next few years, the painful dislocation of families from District Six and the ensuing protests dominated the news, as some 60 000 people were moved.

As the removals ground on, the silence in my school and our Constantia community was deafening.

When I was in high school in the mid-1970s, the construction of remote dormitory townships for coloured families started on Mitchells Plain and in Atlantis.

By the time I started university, the year during which Black Consciousness activist Steve Biko was beaten to death in a police cell in Port Elizabeth, the final clearing of District Six was still taking place. It had been 30 years of vast social engineering, the relentless imposition of an idea that was ostensibly about racial separation, but was in fact a cruel system of domination and exclusion – a new form of slavery.

Looking back at the history of the city and how it intersected with my own awoke uncomfortable memories but also reminded me of how seemingly insurmountable obstacles can be overcome. And Cape Town has a rich history of successful community resistance against oppression.

While openly political organisations were quickly banned, civic, women and youth groups focusing on practical, on-the-ground issues such as gangsterism, drug abuse, housing and social services sprang up around the Cape Flats during the 1970s and 1980s. When the UDF was launched in Mitchells Plain in 1983, I joined a crowd of thousands to listen to a succession of seasoned community leaders such as Allan Boesak and Frank Chikane, who proclaimed that we'd reached a turning point in the struggle for freedom. Politics seemed to have come alive again.

The Cape Town of my childhood was dystopian, an apparent idyll within the comforting arms of Table Mountain whose underbelly was silent violence. The cold hard truth is that we didn't do enough, because our middle-class lives were able to continue largely unaffected. Despite some muted protest, the cocktail-sipping Southern Suburbs gentry mostly looked the other way. We edited our memories of events so that the uncomfortable parts of the past were elided. We lived with little dishonesties every day.

But by censoring out apartheid crimes, we entered a dangerous dance of deception with ourselves. We all lost something through the trauma; our lives were emptier, incomplete. And being aware of this monumental emptiness in our lives was a mark of Cain among my people, who'd learnt to lift their gaze beyond the squalor of the Flats and see only the Hottentots Holland[13] in the blue distance.

A friend and much-loved poet, the late Stephen Watson, who lived near the small fishing harbour of Kalk Bay, wondered about the emptiness of Cape Town, what he referred to as a cultural 'day zero'. Despite all its beautiful landscapes and architecture, Watson observed in 2009 'a species of vacancy about the place, an underbelly of melancholy to it, no matter how copiously and cheerfully sunlight might pour down on it'. This cultural vacancy went hand in hand with a spatial vacancy, he wrote: Cape Town was a 'colonial city that has not yet managed, through architecture, to tame and humanise the space around it; and which, still existing like some permanently unfinished building, works to infect all space around it with its incompleteness, its emptiness.'[14]

Rereading Watson's sad words now, I was struck by how incomplete the Cape Town project still felt – the unacknowledged memories of a painful past, the dislocation that still persists, the hovering between different worlds and visions. My Cape Town, the city of my childhood, was a city of separation and contrasts, a city caught between comfortable modernity

39

and degrading poverty, between those that had everything they could ever want or need, and those who had nothing at all. It's in a no-man's land, an in-between world. The city is poised between west and east, between its settlers with their dreams of a European port city on the trade routes to the East, and its slaves and migrant labourers from Africa and Java whose lives and dreams were stolen.

Twenty-five years after South Africa's transition to democracy, the compartmentalised picture of the Cape drawn by the apartheid planners has endured in many ways.

A few years ago, I was struck by a digitised map of Cape Town using population data from the last census, which graphically showed how segregated the suburbs of Cape Town remain.[15] The more affluent white suburbs were clustered like pearls around Table Mountain and spread out eastwards towards the elegant winelands of Paarl and Stellenbosch. The map showed that some suburbs, like Woodstock, Rondebosch East, Pinelands and Kensington, were starting to become more racially integrated and multicultural, but the rate and pace of integration, a full generation after the end of apartheid, was pathetically slow.

The apartheid dividing lines formed by the Bellville and Southern Suburbs railways formed a cross on the landscape, and the charm faded when you looked at the barracks-like townships on the Cape Flats, strictly demarcated into the African townships of Langa, Nyanga, Gugulethu and Khayelitsha, and the coloured suburbs of Athlone, Bonteheuwel, Grassy Park and Mitchells Plain. Here, still, corralled on barren sand, were all the brown and black people of the Cape, once deemed unsuitable to live in the leafy suburbs around the mountain. These are the descendants of the slaves and mulattos who planted the wine estates, manned the docks and built the city out of the sand and rocks on this otherwise desolate peninsula.

Although government edicts no longer compel residents to move, other forces seem to perpetuate old spatial patterns. Two friends of mine, Zackie Achmat and Mike Evans, have been involved with an NGO called Ndifuna Ukwazi (from the Xhosa for 'I want to know' or 'dare to know'). Ndifuna Ukwazi is trying to stop poor black people being forced out of the city because of rising rents, gentrification and unfair rental practices. Their argument is that urban exclusion is driven by powerful business interests, poor government policies and regressive ideas, which they see as replicating spatial apartheid, poverty and inequality in Cape Town. Among various campaigns and protest actions, they've launched Reclaim the City, a community-based alliance of tenants and workers campaigning against the displacement of poorer black people from well-located areas. 'We believe it is time to take the struggle for housing to the centre of the city, to the heart of power, to the people who should live there, and to the land that matters. Land for people, not profit!' they proclaim.[16]

Through the multiple planning and land controls at its disposal, Cape Town's local government has in its power the ability to either seek to integrate a deeply divided city, or let apartheid divides perpetuate. During the peak of the water crisis of 2018, I was struck by the fact that the question of land, property development and social housing had emerged at the centre of the competing narratives supposed to justify the spectacular political drama pitting Mayor Patricia de Lille against her rivals within the DA. And my being refused access to City records and officials seemed to fall in line with Cape Town's old tradition of selective memory. As Carine Zaayman had told me, absence and silence themselves were signs of something. The City's decision just raised further questions: what was really hiding behind the 'high risk' and 'significant impact'?

Ironically, the City's rejection, after it was made public through the *Sunday Times* article, opened some unexpected doors for me.

4

Between a rock and a hard place

~~~

It was a midwinter's day in a chilly Cape Town, and even though Catherine Stone and I were in a cosy dining room in Tamboerskloof at the foot of Table Mountain, the story she was telling me made my blood run cold.[1]

Stone was head of spatial planning for the City for eight years. She was widely respected for her work on the physical layout of the city, organising urban development so that residents could easily move around the city. She explained that she'd worked on planning policy, which involved pushing for an ambitious spatial-integration agenda. As in any well-run city, housing and private developments had to comply with spatial and zoning plans, or growth would be haphazard and uncoordinated, but she wasn't involved in zoning or granting development permissions, which are typically more conflictual. Theoretically, this should have kept her out of the firing line. But it didn't.

After the *Sunday Times* article, I'd been contacted by a surprising number of people with stories of political purges in the City administration, including many former municipal employees. In all, 311 managers had been issued with 'restructuring' notices in 2016.

Initially I was a bit sceptical. Any administration has its fair share of disgruntled staff, and if you poke around in any government bureaucracy, there are always underperformers who allege victimisation. During my previous investigations into dysfunctional municipalities, the difficulty had always been separating out the petty grievances and grudges from genuine maladministration. What struck me about the bulk of the whistleblowers I met in Cape Town, however, was that they seemed to be highly competent and committed civil servants.

I contacted Catherine Stone after her name kept coming up in these conversations. She wanted to move on with her life and was reluctant to talk about her experiences, but what she told me eerily echoed the many other discussions I'd had with current and former City officials.

Stone had been the quintessential City bureaucrat – precise, professional, hardworking, collegial and socially minded. I met many property developers who'd worked with her, and while some disagreed with her decisions, none could fault her skills and commitment. In 2015 she'd been one of five recipients of the inaugural Mayoral Award, handed over by the mayor in recognition of dedication to the job, at a gala event at the prestigious Table Bay Hotel in the V&A Waterfront.

Mark Noble, the head of property development for the V&A Waterfront, the largest property development in the centre of Cape Town, said that, based on his experience, planners like Stone were highly competent experts who were a great asset to the City. While she might have at times been considered by some developers as a bit dogmatic, Mark didn't experience her as obstructionist.[2]

Yet Stone's job had been inexplicably 'restructured' in 2016.

Stone had known there were ambitious plans to completely reorganise the City's administration, but she hadn't thought it would affect her vital planning department. She'd kept tabs on the process through one of her colleagues who was part of the committee drawing up the grand reorganisation plan to be tabled before the city council. The week before the proposals were to be tabled, her colleague had reassured her that her planning division was safe, and that her job had in fact grown in responsibilities.

Yet, at the last minute, an alternative restructuring plan had been tabled – one that dismantled the entire planning department and amalgamated its function with transport, affordable housing and environment into a powerful unit known as the Transport and Urban Development Authority (TDA). The new organogram was approved, and Stone's job was no longer part of it. Her planning department had been wiped out and her staff distributed across different divisions, slotted into unwanted poky corners in open-plan offices.

Stone arranged for mentors and coaches for her managers to assist them to adjust, but when Melissa Whitehead, who was heading the newly established TDA, found out about the mentors, she put a stop to it. There would be no coaching for these planners.

New job descriptions were issued. A new management position was available, which, according to the Human Resources department, was very similar to Stone's previous job. This meant that she should automatically have been transferred into the post. Instead, the city manager ruled that the post had to be advertised, and that Stone had to reapply. When she asked for written reasons, he didn't respond.

So she applied, and was interviewed for the job. The panel included Melissa Whitehead and Ernest Sass, a former politician turned executive director responsible for social services. The interview panel concluded that Stone was incompetent and not suitable for the job.

Japie Hugo, the executive director for economic, environment and spatial planning, and Stone's former boss, was enraged, questioning Sass's own competence. 'How could they not appoint her to a job which she had done highly successfully until then?' he asked rhetorically in his thick Afrikaans accent when we met.[3] 'This really broke Cathy's heart.'

Stone was issued with a retrenchment letter.

'Were they retrenching planners?' I asked Hugo.

'No, they were retrenching people they didn't want around.'[4]

By then, Stone was tired, and she took the financial package that was being offered. 'I realised Melissa was going to get rid of me one way or another,' she said, adding that she wasn't sure whether to chalk this up to a personality clash or a political move.[5]

Hugo was also pushed out as part of the 'restructuring'. Sitting in his beautiful home in Camps Bay, with spectacular views over the ocean and up to Lion's Head, he told me about his long career in spatial planning, which spanned both the private and public sectors. He'd worked as a senior planner with private developers and in various municipalities. By the time he'd become executive director for economic, environment and spatial planning for the City of Cape Town in 2012, he'd already been involved in two complete overhauls of urban-planning frameworks – one in Johannesburg and the other in Cape Town. He spearheaded the implementation of the third, in Cape Town, following the adoption of the new Spatial Planning and Land Use Management Act in 2013.

As an executive director, Japie Hugo was on a fixed-term contract, which ended in 2016. A few months before the contract expired, it had become clear to him that he wouldn't become the new head of the TDA: before the ink was dry on the reorganisation proposal, Whitehead was already issuing instructions to the planning staff. When Stone complained to Hugo that Whitehead was interfering in matters that fell directly under him before the restructuring had even been implemented, he decided to let it go. 'I'm not going to fight her,' he replied. 'Just take her instructions'.[6]

Hugo decided to apply for the newly created function of executive director in charge of the City's considerable and highly valuable property portfolio. Given his extensive experience in private-property development, he was certain that nobody within the administration was as qualified as he was for the position. To his surprise, however, he wasn't offered the job. 'It seemed as part of a preordained plan,' he wryly remarked.[7]

When Hugo's contract came to an end, he left the City administration and started consulting. His new work was going well, he said, and he spoke passionately about a large new mixed-use development he was working on in the winelands area.

Stephen Boshoff, another former executive director, who worked with Hugo over many years, described him as professional but circumspect, able to work under almost any administration. Hugo was someone who picked his battles carefully, Boschoff said: 'Forget about Cathy; if they couldn't tolerate Japie, then they've really got something big to hide.'[8]

Further conversations fuelled my concern that the City administration had been bleeding valuable expertise and experience for no good reason. Why were seemingly competent civil servants being pushed out?

I met Jens Kuhn, the former head of housing development, in the tea room in the Company Gardens, not far from the old Slave Lodge. Having worked as a town planner and then moved up through the system to become a director, he had a wealth of experience as a local-government official. Wiry and weatherbeaten, with a quirky, irreverent streak, he made no pretence about understanding politics, which he saw as encroaching on – and ultimately ruining – the administrative terrain in which he operated.

Kuhn explained that for the past seven years his job had been to secure land for affordable housing. He would arrange for the land identified either to be purchased or, if it was already owned by the City or the Department of Public Works, to be reserved and transferred to the housing programme. Once he'd secured any piece of land, his team would then determine which type of housing was the most appropriate for it, from temporary transit units during construction in informal settlements to medium-density housing development which could transform the city.[9]

The work was mostly technical, but Kuhn would occasionally have to engage with politicians from the mayor's office, the mayoral committee or the city council. He tried to politely explain to City politicians why some of their demands weren't good ideas, but ultimately he felt that he simply couldn't do the 'oozing and schmoozing' that they apparently expected.

With his frank and direct way of speaking, I could see that he wasn't someone to shrink away from speaking his mind, and in the last round of restructuring in the City administration in 2016, he'd objected quite strongly to the idea of creating subcouncils and 'mini mayors' for the different regions of the City, which he thought would fragment and even paralyse decision-making. This had been an apparently fatal move.

'You were told to go?' I asked.

'Got a letter. Was made redundant.'[10]

Like Catherine Stone, Kuhn had been offered a package to leave: his job had disappeared, his job description written into another post. He'd thought that his retrenchment was illegal, but it was clear to him that the mayor's office wanted to get rid of him, and he wanted to get on with his life rather than get bogged down in the Labour Court.

Kuhn leant across the table. 'I don't know if you've heard from my colleagues, but we had eight directors who were told to just go. I'm not the only one. No reason, nothing. "Here's money, go away."'

Kuhn was appalled at the haemorrhage of administrative capacity that this created. 'The one thing you do need in the City is local knowledge,' he pointed out. 'You can't just employ people from anywhere in senior positions. Even if they're competent, it takes four or five years to learn all the nooks and crannies in the City, and during that learning period, delivery gets put back.'[11]

I continued meeting the flotsam and jetsam left by the restructuring shipwreck. In the end, I interviewed about 50 people both inside and outside the administration, current and former officials, as well as people from the private and NGO sectors who'd worked with the officials involved.

Not everyone had been retrenched: some believed that they had been bullied into leaving. The mournful-looking Seth Maqetuka, who'd worked as executive director for human settlements for the City of Cape Town, and was now working as a senior adviser on housing policy for National Treasury, squeezed me in between meetings.

He was clearly experienced, having previously headed human settlements in the Nelson Mandela Bay metropolitan municipality. Nelson Mandela Bay had been a tough assignment, as I knew too well, but Maqetuka hadn't been prepared for the political minefield that confronted him in Cape Town when he joined the administration there in 2011.

He told me about a purge of the housing staff that had taken place in 2014.[12] It all began when, in line with her official objective to address the city's housing backlog while promoting spatial integration, Patricia de Lille said she wanted more houses built, on better-located land, using the same budget.

Maqetuka put a plan on the table to provide affordable housing closer to jobs and amenities, and brought in top consultants to build the case. But when it came to securing more centrally located land – and conducting difficult negotiations with affluent neighbours pushing back against bringing lower-income residents to their part of town – the political support he needed from the mayor's office wasn't forthcoming. The strategy to build houses in better locations was there on paper, but Maqetuka found that there was little appetite from political leaders to pony up the necessary funds or tackle the obstacles that came up when turning the strategy into reality.

Maqetuka cited examples that he said were typical. To relocate residents from the informal settlement of Imizamo Yethu, which had been ravaged by fires, he'd asked his staff to identify land in the Hout Bay area. Yet his proposal was quashed and he was told by the Council's human settlements portfolio committee to look further away because 'this is going to create tensions within Hout Bay'.[13]

When Maqetuka proposed building an integrated settlement in Strandfontein, he faced similar obstacles. He drove with Mayor De Lille and Helen Zille, then Western Cape premier, to visit the area. After he presented the proposal, Zille and De Lille stepped aside to discuss it. The mayor later told him that the proposal couldn't work. 'We feel that it's just going to create racial and political tensions,' she explained. 'Let's look at other pieces of land.'[14] The alternative was in Delft – much farther away.

At the same time, managers in Maqetuka's department remember how the mayor used to scream at him over delivery issues. De Lille also frequently hinted that the councillors on the human settlements portfolio committee didn't think he was doing his job properly. 'I'm under pressure; the councillors don't want you,' she would tell him. 'I don't understand what it is, because you're doing your work. Perhaps you're not seen to be delivering in their areas, for their constituency.'[15]

Maqetuka thought that the real issue was that the mayor didn't trust his management team. Soon after starting his job, he'd reorganised the department and appointed four directors in charge of various aspects of housing delivery. De Lille felt that they were loyal to the previous mayor, Helen Zille, and not to her, and fretted that they still supported Zille's programmes. Maqetuka came under increasing pressure to get rid of his directors, but he had no cause to do so. 'They were very good professionals, and they were doing their work. When I came to assess them, I just didn't have any reason to fire them, and I told her so.'[16]

According to Maqetuka, the mayoral committee member in charge of human settlements then tried to pressurise him. Then De Lille appointed another mayoral committee member, and Maqetuka felt he was being driven out. 'I wasn't happy. It felt like unnecessary pressure, and I was sick and tired of the interference. I needed to get out.'[17]

Maqetuka resigned in January 2014.

De Lille then made her move. She fired the mayoral committee member for human settlements – it was the second time she'd replaced this mayoral committee member: Ernest Sonnenberg was the first under De Lille, and she'd replaced him with Tandeka Gqada, who was then replaced by Siyabulela Mamkeli – and the chair of the city council's portfolio committee for human settlements. This amounted to a comprehensive purge of the political leadership in charge of housing.

All the directors who'd worked under Maqetuka were suddenly vulnerable, and they were immediately targeted with a 'restructuring' process. Even though the re-advertised job descriptions were similar to the old ones, when the dust settled, all four directors had lost their jobs. It seemed uncannily similar to the way the planning department would be dismembered two years later.

Former housing officials were mystified as to why they'd been pushed out. I wondered whether there perhaps had been any issues around performance. 'We were never attacked on performance,' one former official told me, 'and you can't challenge us on that. We performed pretty damned well under the circumstances. I honestly don't know why they got rid of us.'[18]

I was told of the conflicting pressures on officials from politicians and communities, which made working on housing a minefield.

The picture that emerged from these conversations was deeply worrying. It seemed that the political leadership – and primarily the mayor and her office – no longer considered senior officials to be technical and policy advisers, but rather pliant foot soldiers expected to jump at their beck and call, and who became disposable once they were perceived not to be doing so. 'De Lille was frightening, in the sense that she would let you know your job is on the line,' a senior official told me. 'Whenever I was in a meeting with her, there was very little listening and engaging; it was mostly just bawling you out for whatever she'd decided to shout about. She had an absolute inability to listen. Instead, she manipulated the administration and did things designed to get her way.'[19]

One of the directors in the department, Shehaam Sims, had previously been a politician herself, working as De Lille's mayoral committee member for utility services; in fact, she'd thrown her hat into the ring for the mayor's job, and had lost to De Lille. Sims used to joke that she'd take any job if she could earn more than the mayor – which apparently a director did. This joke might have inflamed De Lille, although it hardly seemed sufficient to behead an entire department.

I made the trip to Oudtshoorn in the Klein Karoo, where Sims was now working. Oudtshoorn is the centre of a dry but starkly beautiful ostrich-farming area, and Sims was the executive director for human settlements for the municipality. Instead of in the smart council building, she'd set up the housing office in a coloured township called Bridgton. The offices did look a bit sparse, but the location in a poorer coloured township was symbolically important.

Extremely welcoming and animated, Sims started our meeting by explaining that many people thought she was a man because of her deep voice and assertive manner. Once she started talking, she was hard to stop.

In Shehaam's opinion, De Lille had had a problem with the senior housing officials because they weren't prepared to deliver according to her timetable. 'If the mayor, for example, wanted something done, then stupid me would say to her, "Mayor, we'd like to do what you want, and we'll give you what you want, but you're being impossible with respect to the time period that you want it in. There's legislation that we have to follow. We can't break the rules. You'll get the glory when it's done properly, but if mistakes are made, it's the officials who'll end up going to jail."'[20]

Sims pointed out that De Lille was trying to deliver as fast as possible, which was her role as mayor. But she said that De Lille also never listened to officials who were trying to tell her that there were procedures to follow.

According to Sims, other housing officials were terrified of De Lille's mercurial temperament, so she was the person sent in to deal with the mayor on thorny issues. 'I'd speak on behalf of all of the cases, but even I wasn't winning any more. You couldn't have two bulls in one kraal. It was certainly her kraal, not mine. And I don't take crap from anybody, it doesn't matter who the hell you are. I chose to resign because I couldn't take De Lille.'[21]

By the winter of 2014, Shehaam Sims and the rest of the housing directors were gone. Sims said she still believed in the DA, 'but it mustn't get into power through doing things in the wrong way'.

In the later restructuring led by Craig Kesson in 2016/17, the unfortunate housing department was broken up into different parts – the construction of new housing was moved over to planning, informal-settlement upgrading was moved to engineering, and the management of the existing housing stock and real estate was sent to the property-management section.

The exodus of good managers spanned several years and continued in 2017. One example was Frank Cumming, a private-sector manager and property developer who'd been hired in March 2017 to manage 'catalytic' property-development projects in the city. Catalytic projects are public or private property-development initiatives that are meant to be spatially transformative and unlock development and investment; the projects are of a sufficient scale to stimulate redevelopment or turn around urban decay, and are designed to have an impact on surrounding properties.

At the end of his six-month probation period in October, De Lille wanted Cumming gone, although he was widely acknowledged as the driving force behind the projects.

Cumming, who'd been leading De Lille's work on inner-city property developments, felt that Kesson's reorganisation was being used to get rid of individuals who had a backbone and were trying to do the right thing.[22] The loss of so many competent and experienced officials, whose principal sin appeared to have been independent thinking, could only have weakened the administration.

My conversation with Sheeham Sims made it clear that, besides the exodus of competence, there was another sizeable problem that threatened to grind the administration to a halt. Officials struggled to reconcile the municipality's pro-business entrepreneurial approach with its obsession with compliance and clean audit.

In theory, each expectation made perfect sense. Cutting red tape ranked high on the agenda of DA leaders, who argued that the City's planners were overly bureaucratic and anti-business in their review of development applications. The Western Cape government had gone so far as to set up a dedicated Red Tape Reduction Unit in 2011, which was meant to assist businesses by cutting bureaucracy. The key goal was to create a supportive environment for business by reducing the complexity of regulatory approvals and administrative procedures.[23]

The City set out to improve its World Bank 'Ease of Doing Business' score, in which economies are rated from 1 to 190, with a high ranking meaning the regulatory environment is more conducive to the starting and operation of a local company.[24]

It was no secret that the DA-led City administration leant heavily towards property developers; it was part of its ideological orientation. This was even enshrined in the City's integrated development plan (IDP), which talked about 'an opportunity city that creates an enabling environment for economic growth and job creation' and committed to a series of growth-oriented partnerships and 'growth coalitions' – collaborations between government and the private sector in areas that showed the best potential for jobs and economic growth.[25]

According to Catherine Stone, it wasn't unusual for some DA leaders in the City to feel that private developers should set the pace and make the decisions, as they were in the best position to assess market risk and work out where to invest.[26] The implicit assumption was that developers were always right, and when officials pushed back on development proposals, these DA leaders sided with the developers. Mayor De Lille, however, seemed to have taken this willingness to give developers a free rein to such extraordinary extremes that it apparently alarmed even her own party.

Stone shared a revealing story about her department's efforts to bring private developers into a place called Monwabisi, which is a coastal node south of Khayelitsha. In line with the overall objective of spatial integration, City officials wanted to bring a range of income groups and housing to that part of the city. Developers, however, were likely to consider the area risky, due to its location and little existing private investment. Stone explained that the best way to attract private investment was to de-risk it, so the City conducted market research to figure out what would move the needle for developers, from upfront infrastructure investment to prior development approvals and rezoning.[27]

When Stone and her team presented the market research to De Lille, she trashed it and questioned the need to pre-judge what the private sector might want. 'How dare you present this research to me?' she fumed. 'The private sector know what they're doing. Just put this thing out to tender.'[28]

Mapule Moore, the former head of finance for the then newly established TDA, concurred with Stone. 'The mayor thinks the market knows best, and the City planners are just interfering busybodies [who] should stand back and let the market lead the way.'[29]

At the same time, the DA leaders put a lot of emphasis on clean audit and anti-corruption measures. In the context of a corruption-ridden South African state, this was reassuring. There was one significant problem, however: going by the book of convoluted municipal regulations didn't sit easily with cutting red tape and being entrepreneurial.

When I talked to Frank Cumming in 2018, he berated the compliance culture in the City, which held back officials who were trying to get things moving. 'Look, we're a DA-led municipality, so we're obsessed with reporting, management control and sticking to the book – to an extent that's unhealthy. We're so obsessed that we actually can't see the wood for the trees,' he concluded.[30]

David Marais, who'd worked with Cumming on property developments in the inner city, agreed that compliance had become the be-all and end-all of the City. 'You're so busy complying you forget to do any work. You end up complying yourself into a coma.'[31]

This paralysing culture didn't seem compatible with the Western Cape government's Red Tape Reduction Programme, which exalted zeal, tenacity, optimism, innovation and an appetite for risk.[32]

In the area of property development, any project carried some risks, and Cumming reasoned that officials needed to be allowed some latitude to make mistakes and learn from them. In an environment obsessed with rules and controls, however, nobody wanted to make a mistake, or risk getting into trouble. City officials were extremely anxious about making procedural errors that could get them fired.

Instead, Cumming explained, most officials either tried to get managers higher up to sign off decisions, which siphoned all initiative out of the system, or remained paralysed.[33]

Cumming had a bit of a reputation of being a cowboy, but other officials confirmed his views. Jens Kuhn, for instance, agreed that the administration and its officials were extremely cautious about following the letter of the law. The problem was, different pieces of legislation sometimes contradicted each other, in which instance officials were damned if they did and damned if they didn't. So they simply did nothing.

One of the experienced housing directors who'd been 'restructured' out of a job had also found the process of delivering housing enormously frustrating because of the obsession with controls and clean audits. Housing projects were extremely complex and typically spanned several years, which required some flexibility to shift funds between financial years and between areas of over- and under-expenditure. These projects also relied on efficient procurement mechanisms to provide the right components at the right time. Ultimately, the housing official found it impossible to manage complex projects with the constraints imposed by a finance department that had become increasingly conservative about financial controls and reporting.[34]

Moore felt that the City administration had been overrun with compliance fanatics, while the administration's restructuring had left many officials utterly confused about their roles, responsibilities and the administration's strategic priorities. 'It's as if the City itself is at war,' she explained. 'Compliance and service delivery ended up at war with each other.'[35]

The focus on compliance created an unbearable level of risk for Moore, and cutting red tape could've had disastrous consequences for her. 'I realised that when the City was fighting political battles, the officials who got targeted along the route didn't matter to them.'[36]

A forensic investigation was started into the MyCiti fare system, in which it appeared that cashiers were fraudulently issuing tickets without payment. This had built up into a R43 million loss to the City.

Moore felt that a witch-hunt was underway, driven by a larger political fight. 'I sat down and made a list of the risks on my table. It was long – I signed every housing contract, I signed every little MyCiti staff card, I signed every bid form for every tender. When you start feeling as if this structure is not properly set up ... then you know it is trouble.'[37]

Moore, who felt that the organisational structure was so poorly configured that she didn't have management control over risks for which she was responsible, was faced with a terrible choice: she could stay and risk being accused of wrongdoing in a City administration gone crazy, or she could leave and maintain a reputation built on 15 years of solid public-finance work. She chose to resign.

The schizophrenia experienced by City officials trying to reconcile getting a clean audit with cutting red tape in a context of byzantine rules and regulations and a reorganisation that appeared to have left a trail of chaos clearly made their jobs very difficult. These contradictory impulses in City administration are by no means the preserve of the City of Cape Town, however. In fact, almost any local-government manager will tell you how difficult it is to reconcile delivery and compliance. Yet, in Cape Town, that tension seemed to have reached a breaking point.

Besides the staff purges and the administrative paralysis, a number of officials were concerned that the most technically qualified people weren't being appointed. Japie Hugo said that in the latest round of managerial appointments, some of the old technocrats had managed to stay, but other new appointments were clearly political.[38]

Seth Maqetuka related how De Lille had interceded regarding a director he was appointing, trying to push a young candidate who she felt would add value to the department. Maqetuka said he would look at the young man's CV – he had a bachelor's degree from the University of Cape Town (UCT), but no management experience whatsoever. Maqetuka now found himself in a tough position: the mayor clearly expected him to appoint her suggested candidate, but he was determined to resist. 'There's no way I could put a guy at a director level who I knew wasn't director material.'[39]

Maqetuka went ahead and appointed someone more suitably qualified, but he could sense that the mayor was unhappy, although she never expressed it to him directly. He thought this contributed to the undoing of the human-settlements department.

The common view among the staff was that some of the people who ended up being appointed after the restructuring launched in 2016 weren't fit for purpose, and that De Lille had used the reorganisation to appoint senior administrators who would support her and do her bidding.

While I have no axe to grind with the DA, my conversations with City officials painted a picture very different from the efficient and clean governance image that the City had been trying so hard to project. I was reminded of the Cape-Dutch-style gable above the cellars in the Groot Constantia wine estate, not far from where I grew up.

As a child, I'd been fascinated by the opulent facade depicting a chiselled boy sitting astride an eagle, pouring abundant wine from a jar for an assembly of playful putti. The relief sculpture, commissioned by the wealthy Cloete family who'd once owned Groot Constantia, had been made by a Netherlands stonemason and sculptor, Anton Anreith, who was popular in late-18th-century Cape Town. But there was a deep crack running up into the facade, and the idyllic vision seemed at risk of collapse.

The Cape Town City administration wasn't quite collapsing, but it seemed to have nonetheless become frighteningly dysfunctional, neutered by the exodus and purge of competent and experienced staff and reorganisations that had dismembered entire departments and sown confusion and paralysis of epic proportions, as well as schizophrenic expectations that administrators somehow combine an entrepreneurial spirit on the one hand and obsessive compliance with bureaucratic requirements on the other.

This was the state of the City administration as Cape Town faced its devastating water crisis.

But was this an exaggeration projected by disgruntled bureaucrats resisting change? There was one way to find out: surely dysfunction of this magnitude would affect delivery. And, unfortunately, it did. In a city saddled with a shortfall of some 350 000 units,[40] public housing in the City of Cape Town took a catastrophic plunge, from over 12 400 houses delivered in 2012/13 – before the human-settlements department was gutted by a reorganisation – to 6 681 three years later. Although the City's annual report failed to disaggregate data for 2017/18, a quick calculation suggests that fewer than a thousand units had been built that year, a number so ludicrously low that it hardly seems possible.[41] When I pointed out this discrepancy to City officials I was referred to the office of the mayoral committee for human settlements, from which I received no response.[42]

Infrastructure services – the number of new water, sanitation and electricity points – took a similarly dramatic nosedive between 2013 and 2017, before showing some signs of modest recovery in 2018.

Ironically, the administrative paralysis that had taken hold of the City administration was also hurting the very private sector that the DA leadership was so keen to encourage. When I met with Deon van Zyl, the chair of the Western Cape Property Developers Forum (WCPDF), he painted a graphic picture of how the dysfunction was affecting his industry. State-funded infrastructure and construction work is a mainstay for the industry, especially during a recession, but he estimated that some R13,2-billion worth of investment was being held up by the City, threatening to sink construction and property-development companies and putting some 2 500 construction jobs at risk.[43]

'We've got a procurement crisis here because of this audit culture,' he said, pointing out that it took 9–12 months to appoint a consultant, and anywhere up to 16 months for a contractor. 'It's a time bomb, and the time bomb is for me concerning because Cape Town is being presented as the example. And it is, when it comes to clean governance, clean pavements and so on. But what happens when this time bomb blows?'[44]

The World Bank's Doing Business service noted a significant deterioration of the efficiency in obtaining building permits in Cape Town between 2015 and 2018 – although the City still outperforms South Africa's other metros.[45] At the same time, the auditor-general reported a deterioration of financial controls.[46] And while the City managed to obtain a clean audit in 2017 – something many other metros could only dream of – irregular expenditures recorded a sharp uptick between 2016 and 2018, while debt recovery declined.[47]

The most significant deterioration, however, was in capital expenditure, which was 25% under budget. This was not good news for the City, or for the DA's claims of efficient management.

The City was still in good financial health and performing far better than other metros, but delivery was clearly deteriorating. This was no doubt enormously frustrating for the political leadership – and first among them the mayor herself. As the City's administrative wheels ground to a halt, her explosive temper, which she seemed to have largely kept in check during her early years in office, took a turn for the worse.

Yet who else but the political leadership was responsible for this carnage? And what could possibly have justified it?

5

Death by restructuring

espite having been officially locked out of the City of Cape Town's administration, I was able to enter its gates through the eyes of its victims, the casualties of its organisational machinery. This gave me a troubled perspective on the metro, but it also meant that my enquiry started from a very human place: the experience of its staff when confronted by the whirring blades of the machine.

Armed with their stories, I felt I was inside the City walls, but not the citadel itself. My immediate interest was in the mechanism and rationale that had been used to purge the housing and urban-planning staff. How had the City leaders been able to do this? And, more importantly, why had they embarked on what seemed to be a wholesale overhaul of the administration?

Patricia de Lille had co-authored a self-congratulatory book, *View from City Hall*,[1] which elaborated on the scheme to re-engineer the City administration, including its planning, financing, implementation and performance-management systems. I read the whole book in search of insights into her motivation and caught myself losing focus as the text described increasingly complicated strategies and tools such as 'systems integration linking budgeting' and 'financial releases and management visibilities.'[2] It read like a management-consultancy report with ever-increasing complexity cloaked in obscure jargon.

De Lille's co-author and the real architect of the City administration's restructuring was her chief of staff, Craig Kesson, the bright, ambitious, Oxford-educated operator whom I'd met at the gala dinner in 2018. Kesson had impressed the DA leaders around Helen Zille, especially the 'old guard' wing of the party who hailed from Democratic Party (DP) and Progressive Federal Party days, who'd 'deployed' him to the City of Cape Town in 2016 as a political minder to De Lille. His role was to ensure that De Lille, who'd only recently joined the DA ranks and was known for her fiery independence, stuck to party policy and didn't do her own thing – which must have irritated De Lille enormously. I'd encountered similar deployments of mayoral advisers in ANC-controlled cities, and their relationships with their charges were typically fractious.

A former city manager described Kesson as 'a political animal', although he felt he'd become less of a party apparatchik the longer he'd served in the administration.[3] Kesson was extremely bright and capable, which partly made up for his youth and inexperience, but he'd clearly made some enemies.

When I asked former City officials about Kesson and his restructuring, one of them exclaimed, 'Talk about hubris and arrogance! Craig is a young man without a huge depth of experience in government. Perhaps he's well intentioned, but he initiated a massive restructuring in a City that had only just stabilised from a restructuring a few years previously. It made matters worse. I'm not sure where he is now, but he has to live with the consequences.'[4]

There was ostensibly some justification for reorganising the City administration. The Cape Town metropolitan municipality had been officially created in 2000 by combining six local municipalities and one metro, which had themselves been fashioned out of some 27 white, black, coloured and Indian municipalities inherited from the apartheid era. Trying to align so many separate administrations and conditions of service had been very complex, and the process of amalgamation therefore turbulent. The deal with trade unions was that no one would lose their job, which resulted in massive duplication of functions and the persistence of separate organisational cultures.

Although by 2016 the DA had been in power in the city for a decade, De Lille and Kesson argued that the administration still lacked a unified culture. In addition, they argued that the City administration was 'designed to satisfy its internal imperatives first, and its service-delivery imperatives second.'[5] This was in line with an ideological view of public administrations as overly bureaucratic and inward-looking, when they should rather be modelled more in line with private-sector principles to better serve city residents. Even though I find that position somewhat simplistic, it's not entirely wrong: bureaucracies can always be more responsive to the people they're meant to serve, and often benefit from streamlining their own processes. During my stint in government, I experienced first-hand how frustrating and inefficient public bureaucracies can be.

De Lille and Kesson's next justification for restructuring, however, seemed far more questionable. In their book, they intended the relationship between politician and civil servant to be far more top-down than had been the case up to then. According to them, the politician – and first among them the mayor – carries the democratic mandate of the people and must therefore pull all the strings. Their argument was tied to the fact that the mayor is tasked by law to present the budget to the city council.[6]

The authors took issue with the pre-existing system in which the mayor acted on the basis of technical advice in the form of memoranda submitted by the city manager and the administration. They argued that the mayor needed to have her own policy capacity, rather than relying on the administration's, and that strategy should sit in only one place: the mayor's office. The administration's role therefore shrinks to execution, for 'the civil servant cannot initiate action without the politician's direction and sanction that it is consistent with the mandate'.[7] They didn't seem too concerned that this would divest all their highly paid and experienced senior managers of strategic thinking and initiative.

In De Lille's mayoral committee, senior officials would sit at the back while the politicians would read out decisions.

The City boasted that the mayoral committee was completely open and transparent, a place where senior officials could raise any point. In reality, all decisions were taken at a prior meeting with only the politicians present, so officials were unable to provide any input, point out blunders or mistakes, or advise against courses of action. This led to some bizarre outcomes, such as when the mayoral committee approved a rezoning of land that the owner hadn't requested.

In De Lille and Kesson's view, creating a unified administration optimally configured to deliver on the democratic mandate vested in the mayor also required a complete reorganisation of all departments and jobs. I have some sympathy for the impulse to comprehensively overhaul inefficient administration but I've also learnt that, while it has its place and time, this 'big bang' approach can have devastating effects if wielded incorrectly. Wholesale restructuring can easily turn into chaos, confusion and deconstruction.

Whittling down the pompous and lecturing prose of *View from City Hall*, the real focus seemed very simple: centralising power in the mayor's hands.

The grand plan had been set in motion soon after De Lille became mayor in 2011. All policymaking was centralised into an SPU that was established in the mayor's office. The new unit was meant to become 'a strategic centre', 'a central control point' that would provide direction, ensure that direction was being followed, and examine where course corrections were required. The new structure, headed by Kesson himself, reported directly to the mayor and the city manager, giving it both political and administrative authority.[8]

In staffing the SPU, Kesson wanted 'systems thinkers' – people who could understand complexity, as well as vast government systems and processes.

The SPU grew to a staff of approximately 60 people, who started vetting and questioning all major policy and budget decisions, even when not within their area of expertise. They were a generation of mainly white, smart but young Oxford graduates or Rhodes Scholars, whom one official described as 'prickly know-it-alls', parachuted into a complex environment and an administration already traumatised by successive waves of restructuring. Their belief in their own policy prescriptions in service to a centralising agenda, combined with their inexperience in government, succeeded in irritating and alienating civil servants, who referred to them derisively as 'the laptop boys'.[9]

The first crack team of policy analysts started working on the City's strategy and policy agenda in June 2012. Every policy had to be reviewed and, where necessary, revised or updated. A transversal management system was set up, with 'transversal objectives' given to all the managers. Each department was told about what should be regarded as strategic priorities.[10] Focused on how to better align budgets with strategy, the SPU extended its reach into what financial allocations departments were to receive, and how they were meant to prioritise projects. Even in my most authoritarian moments as a senior manager in government, I'd never dreamt of this level of control.

'You are not responsible for policy,' a senior official remembers De Lille bluntly telling her. 'We will develop the policy. You're just meant to implement it'. The manager was dumbfounded. 'I wanted to say, "Just sit me down, explain the agenda, help me understand what it is you want and what the purpose is, and let's engage, let's debate, knowing that I've got to respect what your call is, but I'm a professional to whom you pay an absolute fortune to intelligently engage." But that wasn't the message with De Lille. Instead you were expected to just shut up and listen.'[11]

Unsurprisingly, this level of micromanagement, coupled with the lack of constructive engagement with the administration around policy, infuriated staff. And rumours immediately started circulating about the true intentions behind the SPU; some described it as a politburo with commissars who would enforce ideological purity.[12]

Any policy decision had to go through the mayor's office and the SPU, which created a logjam in the mayor's office. Officials described to me how, as more and more authority was taken away from line departments and the council's portfolio committees, critical decisions weren't being made. Decisions about reallocating budget from areas of underspending, for instance, or signing off on critical construction contracts, would be snarled up in the mayor's office for weeks. 'She's centralising more and more functions under herself, and then not performing them well,' one official complained to me.[13]

In effect, the SPU became a duplicate bureaucracy – one relatively unfamiliar with public administration – which introduced mind-boggling complexity and added another layer of red tape to the City, while at the very same time the mayor and the local DA were campaigning against inefficient bureaucracy.

Having set up the SPU and overhauled policy in the City administration, Kesson and De Lille turned their attention to the human-settlements department. As with any large city, the public-housing programme consisted of a mix – informal-settlement upgrading, single government-funded RDP houses, and social housing. Meeting existing demand, however, would require years and a tenfold budget increase. Kesson and De Lille were therefore not satisfied with the existing programme and believed they could do better. They boasted about their new housing strategy, adopted in 2015, which spoke of investing more in informal settlements as well as site-and-service schemes (where the municipality supplies a plot of land with basic water, toilet and electricity, and residents are expected to build their own structure), building houses in areas of greater density closer to the city, subsidising social-housing companies to create rental units, and more community involvement.[14]

This seemed to be somewhat contradictory and unrealistic – they were advocating less spending per person, at a faster pace, while densifying on better located, more expensive land and consulting more with communities. The staff I interviewed weren't convinced that the so-called 'new' housing programme, aside from some shifts in emphasis, was any different from what was already in place.

At the same time, the strategy argued for property development led by the private sector, with the City acting more as a market enabler. With scarce budget resources, this made sense, but it still needed to be properly guided. De Lille felt that developers knew better than City officials where property development ought to take place. 'So let them lead the way,' she argued to a planning official.[15]

Unfortunately, this didn't square easily with the mayor's claims to an inclusive housing policy. While the most affordable housing was supposed to be covered by the RDP, that left a significant gap: the many residents who didn't qualify for public housing but who were considered too great a financial risk for lenders, and who therefore struggled to access the private-property market. Unless actively nudged by the administration, developers were interested only in the profitable medium to high-end segments of the property market, and letting the private sector 'lead the way' wasn't going to close that significant housing gap. And, of course, spatial integration was of little concern to developers unless it was profitable.

Nevertheless, and I suppose inevitably, De Lille and Kesson felt that the human-settlements department itself needed to be reconfigured – and its staff changed – to better align with their 'new' approach. 'We didn't want to pursue a strategy of just moving people around or changing their job descriptions, and hoping for the best,' they explained to justify the purge of the housing department's top officials.[16]

This felt like an ill-advised shortcut, based on a flawed strategy, with some clever-sounding arguments that obfuscated the real hard work required to speed up delivery and improve spatial integration. By itself, reshuffling the organogram and bringing in new faces was unlikely to deliver the desired results. This did, however, explain the wholesale cleanout of the executive director and all the directors under him.

As my conversations with each of them had revealed, they hadn't been accused of incompetence or told why they were being pushed out. There was a clear sense of hurt and rejection among the staff, who were traumatised by how they'd been treated. And the City had lost some valuable skills and experience. The disruption was catastrophic, as the collapse of public-housing delivery plainly confirmed.

The overhaul of the human-settlements department set the scene for a more ambitious and comprehensive restructuring of the City administration.

In 2015, Patricia de Lille was ready to run for a second term and she was pretty certain she would get it. Having run the city for five years, she now wanted to realign the City government to improve service delivery. According to her, the framework for how the city was to develop in the future was in place, and she could now focus on delivery and implementation. This was when she and Kesson cooked up the idea of using an existing tool to push for a more fundamental change.

The mechanism was a seemingly benign restructuring initiative called the Organisational Development and Transformation Plan (ODTP).

Every five years, municipalities put together a development strategy called an integrated development plan (IDP). This IDP is meant to spell out how they're going to achieve their objectives. These documents tend to be rather tedious, and not many councillors bother reading them. Hidden at the back of every IDP, however, is a chapter about how the local government will structure its administration to deliver on its strategy. By this stage of reading the IDP, most people have fallen asleep, and no one pays much attention to this usually bland section.

However, with the graphic stories of bullying and dismissal still in my thoughts, I sat down and read through the ODTP, interested in how and why a normally routine and benign IDP had turned into restructuring carnage.

The proposal for reform had been written into De Lille's election manifesto for Cape Town, but she hadn't waited until the election in 2016: in the latter part of 2015, the city manager, Achmat Ebrahim, had assembled a team, supposedly of the best officials representing the administration's diversity, to produce a reorganisation plan. This meant that they had been hand-picked, and were therefore likely to come up with solutions that reflected De Lille and Kesson's intentions.

Council gave the green light for developing the ODTP in late 2015. De Lille then gave Kesson and the SPU the responsibility for coordinating the development of the ODTP, adding to Kesson's already extensive powers, and in fact appearing to make him more powerful than even the city manager.

In the months leading up to the 2016 local-government elections, 66 people working in six teams put together a complex new plan that was to fundamentally restructure all the departments and posts in the organisation, and revamp lines of reporting. Overseeing this vast undertaking was a steering committee, supposedly chaired by the city manager, but in reality driven by Kesson and his staff. Kesson anticipated resistance to the exercise, but felt confident that it would succeed.[17]

The DA, with De Lille as its mayoral candidate, was elected back into power in August 2016 with an unprecedented two-thirds majority.

After the elections, De Lille extended her restructuring zeal to her own mayoral committee, in which each of the ten portfolios usually correspond to a functional area such as finance, utilities, planning and human settlements, etc. Instead, she proposed to have six mayoral committee members responsible for specific functions, and four members responsible for particular areas of the city (so-called 'mini mayors'). It was unclear who on the mayoral committee between the portfolio members and 'mini mayors' would bear political responsibility for failure to deliver in any particular area.

The DA federal executive, concerned about the proposal, appointed a task team comprised of five MPs from the national Parliament to investigate. Kesson briefed the team but was unable to clarify how the delegation of powers and duties from council to the executive would work – his reply was that the internal delegations numbered over 400 and were contained in a separate, extensive document.

In a confidential report to the party's leadership, the task team worried that there was a high potential for conflict between lines of authority; the report expressed sufficient concern to recommend that the whole restructuring exercise be closely monitored and comprehensively reviewed within six months.[18]

Unbeknown to Craig Kesson, however, the executive director in charge of transport, Melissa Whitehead, had been working in secret on her own restructuring plans, bypassing formal consultations. She would've needed access to privileged information about the restructuring in order to be able to table her alternative proposal, although it wasn't clear how she'd obtained this information. However, Whitehead had made inroads into De Lille's inner circle and won the mayor's trust.

Whitehead was a tough, driven, no-nonsense manager with a good strategic head, but she had extremely poor people skills. She'd been credited with the success of Cape Town's MyCiti bus rapid-transit system, although some claimed she'd taken the credit for work that had been mostly planned before she arrived.

Some officials painted her as a controlling bully prone to outbursts who left a trail of destruction to get her way. This echoed what I'd been told about her behaviour when she'd worked for the City of Johannesburg. Certainly, Whitehead had a tendency to stand on almost everyone's toes, unconcerned about whom she might aggrieve in her determination to get things done. While this isn't a great management style, I knew from experience that it can easily become your default if you're trying to drive programmes through an unmotivated bureaucracy. I'd probably been a bully myself during my own tenure in government.

Yet this didn't quite square with my own experience with Melissa Whitehead. I'd met her in 2011 when we were both part of a team working on dysfunctional municipalities within the ANC. Although she was clearly not a people pleaser or inclined to flexibility, she was effective, and I didn't experience her as being a bully. And when I met her again in Cape Town in 2018, she appeared rather defeated – although by then, of course, the wheel had turned dramatically against her: she was under investigation and had borrowed against her house to pay her legal fees. Having made few friends within the administration besides the mayor herself, she'd found herself isolated.

Yet, for a while, she'd seemed untouchable. Her transport department, called Transport for Cape Town, consisted of public transport, traffic control and roads. Whitehead wanted to include planning and housing functions under a much larger TDA – the very TDA whose creation had cost Japie Hugo and Catherine Stone their jobs – in order to drive an ambitious reconfiguration of the city based on transit patterns. To do this, she needed to cannibalise parts of the planning and human-settlements departments. But in the process of arrogating a whole lot of functions to herself through the formation of the TDA, she angered a lot of people.

When I spoke to local-government expert David Savage about the restructuring, he was broadly supportive of the idea of aligning public-housing delivery and land-use-control instruments with the transport strategy. 'A lot of cities are moving towards integrating those functions at a technical level,' he said. Since Whitehead was a planner by training, Savage saw the TDA as a credible way of aligning housing and transport investments with an overall spatial plan for the city.[19]

On the weekend before the council meeting that was to approve the restructuring, De Lille phoned Achmat Ebrahim and told him that there was an alternative proposal that she wanted tabled instead. The proposal that was eventually placed before council was Melissa Whitehead's, and differed fundamentally from Craig Kesson's in that it shifted a large amount of power and functions into the newly created TDA, which Whitehead would head. The council approved Whitehead's plan.

Kesson was blindsided. The vehicle for city transformation that he'd been nursing had been hijacked, and Whitehead had made a fatal enemy.

At the same time, the mayoral committee member in charge of the TDA, to whom Whitehead reported, Brett Herron, didn't get on with Kesson either. Kesson had amassed a whole lot of functions as head of probity, which weren't in the original restructuring plan, so Herron frequently took issue with him. These tensions were an ominous foreboding of what was to play out later.

Relations between SPU and TDA officials broke down, and staff reported that Whitehead had instructed them not to talk to Kesson. The promise of better integration through the TDA started to unravel.

The problem was that the City administration had now been reorganised along lines that nobody could understand. It destroyed functional areas and ways of operating that had developed over decades, and entire departments became fragmented. Stephen Boshoff, a former executive director for strategy and development, felt that instead of integrating the City government, as the mayor had intended, she'd deconstructed the administration.[20]

Frank Cumming was flabbergasted at the effect of this fragmentation. 'You can imagine the kind of complexity it introduced,' he told me. 'It's fragmented to such an extent that nobody actually knows whose function is whose.'[21]

He cited a recent report that was sitting on his desk, which related to a function that was sitting elsewhere in the organisation. 'Why am I signing this?' he wondered to himself; 'it's got nothing to do with me.'[22]

Cumming said that the uncertainty and confusion about who was responsible for what meant that whenever a manager was in doubt, he or she requested a legal opinion, which slowed down decision-making processes enormously.

On the whole, staff felt that Kesson's restructuring had made the administration slower, not faster.[23] According to a former city manager, Andrew Boraine, getting City decisions around development or private-sector partnerships had never been so slow.

Even though a few officials I talked to felt that there were solid grounds for aligning policy and establishing a strong transport-planning authority, restructuring fatigue had set in – some officials had spent the previous decade constantly tied up in restructuring initiatives. Boraine told me that the ODTP was the sixth time the City administration had been restructured since the inception of the metro in 2000.[24] Certainly, the City administration seemed trapped in a continuous cycle of reorganisation.

The current city manager, Lungelo Mbandazayo, told me that there was a lot of unhappiness among the staff over the wholesale re-engineering of the entire administration.

But the biggest casualty was the prevailing culture and ethos. The glue that holds complex organisations together, these represent the collective sense of mutual responsibility and the staff's support for each other. Previously strong in the City of Cape Town, they had been whittled away.

Jens Kuhn told me how, previously, when politicians interfered in the organisation, the staff would stand by each other and push back together. 'That's completely gone,' he said with a sad shake of the head. 'No one in the administration is going to cover for you. You're on your own. No one wants to put their head out. They say what they have to, to survive. People in the organisation are just told what to do, and are not expected to be independent decision-makers. Now, if you want cover, you must find yourself some powerful politician to protect you.'[25]

A subsequent report by (among others) the DA's chief whip in national Parliament, John Steenhuisen, concluded euphemistically that 'not all is well with the ODTP process'. The cost savings that the restructuring was supposed to deliver had apparently not materialised, and the first phase was reported to have resulted in a ballooning of the wage bill, pushing it beyond the recommended budgetary limits.[26] The DA councillors in the City complained that the reorganisation had been used as an opportunity to retrench or sideline experienced and competent officials who were seen as not completely pliant to the mayor's will.

The report described the ODTP as 'an ambitious over-reach which is seeking to extend the endless tinkering and fiddling with systems that Council has been subjected to over the last five years to a level that is causing a greater degree of institutional paralysis and service delivery delays and problems'. The report concluded that 'the system must be comprehensively re-examined'.[27]

Sadly for the officials involved and for the City itself, the damage had already been done.

The most devastating effects of the ODTP were felt at the height of the drought and the water crisis.

The City's strategic response to the crisis, the 'water resilience action plan', was developed in Craig Kesson's SPU, and then passed on to another of his creations, the central programme management unit, for implementation.

The water resilience action plan built on an earlier plan set out in De Lille and Kesson's book, separated into emergency, tactical and strategic phases. The water plan included temporary infrastructure solutions such as desalination ships and temporary wastewater recycling, as well as getting businesses and households to change consumption patterns, and changing the way that water was financed.

Unfortunately, the mayor's office had paralysed the line departments that were meant to be responding to the crisis by centralising strategic policy and redistributing functions and reporting along convoluted matrices, as well as restructuring departments – including the water unit – into utter confusion. The opinion of water officials was largely ignored and their competence overlooked. The message to the line departments was clear: 'you should not respond to this; we will do this centrally'. This alienated the executive directors for delivery departments, who sat back and said, 'Well, okay, go right ahead.'

The fragmentation ultimately revealed itself in the City's inability to finance the water response. The plan that Kesson and his team had developed came with a massive price tag, but the lack of engagement with the City treasury and the water department resulted in the plan's not being in line with the City's budget. The chief financial officer (CFO), Kevin Jacoby, who'd been involved only at a late stage, was anxious because the City was already running a deficit, and the plan was going to massively increase expenditure.

In addition, the restructuring had resulted in a curious split of functions that meant that the City treasury department couldn't easily identify the cost drivers behind water infrastructure either. Consequently, the financial models required for the water response were slow to develop.

The situation was partly ameliorated by personal interactions between Craig Kesson, executive director Gisela Kaiser, who was in charge of water, and CFO Kevin Jacoby. But that coordination didn't happen through formal structures.

David Savage was running the City Support Programme in National Treasury at the time, and was pulled in to assist the City with some of the technical work on financing water-supply solutions. Savage is super-bright and forthright, and when he's fired up about something he can intimidate and argue anyone under the table. Over a catch-up chat in a coffee shop in Cape Town, he was pretty scathing about the City's approach to solving the water crisis.[28]

The City had only started procurement for water augmentation in June 2017, when the Western Cape dams were at a dangerously low combined level of 21%,[29] and claimed that the first plants would be able to start producing by August 2017 – a ludicrous prediction for complex water-infrastructure projects.

But Savage was more worried that the metro administration was picking the wrong solutions, based on flawed assumptions that pushed the City to embrace an unnecessarily high-cost approach, which would create an immediate investment burden and land the City with heavy long-term operating costs. 'They thought that they had to invest rapidly and significantly in alternative water stuff, such as small-scale desalination plants, including shipping in barges and so forth. But that doesn't meet the first principle of water finance, which is to focus on the demand side. And if you're going to introduce new sources, you need to exploit your lowest-cost sources first.'[30]

Savage's passion and stridency can easily get people's backs up, and initially the City officials weren't receptive to the feedback. 'That was quite a difficult message for them to hear,' Savage conceded. Eventually, though, he met with the De Lille, and he said he felt quite sorry for her. 'The way the officials were communicating the story to her was as if they were try-ing to set her up. They were giving her a series of changing figures with no financial plan and a sense of almost imminent doom. She was being approached on the sides by people promising the earth but with no capabil-ity to deliver, and certainly not in the public interest. In that situation she felt completely misled.'[31]

As Savage was an independent outsider, De Lille asked him to sit down with her and reconstruct the picture from first principles. 'Within the first ten minutes, I understood that this wasn't a technical issue,' he said. 'It was predominantly a leadership and communication issue.'[32]

The centralisation insulated the mayor from technical expertise, which, ironically, left her unsupported when faced with a crisis.

6

Factory flaw

~~~

Looking into the innocent-sounding ODTP, I was struck by the dev-astating impact of the wholesale reorganisation of line departments. Patricia de Lille had managed to centralise a lot of power in the mayor's office – and destabilise the administration in the process. What had made this possible? Had the seeds been planted before she became mayor?

Part of the answer lies in the local-government system itself, and the powers that the legislation gives to executive mayors. The mayor is the head of the executive in local government and accounts to council as the legislative oversight body.

I bore some responsibility for introducing the idea of executive mayors in the late 1990s when I was a senior civil servant in charge of regulating local-government matters. Back then, mayors were largely ceremonial, and the real power vested in town clerks as administrative heads governed by an executive committee composed of councillors appointed by political parties in proportion to their representation in council. The idea of executive mayors, inspired by the US style of city governance, was a way of introducing dynamic, strategic leadership into ossified, apartheid-era bureaucracies.

The South African constitution didn't allow for directly elected mayors, but government did set out to enhance executive powers. For instance, executive mayors could appoint a mayoral committee, which was meant to function a bit like the president's cabinet in national government. All the work of council portfolio committees would flow through the mayoral committee and the mayor, before being presented to council for decision. Mayors were responsible for tabling the annual budget to council, which gave them enormous power over budgetary decisions.

In 1997, when I appeared in Parliament to present the legislation creating the option of executive mayors, the opposition DP (the forerunner of the DA) rubbished the concept as an inappropriate importation. Ironically, they were concerned that the model of executive mayors would allow the ANC to massively centralise political power in municipalities, instead of working through the more collegial multiparty executive committee.

Cape Town formally adopted the executive-mayor system when the ANC took control of the Western Cape province in 2004, and when the DA unseated the ANC in 2009, the system was retained.

When Helen Zille was mayor and the DA headed a coalition of political parties, however, the city council seemed to operate in a fairly collegial way, conducting most of its business through established committees. For her part, De Lille fully embraced the executive-mayor model when she came into office, and argued that if the mayor was meant to fulfil her role as the chief adviser to, and leader of, the city council, she needed capacity to do so.

Besides the centralising door that the law itself opened, part of the problem was also that, since the inception of the metro, the role of the city manager had been downplayed. As head of the administration, the city manager is supposed to steer the ship, while the mayor focuses on being the political leader. But in Achmat Ebrahim, De Lille had inherited a pliant city manager, initially appointed by Helen Zille, who played more of an administrative and compliance role than a strategic-leadership one – which in fact suited the political leadership, who wanted to drive strategy themselves. So in De Lille's time, the centralisation of power within the office of the mayor was in part a response to the vacuum left by the city manager – a vacuum for which an earlier DA administration was responsible.

Without strong leadership from the city manager, however, the departments under him became much more insular. As David Savage remarked, 'When you take the centre away, you're going to harden the borders of the silos.' Savage thought that stripping the city manager of strategic coordination and centralising it in the mayor's office was intrinsically flawed, because the administration would become unable to self-coordinate or assert itself in relation to the political sphere: if the political leadership destabilised for any reason, the administration wouldn't be able to insulate itself from the storm and stay the course.[1] In other words, this would significantly weaken the administrative machinery and make it far more vulnerable to political ebbs and flows – which unfortunately is exactly what happened.

I also wondered to what extent the previous mayor, Helen Zille, had laid down the template for later centralisation under De Lille. The officials I spoke to had mixed views about this. Stephen Boshoff pointed out that it was Zille who'd started the practice of creating an office around herself – although during her tenure this was limited to about eight staff who were mostly former journalists, focused on strategic communications and building Zille's image.[2]

When she first got into City Hall, after several years of ANC rule, Helen Zille seemed to distrust the administration to some extent. She replaced the city manager and other senior administrators – perhaps she felt that she couldn't fully trust the incumbent senior officials, or perhaps this was part of her ideological makeup, her sense that public-sector bureaucracies are inefficient machines that couldn't be trusted to deliver. Zille was determined to create a model of good governance that would be a shining beacon when compared to some poorly run and corrupt ANC administrations.

This would allow the DA to solidify its hold on the Western Cape electorate. Boshoff jokingly referred to Zille as 'the queen, the great white queen, the white hope'.[3]

She also did bring a very hands-on leadership style to City Hall. Lungelo Mbandazayo, who worked under her, felt she micromanaged the administration but with good results. 'Helen always gets things done,' Mbandazayo said. 'She is not the person to just refer you to someone else. She will always follow up. She doesn't leave you in the lurch. If you want something done, she will follow up until she gets what she wants. I didn't have a problem with that.'[4]

This hands-on, get-it-done attitude was in line with the Helen Zille I remembered. Back in the 1980s, when I was involved in the ECC, various church and peace organisations had joined the call to end mandatory military service. These organisations included the Black Sash, which ran advice offices for black people being victimised by petty apartheid laws. One of the Black Sash women with whom I worked on the ECC was Zille, back then an outspoken liberal journalist. She struck me as highly principled and hardworking, even though she didn't like the ideology of the ANC and its internal allies, such as the UDF.

I benefited first hand from Zille's steely determination during my stint in jail in December 1986, when she campaigned for the release of those of us who'd been arrested for organising an ECC event during the country-wide state of emergency. And while we were behind bars, the Black Sash made sure we were legally represented and properly fed.

I had some trouble reconciling the warm and engaging young woman I recalled with the hardnosed, somewhat shrill public image that she later projected as a national politician, but when I visited her in the Western Cape provincial premier's office in November 2018, she was as personable and warm as I remembered her to be. After she had walked me into her office, greeting the security guards and support staff on the way, we

81

reminisced a bit about our struggle days, and later she couldn't resist sharing photos of her two sons and her 2-year-old granddaughter.

When I advanced that she'd micromanaged the administration when she was mayor, she didn't disagree – but she also suggested that she'd known better than anyone in the administration how to run the city. In this, she was perhaps similar to Patricia de Lille.

Suzette Little, a DA councillor who worked with both mayors, argued that they have much in common. 'She and Pat are genuinely the same person. You can't control them; they will achieve whatever they put their minds to.'[5] Little was equally fond of both women for being dynamic, driven and feisty.

Nevertheless, according to officials who worked with both mayors, Helen Zille appeared to have relied on the City administration for support much more than Patricia de Lille did, and had been willing to listen to civil servants on technical issues. Most argued that Zille didn't really centralise the administration: she respected the existing system of delegations and didn't spend much time trying to reorganise the institution.

Seen through the eyes of officials who worked with her, Zille came across as hardworking, prone to micromanagement and on occasion abrasive, but fair. Officials felt that they could engage and even disagree with her. Catherine Stone told me that Zille flew off the handle a few times, but that afterwards she was still able to have coffee with her, and if she could present a coherent technical rebuttal, Zille had the grace to say 'you're right'.[6]

Lungelo Mbandazayo said that Zille didn't work through hierarchies, and if she wanted to speak to someone, she would phone them directly.[7] She was driven by solving problems – directly if necessary.

She also gave business leaders and communities direct access to her, which meant that issues didn't work their way through the system in a traditional way. Stephen Boshoff called it a very 'knee-jerk' administration, which had its pros and cons.[8]

So despite being leaders from the same political party and sharing some personality traits, it appears that Zille and De Lille were very different in their approach. Zille was pragmatic and had no interest in any grand re-engineering of the administration. She might not have fully trusted the City administration and often thought she knew best, but she seemed more willing to listen. And although I couldn't find any definitive indication that she sought to amass power in her office, her overbearing and micromanaging tendency might nonetheless have laid some basis for De Lille to embark on her centralising mission.

But this wasn't the first time the DA had been in power in the City, and an earlier period of interference had perhaps also contributed to the situation.

Back in 2000, the DA had won a majority in the first elections for the newly established Cape Town Metropolitan Municipality. Their mayoral candidate, Pieter Marais, was a colourful politician who'd served in the discredited apartheid-era tricameral Parliament. Marais' candidature had come about as a result of an opportunistic merger between the New National Party (NNP, the rebranded version of the NP that had ruled during apartheid, to which Marais had hitched his wagon) and the Democratic Party (dating from 1989, although the party existed under other labels throughout the apartheid years, when it was the Parliamentary opposition to the ruling NP's policies) to form the Democratic Alliance as a solid opposition block to the ANC. This strategy proved successful in Cape Town, giving the DA a narrow majority on the council. (Because of a legal technicality, the NNP and the DP remained separate entities nationally in order to preserve their Parliamentary seats.)

The Cape Town metro had only recently been created, and there was an enormous amount of reorganisation to be done. A powerful corporate centre was set up to manage this process, and top officials were seconded to it, under the overall leadership of Ben Kieser, who was head of the legal section. According to Victoria Johnson, a former city official turned whistleblower, Kieser was 'ambitious and strongly politically connected, primarily on the NNP side of the DA, and was intolerant of those standing in his way'.[9] Kieser was good at his job, and quickly became a key player in the mayor's inner circle, although the top management structure of the City hadn't yet been appointed, and it would take some time before this was finalised. This initiated a pattern of political apparatchiks cutting across traditional structures, which was to be repeated later on a much grander scale.

As one of his initial projects, the mayor wanted Adderley Street and Wale Street renamed after Nelson Mandela, the first president of democratic South Africa, and FW de Klerk, the last president of the apartheid government. De Klerk's nomination was contentious, as not many black people considered him someone to celebrate, even if he had peacefully handed over power to the ANC. Unfortunately for the mayor, when the proposal was advertised for public comments, the overwhelming public response was therefore negative.

As objections flooded in, the mayor's spokesman, Johan Smit, announced that 500 letters of support were about to arrive.[10] In response to a staff comment that this made the public participation a farce, Kieser had said that the renaming would be pushed through regardless of objections. 'Fuck the public,' he said; 'it's going ahead, no matter what.'[11]

On the last day before the comment period closed, Smit handed in the almost 500 pledges of support, allegedly saying, 'This is how you win elections.'[12]

On closer examination, the letters had similar handwriting. In addition, the staff processing the public comments were instructed straight from the mayor's office to categorise the letters in ways that would obscure the number of objections.

The *Mail & Guardian* ran a story alleging fraud in the street-renaming process – it seemed that someone high up in the DA had leaked the information as part of an internal political battle. Staff were bullied and intimidated to prevent further details getting out.

Eventually, an independent enquiry found evidence of fraud and recommended that the matter be reported to the police. Smit and Kieser faced disciplinary enquiries during which all the facts of the street renaming came to light. Smit's contract had already lapsed and wasn't renewed, and Kieser resigned before he could be dismissed.[13]

The DA proceeded to expel Marais from the party, but the mayor launched a court challenge, which resulted in his being reinstated – a few hours after which, having served barely a year as Cape Town's inaugural mayor, Marais resigned, and the NNP left the coalition with the DA to join the ANC.[14]

This unhappy saga that unfolded in the opening years of the new millennium ended the DA's first experiment with political power in the city, ushering in a fractious period of ANC rule under mayor Nomaindia Mfeketo which succeeded in alienating ANC voters, especially in the coloured community.

The parallels with the DA's internecine battle while De Lille was mayor, which led to another political split, were striking. What the saga revealed was a penchant for centralised control to suit a political agenda, as well as for a climate of fear and secrecy, which somewhat echoed De Lille's misguided reorganisation.

Yet it was also a story of outright dishonesty and hubris.

Were these elements to be found as well in the current administration? I wondered whether there were perhaps more parallels to be made.

7

Where angels fear to tread

∿∿∿

'This is what happens when bad development decisions are made,' said John, a retired Capetonian I encountered collecting plastic waste while walking along Bloubergstrand in September 2018.

This, the West Coast, was the most beautiful open stretch of coast north of Cape Town, with a picture-perfect view across Table Bay to the city centre, cradled like a jewel between Table Mountain, Lion's Head and Devil's Peak. Robben Island, where Nelson Mandela was incarcerated for 18 of the 27 years he spent in jail, floats like an ominous mirage on the horizon. The kilometres of windswept coastal plain continue northwards, past Koeberg nuclear-power station, past the desolate apartheid settlement of Atlantis, all the way to Saldanha Bay and the birding paradise of Langebaan lagoon.

Marring the landscape was a breeze heavy with the smell of sewage. 'Where is it coming from?' I asked John, who was busy putting plastic waste into a refuse bag.

'I've lost count of the number of sewage spills in this area,' he said. 'There are at least ten that I counted in the last few years, but the people who've lived there from the start say it's always been like this.'

My new friend pointed to the extensive new development alongside us,

Big Bay, which he said was the cause of the problems. 'When the development was planned in the 1990s, the environmentalists were up in arms about developing in such an environmentally sensitive area, and the City's planners pointed out that there wasn't sufficient bulk-sewerage capacity. But then the politicians were corrupted by the developers, and the property development was pushed through.' A decade later, the development had predictably resulted in environmental degradation and concerns about human health.[1]

According to the City's own assessment, the persistent sewage leaks, illegal pumping of leaked sewage water into the stormwater system, and poor management of the retention ponds were 'hazardous to human health'.[2] Seepage onto the dunes had caused the beach to lose its Blue Flag status – a sought-after certification granted by the international Foundation for Environmental Education for meeting its stringent standards for quality and safety.

'This is the social and environmental consequence of corruption in property deals,' said my new acquaintance.

My interest was sufficiently piqued that I read up on the development. The Big Bay corruption scandal had tarnished both the ANC and NNP in the early 2000s.

Big Bay sits on the Bloubergstrand coastline, with the most incredible views across Table Bay. It was prime development land but environmentally sensitive, which required proper controls to avoid devastating consequences. The Blaauwberg municipality also lacked sufficient bulk-sewerage capacity to service new developments.

In 1999, the year before the amalgamation of municipalities into the Cape Town metro, the NNP-controlled Blaauwberg Local Municipality appointed a consortium known as Rabcav, comprising Rabie Property Developers and the Cavcor Property Group, to facilitate the development of the municipality's landholdings as a public-private partnership. They drew up a new development plan for the Big Bay area, which included a hotel, houses and an entertainment and commercial node in an area that had originally been earmarked for public amenities and dune conservation.

I spoke to an environmental expert who'd looked into this deal, who said the development should never have been approved. He was highly critical of the environmental impact assessment, which was done by a consultant who'd been doing a lot of work for the provincial department.[3] Officials had complained about pressure from NNP politicians in the province and the municipality.

In 2001, environmental authorisation for the development was granted by the provincial government, then controlled by an alliance of the NNP and the DP, against the advice of its own environment department's officials and legal adviser. The legal adviser's memorandum subsequently went missing from the files.

Independent consultants who subsequently reviewed the province's environmental-impact assessment of the Big Bay development were surprised by the 'extreme lenience' shown to the developers.[4] When an appeal was lodged against the environmental authorisation, the conditions were further softened by David Malatsi, the provincial minister in charge of environment and planning – who was, in 2006, convicted of corruption and sentenced to five years in jail for accepting a R100 000 payment in 2002 from the developer of Plettenberg Bay's Roodefontein Golf and Country Estate to approve the development, despite concerns. Malatsi also ignored the provincial planning advisory board's recommendation that the development plan for Big Bay be substantially amended.

This sequence of seemingly irrational decisions made sense when the NNP chair of the City of Cape Town's Blaauwberg subcouncil, George Mellet, reported in a party caucus meeting that the Rabcav consortium had made a 'substantial' donation to the NNP. 'We're among friends here,' he reportedly said.[5] Mellet subsequently sidelined the City's officials altogether on Big Bay, and dealt directly with the provincial planners and the developers.

Gerald Morkel, the provincial premier from 1998 to 2001, had a close association with John Rabie: the property developer had sold him land in Westlake at a substantial discount and had also contributed some R100 000 towards his legal fees.[6]

John Rabie, the head of Rabie Property Developers, claimed that his company donated to all political parties, and that no specific financial contribution had been made to the NNP as part of the deal. The NNP's financial records were mysteriously destroyed.

The scandal washed over into the administration of Nomaindia Mfeketo, the ANC mayor who took over City Hall in 2002. Mfeketo found herself hamstrung by a bitter ANC factional battle pitting an Africanist wing (of which she was part) against the ANC provincial chair and subsequent premier (from 2004 to 2008), Ebrahim Rassool. Weakened and controlled from the provincial party headquarters, Mfeketo started bringing in dubious political advisers who quickly established patronage networks on the back of existing irregular deals.

The ANC mayor was excoriated for selling 14,5 hectares in Big Bay to 17 black-empowerment companies at a major discount and without open tender. Following a public outcry, the sale was scrapped, and the tender process restarted. Rabcav recommended approving a R147-million bid from Irish-owned Earthquake, which Mfeketo rejected in favour of a R115-million tender from empowerment consortium Jonga Entabeni headed by Tokyo Sexwale. Under an ANC government in the City, it seemed that the financial interests behind the deal were being reconfigured. Tokyo Sexwale was to emerge as a player in some of the later property deals linked to De Lille.[7]

Big Bay wasn't the only controversial development, however. Not far from the beach where I'd met John, closer to Koeberg nuclear-power station, lay a more recent (and failed) property development known as Wescape. Wescape had been one of the projects about which City planners such as Catherine Stone and her boss, Japie Hugo, had raised concerns, and which had ultimately contributed to their demise.

I was advised by an investigative journalist to look at the development. 'Wescape was the first real sign that something was wrong in the De Lille administration,' she'd said. 'It laid down a template for what happened in later developments in places like Philippi.'[8]

Now I was more than intrigued.

Wescape was meant to be a massive development of 200 000 units built on 3 100 hectares of farmland, a mini-city of some 800 000 people about 25 kilometres north of the city and 11 kilometres south of Atlantis. A large proportion of the units was supposed to be affordable housing,[9] which would address almost a quarter of the housing backlog in the city. This is what initially attracted De Lille to the project soon after her election as mayor in May 2011.

When I met with Gita Goven, the chair of communiTgrow, one of the Wescape developers, she argued that such developments were the only viable way to accommodate the massive growth in Cape Town's population expected over the next few decades. According to her, lengthy application processes meant that multiple small developments on vacant or underused land in the city itself – known as infill development – were impractical; in any case, she argued, the cost of land in the city centre was prohibitive. This was compounded by ageing and under-capacitated infrastructure.

'I've been involved in doing low-income development projects for 30 years, and it's been an uphill battle to unlock inner-city land that's afford-able to people who really need housing,' Goven explained.[10] As a result, she'd found it virtually impossible to overcome spatial segregation in the city. The West Coast was the only realistic future growth path for the city, she said, and jobs would be created in the construction and servicing of the development.

Logical as it sounded, this view was disputed by a number of planning experts. They countered that infill development closer to the city centre, while difficult to achieve, could be done, and that densification and spatial integration should remain the priority for the City.[11] The higher costs of infill development, they advanced, were offset by lower servicing and transport costs, as well as economies of scale in social facilities, greater access to work opportunities, and business benefits from agglomeration effects. In addition, the City could further facilitate spatial integration and infill development by repurposing publicly owned land closer to the city centre, scaling up the subsidised rental-housing stock and requiring that a portion of new property developments in affluent areas be earmarked for affordable housing.

These planning experts also questioned the developers' argument that the comparatively more affordable land up the West Coast would draw additional investment: nearby Atlantis, one of the apartheid era's 'deconcentration' nodes aimed at shifting black people away from urban areas, had no shortage of cheap and vacant industrial land, but had managed to attract only 1,2% of investment in Cape Town between 2005 and 2012. If Wescape failed, it would leave Cape Town with another remote and economically dependent dormitory town.[12]

Besides the dubious catalytic-investment argument, the proposed Wescape development was in a nuclear-evacuation zone. Given its proximity to Koeberg nuclear-power station, there were worries about whether the emergency-evacuation plan could be implemented – the Fukushima Daiichi nuclear disaster of 2011, when a tsunami flooded the emergency generators resulting in a coolant loss that led to three nuclear meltdowns, and the fact that it had taken Japan a week to evacuate 100 000 people from the prefecture, was still fresh in everyone's memory.

Further objections included the loss of agricultural land and beautiful landscape – the proposed development also fell outside the urban edge, which defines the city's limits and stops urban sprawl. In addition, the massive bulk infrastructure required for the project, the cost of which was estimated at R1,5 billion, would tie up the City's budget for years. And the rail and transport connections were inadequate, which risked leaving Wescape residents without easy access to the city.[13]

Finally, the development would be managed outside of City control. The main property developer in the consortium behind the project, David Lee Pearson, claimed that the company would control everything that happened in the 31-square-kilometre area: 'Every business activity needs our approval. We control everything, even the utility company.'[14]

Jens Kuhn had scoffed at this. 'In the back of their mind was the idea that they could run this thing like a security estate, like a private little town where they had full control of the body corporate, maybe even ownership. That was never going to work,' he said.[15]

Yet the developer submitted an application to amend the City's urban edge and Cape Town Spatial Development Framework (CTSDF) in October 2011, just after De Lille first became mayor.[16] After advertising the proposal for public comment, the City recorded 13 objections, including from Eskom, the National Nuclear Regulator, and the City departments in charge of emergency services, utilities, environmental resource management and city parks.[17] Besides the project's obvious location and infrastructure flaws, the proposal lacked sufficient detail[18] and many City planners were therefore against it.[19]

Patricia de Lille, however, said she was 'excited' about the huge development, which she believed would 'unlock opportunities',[20] and she pushed hard for it to go through, against overwhelming opposition from almost all the City administration's technical departments.

A large team of officials was assembled to engage with the developers, which raised eyebrows. The City's then mayoral committee member for energy, environment and spatial planning, Johan van der Merwe, defended the creation of the joint team, saying that this was done for all developments in the city.[21]

The City's spatial-planning and land-use management directorates within the planning department assessed the development application, and recommended rejecting it. In August 2012, Japie Hugo and the new mayoral committee member for his portfolio, Belinda Walker, signed off on these conclusions, which were then sent to council.

The council's economic, environment and spatial planning portfolio committee, which was tasked to review the recommendation, met in November 2012. Based on the minutes, the discussion on Wescape appears to have been astonishingly one-sided.[22] None of the concerns and objections raised by the City's own officials and members of the public was dealt with, and the discussion focused entirely on the need to address the city's housing backlog. A city can have multiple development nodes, it was argued, and Wescape was the logical direction in which the City of Cape Town had to expand.

Members of the portfolio committee stated that the City's departments in charge of health, economic development, roads, stormwater and solid waste hadn't objected to the development. What they failed to mention was that some of these departments *had* initially objected, but had withdrawn their opposition under political pressure. Nor did they mention the crucial objections raised by other City entities and departments.

Ignoring the recommendation of the City administration's own experts, the portfolio committee recommended to the city council that the spatial-development framework, which set out the urban edge, be amended to accommodate the project.

But portfolio committee members hedged their bets by also asking for a legal opinion, as well as more details on the development's operational viability and next stages.[23] They also requested further investigation into the Koeberg evacuation zone, the financing of the bulk infrastructure, the public-transport arrangements, and whether the economic growth and job numbers were credible.

It goes without saying that all of these issues should have been investigated prior to the agreement to amend the urban edge for the development project.

De Lille, however, overruled the caveats of the portfolio committee, recommending that the city council support the application to amend the urban edge without any conditions – which the council duly did in December 2012.[24]

Fortunately for Cape Town, the development then ran into financial trouble. The first problem was the principal character behind the development, David Lee Pearson, a mercurial, persuasive businessman – and a fraud. Supposedly a Buddhist, he regularly pitched up at important meetings dressed in a caftan. But he was also exposed as a delinquent borrower who lied about what he owned or controlled, and who'd taken large sums from private investors and not repaid his debts.[25]

Pearson's modus operandi was to channel his dealings through myriad companies, which closed down or vanished every time he felt some heat from lenders or investors. In 2015, he was taken to court by Absa after having failed to pay back over R3 million to the bank, and then he defaulted again on the settlement agreement.

On 18 January 2016, the executive of the consortium behind Wescape eventually decided that 'Mr Pearson should no longer be involved in Wescape, although he is still completely committed to seeing Wescape become a reality'.[26]

And there were broader concerns about the finances of the project itself. Japie Hugo thought that Wescape never had any real money behind it.

The developers didn't actually own any of the land; they had simply taken options to purchase the land if the development came off. And most of the consultants they'd hired had worked at risk, and would earn fees only if the development proceeded. 'It was just a lot of hot air,' Hugo said.[27]

Frank Cumming, who'd been in charge of several property developments for the City, was apoplectic when I asked him about Wescape. Two of the original four parties behind the development had gone insolvent. 'On what basis would the mayor elect to approve this massive scheme when the development partner has no substance?' he asked.[28]

The development ran into further trouble when Eskom and the National Nuclear Regulator, whose views on the nuclear-evacuation zone hadn't been considered, challenged the city council and Western Cape province's decisions in court. (At the time the planning legislation vested the final decision to amend the urban edge with the province.)

The City leadership started to backtrack. In an affidavit, De Lille denied that the City had taken a decision to amend the urban edge: council, she said, had merely made a recommendation to the provincial minister.[29]

The Constitutional Court, meanwhile, issued a very significant ruling on land-use-planning powers: provincial governments could not take decisions that rightly belonged to the municipality. This curtailed provincial authorities' frequent involvement in property-development decisions, although they still wielded power through environmental and heritage considerations.

The momentum behind Wescape ground to a halt.

At the time of writing, I understand that Eskom was still litigating around the new CTSDF and its lack of provision for protecting the nuclear-evacuation zone.

The last communication I was able to find from the consortium behind Wescape dated back to 2016, and the last post on their Facebook page[30] is even older, dated January 2014.

The hype around and public profile of the development have turned into a distant memory.

The Wescape saga raises a number of questions. Why, for this project, did the City's political leadership ride roughshod over the technical advice of officials and the recommendations of Belinda Walker, the member of the mayoral committee?

There may be times when development needs a bit of push to get through the complications that bureaucracies tend to create. It may well be that De Lille's decision to back the development was originally motivated by a genuine concern over the housing backlog – even if the project would have done little for spatial integration. But in this case, the warning lights flashing from multiple quarters must surely have alerted politicians that the project was deeply problematic.

The financial dealings behind Wescape – empty promises, false declarations of assets and value, unpaid debts – speak to financial practices that could easily have extended into other areas. The facts didn't add up, and there appeared to be other factors at play.

Even though the project stalled, what Wescape appeared to do early in the De Lille administration was lay down a template for political behaviour that was to have even more disastrous consequences in other developments. The real casualties were to be the officials who'd proffered their advice, and the planning tools such as the urban edge that they administered.

Unfortunately, Wescape was not an isolated case.

8

The promised land

〽️

'Just look at this land!'

Farmer Nazeer Sonday waved at harmonious rows of deep-green vegetables on a large flat and sandy area in Philippi, southeast of the Cape Town city centre. 'It's a special place to be farming in a time like this.'

In spite of the drought that was gripping the Western Cape at the time, Sonday's crops were thriving on water drawn from the aquifer beneath the land. The proximity of the aquifer to the surface is the key to the agricultural productivity of the area, and the farming land in turn is an important recharge zone for the aquifer. Said Sonday, 'Our land is valuable for us as farmers, but it's also very valuable for Cape Town and all its citizens. We supply the city with 200 000 tons of vegetables a year, and we're the guardians of the Cape Flats Aquifer, which has enough water in it to supply the city with 30% of its water needs.'[1]

Prodded by what I'd found out about Big Bay and Wescape, I'd set out to look into other property projects. The single greatest flashpoint had been in the Philippi Horticultural Area (PHA), where two deals in particular stood out. I was hoping that Sonday could assist me to understand what had gone wrong and why.

It was August 2018, and I'd driven through dismal, dusty and rundown suburbs on the Cape Flats to visit Sonday's farm and take a tour of his lands. Standing in the middle of his fields wearing his trademark leather hat, shorts and boots, Sonday fretted that the farming area was under severe threat.

The PHA is one of the last few large pieces of land in the Cape still unbuilt, and both communities and developers had been eyeing it out for housing and development purposes. Sonday observed that the very authorities who were meant to be protecting the area were colluding with developers. 'If you look at all the decisions made by the City and by the province in the last ten years, then you can see how they're just steadily trying to turn this land over to developers.'[2]

In 2012 Sonday had organised small-scale farmers and various civil-society organisations into the PHA Food & Farming Campaign. This followed the success of the nearby Princess Vlei Forum in halting City plans to commercialise a large public space next to the PHA and forcing a reluctant City administration to collaborate with them on the development and improvement of the area.

The Princess Vlei Forum acted as a spur to the farmers and agricultural community in Philippi to build a 50-strong coalition of organisations to campaign against the multiple developments that were slowly whittling away the remaining agricultural land. 'We feel we're under severe pressure in the PHA in protecting our area. I spend half my time having to fight to be able to keep this area alive. I would much rather be farming. But in order to keep farming, I have now become a fulltime activist,' said Sonday.

He thought that De Lille was fanatically pushing two particular property deals in the PHA, and the Food & Farming Campaign's attempts to convince her otherwise had been disastrous. 'I'll never talk to those farmers again,' the mayor had allegedly said at one stage. 'When they came to see me, they had dirt under their fingernails and dirt on their shoes. They were rude to me.'[3]

Sonday was perplexed: 'What does she think farmers do?'

Philippi has for decades been the forgotten suburb of Cape Town, bounded by the arterial Lansdowne and Strandfontein roads and Vanguard Drive, and pressed in on by the large informal settlements of Crossroads to the north, Weltevreden Valley to the southwest, and Philippi East to the east. As a place of refuge from apartheid policies and political repression, Philippi has been under serious pressure from competing land uses.[4]

When farms in Mitchells Plain were bulldozed in the 1970s to make way for the new township, many of the farmworkers moved to Philippi. Other people also fled to Philippi as they were forced out of 'white' areas during the apartheid Group Areas Act removals. And economic refugees from apartheid's failed 'bantustans' (ten 'independent homelands' set aside for black inhabitants of South Africa) had also flocked in, and invasions on unused land became commonplace.

The smallholder farming area to the west known as the PHA, a food-production area established 150 years ago by German settlers, stands within this pressurised area.[5] The PHA was granted protection in 1967 by being designated as a horticultural area within the Cape Town guide plan (an early form of spatial plan in terms of the Physical Planning Act). Much of the land is farmed, but some parts have become degraded due to illegal land use and rubble dumping (according to Sonday, a result of deliberate neglect by the City) and increasingly expanding informal settlements. The area has also suffered from steady inroads over the years; in the 1970s Philippi East was rezoned from farming to industrial use and became an industrial node.

Eight studies, some conducted by the City itself, have confirmed the area's importance in terms of food security, agricultural production and protection of the Cape Flats Aquifer, and highlighted its social and cultural significance.[6] A 2009 report concluded that the PHA was critical in addressing the City's food insecurity, and offered 'far more to the City than can be quantified in terms of land, housing and other value assertions'.[7] Another study, from 2012, highlighted the importance of the Cape Flats Aquifer as a source of water for the city, and how developing the area and paving it would prevent rainwater from being absorbed into the soil, which in turn would threaten the aquifer. It recommended that the urban edge be clearly defined, and the PHA secured as an agricultural area.[8]

Sonday was very worried about two developments that were threatening the PHA. Back at his home, he rolled out a map and showed me how the original footprint of the PHA had been eroded, as well as the projected impact of the proposed developments. In the southeast quadrant of the PHA, 472 hectares of land had been earmarked for a development called Oakland City, which would include some 30 000 houses and a privately run prison. In the southwest quadrant, another 280 hectares were targeted for more upmarket housing and retail and a private school, driven by a company called Multi Spectrum Property (MSP). Philippi had also been identified to become a central node in the city's transport network, with six bus-rapid-transit routes intersecting at a major station.

With Sonday's assistance and some excellent investigative journalism from the *Daily Maverick*,[9] I was able to build up a detailed picture of what happened in each of these developments. I was flabbergasted by what I found.

For the Oakland City project, pension funds had been hoodwinked to invest on the basis of inflated land prices. Yet provincial and City authorities seemed to have pushed hard to move the controversial project forward.

The main character behind the development, Wentzel Oaker, was a controversial Cape Town businessman who had used his links to trade unions to advance various schemes, including buying out a textile and clothing company as a 'business rescue' and then asset-stripping and liquidating the factory. In the case of Oakland City, Oaker had bought 472 hectares of agricultural land in the PHA for R36 million in 2007, and then repackaged it as an 'investment opportunity' for six retirement funds linked to trade unions at a 'discounted price' of R260 million – a scheme that involved a confusing number of entities and a dodgy financial structure. In addition to the further capital they were required to 'invest', between them, the retirement funds sunk R519 million in the development – long before any development rights were granted or any construction took place.[10]

Oaker then set about acquiring the required development rights, which involved getting the agricultural designation of the land changed, the CTSDF amended and, finally, the land rezoned. This was a standard sequence of approvals required for any development in the PHA. The first two steps involved changes to policy and didn't confer any development rights, which were only finally given when the land was rezoned.

Despite opposition from the national minister for Agriculture and the City of Cape Town, the DA's provincial minister in charge of planning,[11] Anton Bredell, excised Oaker's land from the PHA by amending the CTSDF in May 2011.[12]

The only positive element was that Bredell then drew a line around the rest of the PHA, saying that it needed to be preserved at all costs. This line was crucial, as it constituted the basis on which City officials were to reject subsequent development applications. Despite this, however, the PHA has continued to be whittled down, from its original 3 000 hectares to 1 900 hectares as of April 2018.

Proceeds of the deal – some R200 million – were then taken out of the scheme by Oaker as 'profits'. The pension funds were sufficiently alarmed to trigger an investigation by the Financial Services Board (FSB), which concluded that the whole deal constituted 'an unlawful (unregistered) collective investment scheme business'.[13] In addition to the R200 million he'd pocketed at the stroke of a pen, Oaker had been earning a 2% commission on the value of the development. The ruse had involved a steady increase in the valuation of the properties – the last valuation before the FSB intervened stood at R981 million, inflating the value of the land by over 2 000%. A further R300 million had been lost through other entities and dubious financial accounting.

Two of Oaker's entities, Rockland Asset Management and Consulting and Rockland Targeted Development Investment Fund, were placed under FSB curatorship in August 2012, and this was extended to another entity in 2013. After liquidating Oaker's entities and putting the development under the control of the retirement funds, the curator appointed by FSB was able to recover 80% of the funds.[14]

The pension funds and the curator were determined to continue with the development in order to make good on a bad investment. On the back of Bredell's decision, they lodged a rezoning application with the City in 2011. De Lille was now in power, and, unlike her predecessor, Zille, she seemed to be fully behind the Oakland City project. De Lille may have been genuinely trying to favour the union-linked pension funds in her efforts to bolster her political constituency.

When the rezoning application was discussed between the developer and City officials, promises were made around affordable housing and the rezoning went through remarkably smoothly. But when the planning department tried to hold the developers to their affordable-housing commitments, the spatial planning and land-use management committee said they couldn't do this. There may have been technical reasons for this, but it didn't make sense if the City's purpose in supporting the development was to promote access to affordable housing.

The PHA Food & Farming Campaign appealed against the rezoning decision, but lost in June 2017. The reasons given included that the proposed development 'align(ed) with the principles in, and contribute(d) to, achieving objectives set out in the Integrated Development Plan, Economic

Growth Strategy and Social Development Strategy', and that the property was located within the urban edge – in other words, it was no longer part of the PHA in terms of planning law.[15]

Nevertheless, the pension funds are now trying to sell the land and exit the project, which they no longer consider as financially viable.[16] Many developers seem to agree, as there's apparently only one buyer interested: Wentzel Oaker. Oaker's latest move appears to be trying to sell the land to the Housing Development Agency, a national public-sector body that acquires and develops land for human settlements, on land where the water table is too high for gap housing (a higher water table can be dealt with but it makes the development more expensive, not suitable for lower income brackets).

When reporters asked Brett Herron, then mayoral committee member in charge of transport and urban development, why the City had continued to support the development, he replied that once the Western Cape province had decided to excise the land from the PHA, rights had to be granted if all submission requirements were met, which they eventually were.[17] This was not strictly correct, however: the City could have exercised its own discretion in granting the rights.

The story of Oakland City had been quite revealing. Not only were the financial dealings highly irregular, but the sequence of events suggested untoward political influence.

The other major development in the PHA was led by MSP and Uvest, two well-known developers with a string of residential and commercial developments to their names, mainly in the Durbanville area. Uvest grew out of its forerunner, MSP, and the two companies have remained intertwined. MSP's website claims that the company maintains the highest ethical standards, including a strong environmental ethos, in all business dealings.[18] Its behaviour has brought this claim into question, however.

One of the members of the PHA Food & Farming Campaign, Susanna Coleman, told me that Catherine Stone and her department had been the victim of a systematic campaign by developers to discredit them.[19] Uvest had written to De Lille to complain that their efforts to develop in the PHA 'had been frustrated by opposition from certain officials within the City's urban planning departments'.[20] These officials were, they claimed, causing unnecessary delays, and the developer had to 'continuously counter an apparent historically negative predisposition of certain officials'. A lawyer for Oakland City had complained to the province and the City that the planners had been obstructive, displayed a 'malicious attitude' and were out to 'get' them.[21]

Stone had only just returned from maternity leave and wasn't named in the letter, but from that point on, the mayor no longer trusted her. Ultimately, the developers' actions contributed to Stone's being pushed out.

The MSP/Uvest application, submitted in October 2011, was for a mixed-use development on 281 hectares of farmland in the southwest corner of the PHA. The submission applied to amend the recently approved CTSDF, which included the urban edge around the PHA, and wanted a change of land-use designation from 'agriculture areas of significant value' to 'urban development'. The developers argued that they would bring housing and urban development and would act as a buffer for the remainder of the PHA.[22]

This was on land that provincial minister Bredell had only recently declared should be protected in perpetuity as part of the trade-off for Oakland City. In the draft CTSDF (which was subsequently approved by council in May 2012) the land was also delineated as falling outside the urban edge.[23]

When the proposal was advertised for comment, the national and provincial agriculture departments, Heritage Western Cape, and the City's own departments for economic and human development, environmental resource management and city parks all objected, citing food production from the area, concerns over the aquifer particularly in light of projected water shortages, and heritage value.

Once again, Catherine Stone's spatial planning and urban design department led the assessment of the development, and the memo that they prepared for council recommended that the application to amend the CTSDF be refused.[24] The economic, environment and spatial planning portfolio committee agreed with the recommendation.

De Lille, however, asked for an independent study on the city's long-term food security needs and the role of the PHA.[25] Although the economic development department was officially tasked to manage the study, Craig Kesson's SPU took charge of it and instructed his officials that under no circumstances was Catherine Stone to be involved, due to her 'bias'. Kesson was apparently of the view that urban planners overestimated the agricultural value of Philippi.[26]

Japie Hugo, who was worried that the study might go awry, seconded an official to Kesson's office in order to assist.

A tender for the study went out in May 2013, but strangely all references to the PHA were removed from the terms of reference.[27] The reasons for this only became clear later.

Planning officials thought that there would be some breathing space around the PHA while the food-security study was being undertaken. They were wrong.

In June, a team of officials was pulled together to discuss housing initiatives in the area, but the mayor's office instructed them to consider only options or alternatives submitted by MSP/Uvest.[28] Apart from the environmental-protection issues, the City officials were concerned about serious technical flaws in the development. The proposed project stretched over a patchwork of sites that weren't contiguous, which would make it very difficult to put in roads or infrastructure. The land was flat, posing challenges for sewer lines and stormwater drainage, which run on gravity. The site was also waterlogged during winter, due to the proximity of the aquifer. And there was insufficient water pressure in the area, which would compromise firefighting services.

Hugo, who'd been involved in many private developments in his time, was convinced that the whole development was terminally flawed from the start. Nevertheless, the mayor's office sent him a note saying that the MSP/Uvest development was one of the key projects that the mayor wanted his department to work on.[29] What that meant in practice wasn't clear.

De Lille started calling meetings directly with officials to discuss the PHA, to which Catherine Stone wasn't invited.[30]

Japie Hugo was summoned to the mayor's office, where De Lille confronted him, asking why he didn't want to support the development. Hugo told her that he thought the configuration of erven on the site was problematic and that the development was unserviceable. In desperation, he pulled in an official to assess the financial viability of the development, but when he presented the results to De Lille, she allegedly objected. 'Who are you to say it's not viable? That isn't your decision to make. Let the private sector decide if they want to do the development.'[31]

De Lille also met with Helen Zille to discuss the PHA, obtaining an agreement in principle from the then provincial premier of the Western Cape to go ahead with the MSP/Uvest development.[32]

It seemed that all the pieces had been manoeuvred into place to push the project through.

When Japie Hugo went on leave in July 2013, De Lille and Kesson decided to act. Kesson sent an instruction to Kendall Kaveney, who was acting executive director while Hugo was away, telling him that the mayor wanted to review the MSP/Uvest application as 'a matter of extreme urgency'.[33]

The instruction was explicit: the department had to revise Catherine Stone's memo to council, request the mayoral committee to review the application, and submit the application to the council and then to the province. De Lille and Kesson clearly wanted the development to go through.

Kaveney phoned Stone to ask her to revise her initial recommendation.

'Well,' Stone said, 'what must I say in this report? The facts of the matter haven't changed, and the food-security study hasn't been completed. There isn't anything else I can add.' She refused to revise her memo.[34]

Kaveney didn't try to override Stone, and reported back to Kesson that the spatial planning team wasn't in a position to resubmit the memo.

Kesson was furious. He phoned the mayoral committee member for planning and dictated to him the wording of a memo that claimed that the circumstances around the application had changed – that there were land invasions and housing pressure – and that it was therefore necessary to amend the urban edge in line with what the developers had requested. Kaveney was then bullied into signing it, as if the memo had come from his department.

As an act of protest, Kaveney wrote on the memo that 'the Executive Director for whom I act would probably not support the application. The City Manager has indicated that he expects me to sign alongside this note.'[35] This made it clear that he'd been pushed into signing it.

When it came to the food-security study, which wasn't yet complete, the memo simply denied that the study was specific to the PHA.[36] Why the terms of reference for the study hadn't made any reference to the PHA now became evident.

On 13 July 2013 the memo went to the mayoral committee, which focused on 'the urgent need to provide more housing opportunities' while ignoring all concerns raised by the planning department. The mayoral committee overturned the decision it had taken the previous year, and at the end of July 2013, the council decided to shift the urban edge to accommodate

MSP's application, despite significant pushback from opposition parties.[37]

De Lille and Kesson had succeeded in ramming the development through, but they now had some cleaning up to do. De Lille instructed the city manager to investigate Catherine Stone for insubordination, but because Kaveney hadn't overruled Stone by giving her a direct instruction, the internal investigation found that there were no grounds for insubordination charges. De Lille then instructed the city manager to appoint an external lawyer to investigate Stone; the lawyer came back with the same findings – there was no basis on which to charge her.[38] Stone had dodged the axe – for now.

During the latter half of 2013, MSP and Uvest met with a number of executive directors, including Japie Hugo and Gerhard Ras, head of corporate services. In these meetings, MSP confessed that its proposed development wasn't feasible; it now wished to sell the land to the City – a strange about-turn in light of the recent political machinations.

Hugo was exasperated, having only recently been rapped over the knuckles for telling De Lille that the development wouldn't work. He was convinced that MSP had known this all along and had merely engaged in land speculation for possible financial return.

MSP and Uvest met with De Lille and told her that the development wasn't working out – although they didn't reveal the full extent of its unviability. Instead, they told her that they needed to sell a portion of their land to the City in order to finance the rest of the development. This wasn't implausible – five years previously, the City had taken an option on a portion of the MSP land for low-income housing, but the option had expired. During that meeting, De Lille apparently called in Achmat Ebrahim, the city manager, and instructed him to purchase the land.[39]

Jens Kuhn, who'd been involved in taking out the original option on the MSP land, was horrified when he saw what MSP was offering to sell. A portion of the original option, it was the worst part of the site – low-lying, regularly flooded, not linked to any of the arterial roads, and obviously unsuitable for low-income housing. 'It's the piece they couldn't develop,' said Kuhn, 'and there was no way the City could make it work. Putting an island of poor people in the middle of the farming area would be disastrous for everyone.'[40]

According to Kuhn, officials were then put under enormous political pressure to buy the land. City officials valued the site to be worth R18 million, which the developers considered to be unacceptably low. An alternative valuation for the land, if it were to be rezoned as commercial or for mixed use, came out at R52 million and officials were instructed to conclude a sale agreement based on the higher valuation. The City was in essence paying an extra R32 million for development rights that the City itself would issue, for land seemingly unusable for housing. The deal seemed patently illogical.

The officials drafted a sale agreement, which tied MSP/Uvest to securing the land rights – the condition of purchase was that the land be found fit for residential development and accordingly rezoned prior to purchase. Following this, transfer would take place.[41]

The purchase price was paid over to the transferring attorneys, to be held in trust pending the finalisation of the deal. MSP/Uvest then submitted rezoning applications for 15 plots, one of which was for the property that was supposed to be bought by City.

The unusual level of political interest in the development and the micromanagement of the administration continued when MSP ran into trouble early in 2014. Back then, the provincial minister for Environment and Development Planning (then Anton Bredell) still signed off on any amendment to the CTSDF. Bredell's earlier decision on Oakland City had drawn a line in the sand, which had indicated that no further developments would be approved within the PHA. In January 2014, after having received a number of objections to the application by MSP/Uvest, he turned it

109

down.[42] Bredell was on shaky ground, however, as a recent Constitutional Court ruling had determined that land-use planning decisions were the sole prerogative of local government, and the province couldn't presume to exercise those powers.[43]

Gerhard Ras instructed Catherine Stone to prepare a letter for the mayor to sign, telling the Western Cape government that it no longer had any power over the CTSDF.[44] City officials were then instructed to amend the CTSDF to excise the MSP/Uvest land from the PHA.[45] At the same time, De Lille obtained the power to override any decision of the City's spatial planning and land-use management committee whenever the committee recommended against a development.[46]

The food-security study was completed at the end of 2014 and, despite Kesson's efforts to micromanage it, confirmed the vital role played by agricultural areas such as the PHA in providing low-cost fresh produce, especially for lower-income households.[47] The conclusion blatantly undermined the decision to approve the MSP/Uvest development.

This was an embarrassment, and the mayor's office tried to bury the report. Instead of tabling it to council, De Lille used the mayor's recess powers to act on behalf of the council when it wasn't sitting, and on 18 December 2014, the mayor simply 'noted' the report on behalf of the council. There was therefore no discussion on the study.[48]

The mayor convened a mayoral committee meeting in January 2015 at which the conditions attached to the zoning approval for the development were lifted.[49]

In spite of the push from the mayor's office, however, the developers ran into serious problems trying to complete the sale of the land. The new spatial-planning legislation[50] required municipalities to set up an independent tribunal to process certain land-use decisions.[51] Councillors were specifically excluded from participating in the tribunal, although the mayor did remain as the ultimate appeal authority. There was now an independent body able to consider the evidence objectively.

Nazeer Sonday and the PHA Food & Farming Campaign had in the meantime, in 2017, lodged an appeal with the City of Cape Town. Among their arguments was that while other farmers in the Western Cape had suffered production losses during the drought, which had overtaken the region in 2014, Philippi farmers had not.

In May 2018, the municipal planning tribunal overturned the previous decision to rezone the MSP/Uvest land for the development of a shopping mall, a school and a portion of road. The tribunal argued that the preservation of the agricultural integrity of the area was important for employment creation and food security. The proposal was also found to lack 'spatial logic', as this was an isolated ad-hoc development that wasn't integrated with surrounding developments or land use. Assurances regarding any negative impacts on the aquifer were considered inadequate.[52]

The tide seemed to be turning, but other decisions still had to be overturned. In September 2017 the PHA Food & Farming Campaign had petitioned the High Court to review 12 development decisions in the PHA, including the shift of the urban edge.[53] The matter will be heard in October 2019, and Sonday is hopeful. He said the city council seemed to have grown more interested in balancing competing land uses in the PHA. 'The city can't ignore its obligations regarding food and water security, heritage and land reform. These should take precedence over developers' profit,' he said.[54]

It's taken Nazeer Sonday ten years of campaigning, legal challenges and engagement with the authorities to get to this point. 'I'm convinced of our cause; we must have the PHA reserved in perpetuity for agricultural use. Cities all over the world are trying to become self-sufficient in food provision. The vision for what we can do in the PHA is far more exciting than all this fighting. Really,' he says, looking across his own piece of organically farmed land, replete with sunflowers, 'I'd rather be farming.'

9

Between the devil and the deep blue sea

'Look over there,' said Albie Sachs, waving the stump of his amputated arm, as we gazed out of his bungalow in Camps Bay at the translucent turquoise ocean. There was a school of dolphins swimming past, accompanied by a flock of gulls overhead. They were obviously chasing a shoal of fish in the icy waters of the Atlantic Ocean.

Camps Bay is one of the most beautiful beaches in the world, set in a coastal reserve, with an outcrop of grey granite boulders framing the hot white sands and cold blue sea. It's an upmarket suburb, home to some of the richest people in South Africa.

Hidden between the rocks is a small but historically significant inlet called Maiden's Cove. During apartheid, when even beaches were racially segregated, Maiden's Cove was one of the few beaches that coloured families were allowed to use. The nearby coloured communities of Bo-Kaap and District Six had maintained a long tradition of Sunday picnics on the beach.

Now, in 2018, this was under threat.

Albie Sachs, a highly respected former Constitutional Court judge and liberation fighter who'd lost his arm in a car-bomb attack, was outraged that the City had gone ahead and sold Maiden's Cove, which was public open space and a protected reserve, to a shelf company.[1] The plan was to build a boutique hotel, more than 50 upmarket private homes, a parking garage for 750 cars, and a large retail complex. The highest bidder would be given a 50-year lease for the commercial section and full ownership of the rest of the land, for which it would pay as the new houses got sold off. The City was also going to assist the new owners to get the necessary planning permissions.

'The City can't evade or outsource its constitutional and statutory responsibilities,' said Sachs. 'This isn't a piece of municipal land like a derelict building or underused parking area. This is a particularly precious piece of protected public space that the City is obliged to handle as a public trust for present and future generations. The City is legally obliged to enhance, not reduce, access to the sea for the public. The Constitution requires it to heal, not exacerbate, the divisions of the past, and to counteract rather than intensify the racial and spatial divide of Cape Town. What the City is doing is the exact opposite.'[2]

Sachs was also aggrieved about the way the City had consulted with the community of Camps Bay and the broader Cape Town public. Instead of being asked for their views on what should happen, if anything, to the land, the City had put a detailed prescriptive proposal for high-end economic development on the table as a fait accompli, and then consulted the public on the details. 'The coloured community developed an intimate connection with the area in the decades when the beautiful nearby beaches were forbidden to them, and they have in fact been rendered invisible in the processes followed by the City,' Sachs argued. 'They should be the first to engage meaningfully with the City about how the area should be upgraded.'[3]

The project had come about after two business associates with personal links to Mayor Patricia de Lille, Mark Willcox and property developer

Tobie Mynhardt, had presented an unsolicited proposal to the City for a multi-use exclusive development on publicly owned land. Even though the City had supposedly rejected the development, it then put out a proposal for public comment that looked remarkably similar to the one drawn up by Willcox and Mynhardt. De Lille said the City intended to sell the public open space in order to raise revenue. The city's process 'is for the good of the people of Cape Town [and] is a transparent and open one that is trying to find innovative sources of revenue', she said.[4] The City did, however, refuse to give the media the list of bidders for the development.

City officials were alarmed at the privatisation of public open space, and felt that their professional views were being ignored by senior managers and politicians intent on forcing the project through. A City official who raised questions about the development was warned not to oppose it because it was 'a mayoral project'.[5]

The gossip mill in Cape Town spoke of private dinner parties De Lille attended in Camps Bay at which Willcox and Mynhardt were also present. Willcox, who admitted to being a longstanding friend of De Lille's, made donations to various charities suggested by the mayor, and was rumoured to be funding the DA as well. De Lille was also close to the Mynhardt family, and Mynhardt's daughter had thanked De Lille on a number of occasions for her 'support'.[6]

The media asked whether De Lille's personal relationships had influenced her to back the controversial plan, rather than recognising a possible conflict of interest and standing back. In turn, Willcox threatened to sue the journalists over 'unfounded and slanderous allegations'.[7]

For her part, De Lille was furious at the suggestion that there was anything untoward in the relationship, and penned a sarcastic reply: 'Why let the facts get in the way of a good story? ... Patricia de Lille knows a rich person in Clifton who makes money doing stuff; Cape Town is engaged in the process of releasing assets it owns in Clifton; she and her friend must somehow be collaborating on this deal … In this logic, there just has to be something unsavoury about a friendship between a politician and a businessperson. The lack of evidence is a minor detail.'[8]

In October 2017, after the media had enquired whether the tender had been awarded, the City issued a press statement indicating that they'd accepted an offer of just over R1 billion for the land.[9] The winning entity was a shelf company with the catchy name of K2015298271, one of whose directors was Tobias Mynhardt. The agreement included an upfront once-off payment instead of annual income over the 50-year lease period, which was unusual and attracted some criticism.

Albie Sachs was instrumental in pulling together Maiden's Cove for All, a coalition of organisations that opposed the deal, and of which the Clifton Bungalow Owners' Association was a key member. The Clifton Bungalow Owners' Association took the City to court to set aside its decision to sell and lease a portion of the land, but the court never got to decide on the merits of the matter because in October 2018 the City decided to withdraw its opposition to the legal challenge, acknowledging that the consultation process had been flawed. Two weeks later, the developers themselves announced they wouldn't oppose the court application to set aside the project.[10]

The campaign felt vindicated but concerns remained. At the time of the original announcement of the deal, Brett Herron, the mayoral committee member for transport and urban development, had said that 10% of the monies from the deal would be ploughed back into affordable housing. While a botched privatisation of land had been abandoned, the status quo remained, and the City's poor remained largely shut out of Clifton and Camps Bay.

Reflecting on the Maiden's Cove fiasco, Sachs said it revealed a high-handed, arrogant approach to City governance that flew directly in the face of the City's public commitment to consultation, social integration and spatial transformation. 'What worries me is that Maiden's Cove is by no means the first time this has happened,' he said. 'There are a long list of projects where the City is willing to take public land, which by right vests in the people of Cape Town, and sell it to the highest bidder.'[11]

Three examples are a proposed housing estate at Oudekraal on coastal land beyond Camps Bay, which had been blocked in court by environmental groups and the Muslim community, who argued that planning permission should have been refused on the basis of environmental heritage concerns; the City's planning approval for a proposed development on the Sea Point promenade, which would have blocked public access to a well-frequented area, and was overturned by a community-driven organisation, Seafront for All; and the Princess Vlei Forum, which had campaigned and ultimately halted plans to commercialise a large public space adjacent to the Vlei.

Said Sachs, 'We need a different understanding of what public ownership means – the land is held in trust, on behalf of the people; you can't just dispose of it as you see fit.'[12]

The issue of Maiden's Cove and the roughshod way the mayor's office had handled public 'consultation' highlighted another worrying angle to my growing list of questions surrounding high-profile property developments in Cape Town. Whose interests were these developments and the City leaders truly serving?

By the time I got to the Paardevlei development project, my ears were ringing, and I felt that a clear pattern was emerging. But I was in for a surprise.

In June 2015, the City of Cape Town purchased a 684-hectare open piece of land in Paardevlei, Somerset West, some 45 kilometres from the city centre, for R400 million.[13] This was one of the last extensive, unbuilt land plots within the City's developed footprint, and the municipal administration claimed that the purchase reflected its 'commitment to meeting the needs of an expanding population'. The land was zoned for mixed use, and the plan was for the City administration itself to develop it as low-income housing.

The previous landowner, however, was a chemical and explosives company, AECI, and the property had been used for testing various chemical weapons and explosives.[14] According to the City, a lengthy due-diligence process had been carried out and all legislative requirements had been met. Yet there was no sign of environmental or planning studies.

I was initially alerted to the transaction by a human-settlements official, who indicated that the funds for the land purchase had come from the Urban Settlements Development Grant, a national grant to assist metropolitan municipalities in providing infrastructure services and housing to poor households. Although the grant makes allowances for procuring land that would support 'urban development, spatial integration and inclusion', the housing official was concerned that a purchase on this scale, and the plans for the mixed-use development that went with it, didn't comply with the conditions of the grant.[15]

This was a concern that the head of the finance section of the City's TDA, Mapule Moore, shared. The City, which had been underspending on the grant for the last four years, had accumulated about R400 million on which they were earning interest while National Treasury drowned in debt. Eventually National Treasury drew a line in the sand: if the City didn't use the funds within the 2014/15 financial year, it would have to return the money to National Treasury.

Moore suspected that by channelling the funds into a large land purchase, the City had engaged in 'fiscal dumping', which involved shifting unspent funds at the end of a financial year into a seemingly planned purchase.[16] The national minister for Human Settlements had picked up on this and attacked De Lille for financial irregularities.

When in August 2018 I finally got to speak to the head of the TDA,

Melissa Whitehead, and asked her about Paardevlei, she was quite forthright. 'Of course it was a fiscal dump,' she said. 'The City weren't building houses and needed a place to put the money as an excuse.'[17]

In addition, Moore wasn't convinced that the City had done its homework on the site, nor that the site made sense for low-income housing. Residents would have to travel some 20 to 40 kilometres each day to jobs in the city centre, a significant cost for low-income families. Moore did think that the development could make sense as an integrated, mixed-use one with different income brackets, but that wouldn't fall within the grant criteria.[18]

When in May 2019 I spoke to Japie Hugo about the site, he said its primary problem was that it was flat and low-lying, and what was required to develop it made it too expensive for low-cost housing. Nor did it make sense for the City, which was committed to housing development led by the private sector, to be driving a development of this scale itself.[19] The cost to develop such a large integrated development would be astronomical – Moore estimated that it would cost at least R1 billion just to start the development with the highway offramps, road network and stormwater drainage.[20] Yet the deal was pushed through in a hurry at the end of the City's 2014/15 financial year.[21]

In 2017, the Paardevlei project became Melissa Whitehead's responsibility, and she instructed Frank Cumming to pull out the legal documents so she could review the sale agreement. Whitehead was appalled by what she found. The land that had been purchased was highly contaminated from its previous use, and the groundwater on the site had been polluted, probably in perpetuity. In fact, former owner AECI was still operating a dynamite factory on an adjacent site, and although no proper environmental assessment had been conducted, the sale agreement completely indemnified the company from all past and future liabilities.[22]

Whitehead had grave doubts about the motivation behind the deal. The estate agency that had managed the sale of the land – and that had earned a substantial commission off it – was an unknown company without any track record.

When in January 2018 Whitehead found herself facing a disciplinary hearing over her handling of the bus-rapid-transit system, she took the opportunity to flag the Paardevlei transaction and threatened to reveal further information. The contents of the hearing were almost immediately leaked to the rest of the administration and ricocheted around the City.

Any further funds for the project were removed from the 2018 budget, and the project was suspended.

Whatever the real motivation behind Paardevlei, the project seemed fatally flawed and made a mockery of the otherwise rigid commitment to compliance in the City administration.

It also raised a number of uncomfortable new questions. Why was the City directly acquiring land on such a massive scale, instead of pursuing its official strategy of relying on developers? And had this questionable project been overtaken by other interests, directly or indirectly; and, if so, on what scale?

These property-development projects highlighted what appeared to be common patterns. The City politicians, and particularly the mayor, took an extraordinary level of interest in these projects and pushed them hard.

When I looked at the City's development plan, I realised that the controversial developments in Philippi, Maiden's Cove and Paardevlei were all listed as catalytic projects. A transport interchange in Philippi East (albeit some distance from the private developments) would facilitate and catalyse surrounding development; Maiden's Cove was supposedly part of a long-term private-sector investment and infrastructure initiative in the inner-city precinct; and Paardevlei had been purchased, the development plan argued, in order to combine housing and economic opportunities.

The list included two other initiatives. The Foreshore Freeway project was intended to deal with Cape Town's unfinished freeways to unlock economic potential in the area and complete the urban design of the inner city; but it was to come spectacularly unstuck at a later stage. And the Bellville central business district (CBD) revitalisation included a large public-transport interchange. Both projects were intended to leverage private-sector investment. For instance, George Georgiou, who owns large tracts of land on the Cape Town Foreshore (the City planning department rents space from him), is planning on leveraging the City's Bellville project with his own R2-billion investment in office and retail space, affordable housing and transport links.[23]

And the provincial government had added two other projects: the development of the derelict Conradie Hospital precinct, around which the City had initially been uncooperative; and the Two Rivers Urban Park, which had been many years in the planning with little to show for it, and which turned out to be equally problematic. The site, which sits on a floodplain at the confluence of the Liesbeek and Black rivers, is an environmentally sensitive, flood-prone area located on an ancient Khoi burial ground close to heritage buildings such as the old observatory and Valkenberg psychiatric hospital. The new owner of the River Club site wanted maximum development rights, but the planners and the Observatory Civic Association (OCA) feared that the project would divert water and cause flooding in the suburb. City and provincial officials bullied the planning consultants on the project to amend technical reports in order to favour the developer.

In theory, these catalytic projects reflected what appeared to be a strategic shift from the City administration towards fostering property development closer to the city centre, favouring infill projects and, presumably, spatial integration. Yet according to Mapule Moore, the strategic projects were politically motivated. 'If you ask anyone in the property-management unit, they'll tell you they have no idea why these projects were chosen [as strategic priorities]. They wouldn't have chosen these projects on a technical basis.'[24]

So who did choose them?

'The mayor,' she said. 'Who was with her, who was not, I'm not quite sure. But this was very much from her side.'[25]

The pattern of systematic political interference had eroded the capacity and integrity of the City's planning and land-management machinery. In all these projects, City officials had pointed out significant technical flaws or lack of due process, but when they did so, they'd been put under significant pressure to change their opinions. Those who hadn't were marginalised or found themselves without a job when the administration was restructured – the planning team, led by Catherine Stone and Japie Hugo, had been closely involved in the PHA and in Wescape because both projects had required amending the City's spatial plan and rezoning; and Jens Kuhn had also opposed the PHA proposal over the City's controversial land acquisition from the developers.

The planners working on the spatial strategy for the Two Rivers Urban Park, where the River Club development was located, came under significant pressure – from both the City and the provincial authorities – to amend their technical reports, which advised against the project as it was conceived, on the grounds that it was located on a floodplain, which also happened to be of great historical significance. When they refused, their contracts were not renewed and the plan was put on hold.[26]

Although he'd spearheaded the Foreshore Freeway project, Frank Cumming ended up locking horns with the mayor's office after he came under pressure to favour a specific bid – allegedly the mayor's preferred proposal. At the end of his probation period, his contract was terminated as well,[27] although he was later rehired by the City.

Did the City leadership, and particularly the mayor, genuinely believe that these development projects were the best options for the City, to be pushed at all costs past obstructionist and narrow-minded bureaucrats? Were these deals ham-fisted attempts to speed up private-sector-led housing and investment through property development, in part to address the city's crushing housing needs? Or did these projects offer something else for political leaders?

Every City administration faces difficult choices, having to strike an often uneasy balance between addressing monumental housing backlogs as quickly as possible, encouraging economic activity and private investment, and looking after the City's purse, while at the same time protecting the environment, preserving public spaces, looking after cultural and historical heritage, and promoting spatial and socioeconomic integration. These often-conflicting considerations, supported by different constituencies, are tricky to reconcile. No development project can satisfy all constituencies and the interests they represent, and most proposals are likely to unleash fierce opposition.

The City's population is growing fast. The metropolitan area is home to some four million people today, and another 200 000 people are expected to join its ranks by 2023. Yet more than one in five Capetonians have no access to formal housing.[28] At its current delivery speed, the City's housing backlog of some 350 000 units would take over 60 years to clear. This creates significant pressure on the City and its leadership.

At the same time, the property industry is an essential component of urban development. It's the property industry that builds cities and drives urban growth, creating iconic city office blocks, vibrant entertainment centres and stylish housing estates. It's the property industry that creates innovative urban form and design, and that finds the gaps in the market that enable big schemes to come alive. Without property developers, cities would be left with staid government layouts and ageing infrastructure that would impoverish our lives.

Still, it's hard to believe that these particular catalytic projects, with their glaring technical weaknesses and, in some cases, highly question-able financial arrangements, were in the public interest. It's hard to believe that building houses in nuclear-evacuation zones, in flooding areas or on terminally contaminated land makes any sense at all, regardless of the size of the housing backlog; nor does spending taxpayers' money on overvalued land unsuitable for housing. It's hard to believe that these projects, which appear to fly in the face of environmental and human safety, spatial inte-gration, and due process and proper consultation, weren't instead meant to fulfil very different interests.

Yet even in the midst of the political trench warfare that racked the DA in Cape Town between 2016 and 2018, both sides seemed, for the most part, to carefully step around these controversial property developments. In the midst of the slew of allegations and investigations that the political battle unleashed, few words were spoken publicly by either side about these projects (with the exception, as we shall see, of the Foreshore development).

After looking into all these questionable property deals, I felt perturbed and wondered about what interests might be at play. I decided to have a chat with an old friend who'd once been Cape Town's city manager, Andrew Boraine.

Boraine had played a central role in managing the transition from fragmented apartheid local government to the system of today, and was instrumental in crafting the sections in the constitution dealing with local government. Boraine thought a bit about what I told him, then pointed out that deals between property developers and politicians in Cape Town were nothing new. He took me back to 19th-century Cape Town and British colonial rule, when large landed-property interests controlled the Cape Town municipality and made sure its roads, infrastructure and land regu-lation served them.

'Moving on to the 20th century,' Boraine said, 'many mayors in Cape Town had close ties with the business and property class as well as property developers, and tended to act in their overall interests.'[29]

This chimed with what a prominent Cape Town architect had told me, that the elite would meet in the city's private booth at the opera house, where the deals around developments such as Cape Town's first malls were sealed.

Catherine Stone had told me about 2011 research on the impact of climate change on coastal properties which were threatened by sea-level rise. In the records on a development close to Milnerton market from many decades ago, a researcher had dug out letters between the foreign developer and their partners prior to their development being approved by the City. 'It will be approved, don't worry,' the developer had written, long before City approval was granted, suggesting that such approvals were a fait accompli.[30]

Boraine felt that this sort of inappropriate influence in decision-making had been the norm before the modern era. It seemed to me that these old patterns of interaction between property, money and power were taking new forms under the De Lille administration. So would the restructuring of the municipal administration and the centralisation of power in the mayor's office make it easier for land and property deals to be sealed?

This led me to my next question. Cape Town is home to a rich and long tradition of protest around community and social issues, and the civic and ratepayers' movements in the city are very active – Maiden's Cove for All (represented by the Clifton Bungalow Owners' Association) and the PHA Food & Farming Campaign stand as testimony to civic mobilisation and resistance against inappropriate property development, and against a City administration keen to push these very projects past any technical and community objection.

So how did developers handle the usually vocal communities who were directly affected by their projects?

10

How to steal a civic

᨝᨝᨝

In October 2018, I returned to my old student neighbourhood of Observatory. Wedged between Groote Schuur Hospital and the UCT medical school on the mountainside, and the Liesbeek River down below, the scruffy suburb has always been an eclectic mix of working class, students, bohemians and professionals. Back in my university days, radical left students and professors could be seen discussing struggle politics in the bars and bookshops on Lower Main Road.

Abutting the previously 'coloured' suburb of Salt River, the area had retained its non-racial character through the worst of the Group Areas Act period. Black and white activists could come and go unnoticed, making it a haven for underground activities. There was also a wilder side: I used to be able to pop down the road to the corner of Arnold Street and buy marijuana from a Muslim lad, who was no doubt working for one of the gangs controlling the drug trade in the area.

The suburb hasn't changed much since I wandered those streets as an angry and disturbed young student 40 years ago. There's still the same eclectic mix of old and new, the same feeling of social backwater, the slightly dingy bars, coffee shops and restaurants, the same mix of vagrants, students, weirdos and hippies. During my visit, I felt caught in a time warp, expecting at any moment to bump into the same boy with whom I'd fallen in love for the first time.

But I was there for more than a trip down memory lane. I'd reconnected with a fellow medical student, Leslie London, now a professor in the School of Public Health and Family Medicine at UCT.

As young doctors in training back in the 1980s, he and I had attended a Marxist reading group on health and the political economy, debating how the South African health system could be transformed by focusing on primary healthcare. Following the launch of the UDF in 1983, London had been among the neighbourhood lefties who'd set up the Observatory Area Committee, a forerunner of the Observatory Civic Association (OCA), which mobilised community support for the broader struggle against apartheid.

There'd been a lull in civic mobilisation since then. For instance, the Observatory community hadn't raised objections to the new zoning scheme for Cape Town in 2013, which gave the City wide discretion to approve development applications, and was quite permissive on development rules in the area.[1] At the time, there was limited development in Observatory, and no one took much notice. Following the introduction of the new zoning bylaws, the City created an electronic internet portal for submitting building and land-use applications online, which speeded up their processing. The City held a series of meetings with developers to explain their implications, enabling them to navigate the new regime, but no such education was offered for the civic association or the community.

The City had then interpreted the maximum permissible building height – between 15 and 24 metres, depending on location[2] – as an entitlement. In the years between 2014 and the time of writing, developers had been pulling down the old historical Obs houses, and building higher and higher. The OCA had been re-energised to contest these developments:

although most residents accepted that densification should happen along the main arterial road to make space for more people, they were also keen to preserve the character and heritage of their neighbourhood.

Leslie London and many other old friends had become re-engaged when they saw a 'wall of concrete' coming their way. For London the impact was direct – three large apartment buildings went up within 100 metres of his single-storey house.

London told me about property developers who had attempted to take over the OCA, and agreed to introduce me to members who would tell me the story.

The association had always tried to be inclusive, and among its members were business people who were active in the development of the area. Much of the contestation unfolded in the OCA's architecture and heritage subcommittee, chaired by Mark Turok, who'd been fighting to preserve the history of the area for many years.

Discussions in the architecture and heritage subcommittee often became quite heated, and newer members such as Theo Kruger, founder of Two Five Five Architects, and Ebrahim 'Himmy' Abader, who owns Elite Taxis in Observatory, complained to the chair of the OCA that Turok was stifling development and debate. Yet both Kruger and Abader were linked to property developments in the suburb, and the association members realised that they, and not Turok, were the people with a conflict of interest.

Every year, the OCA holds an annual general meeting at which a new leadership is elected. The meeting in October 2017 at first seemed pretty much like any other, although a number of new faces showed up, which the leadership were excited about, as they were always trying to recruit new members.

Kruger and Abader were seen chatting with one or two of the new people, but no one thought anything of this. At one point, when the treasurer, who normally registered new members, had to leave to present the financial statements, Abader offered to take over the registration table. Still, no one was concerned.

After the various reports had been given, the new recruits had mistakenly thought the meeting was over and left, at which point Abader had ushered them back in. Then came elections for a new leadership. The hugely popular chair, Tauriq Jenkins, was voted out and replaced by Theo Kruger. Abader became secretary unopposed, as regular members were reluctant to put their names forward – it's always quite a struggle to get people to stand for executive positions, which are unpaid and quite demanding. Mark Turok was voted out as chair of the architecture and heritage subcommittee and replaced by architectural technologist Tertius van Zyl.[3]

Turok raised a concern about the obvious conflicts of interest, as Abader, Kruger and Van Zyl were all linked to ongoing property developments in the suburb. Kruger had clashed with the large-developments subcommittee over some of his projects, which had been deemed to be inappropriate in scale and impact on the surrounding environment, which is mainly fine-grained Victorian one- and two-storey houses. Abader had plans to convert the Elite Taxis offices into a spanking-new development, and a municipal planning tribunal was scheduled for December to consider his application; he was also involved in another three or four small developments, mostly five-storey apartment buildings.

Turok's point about conflicts of interest was brushed aside.

Once elected, Himmy Abader immediately wanted the OCA to rethink its policies on property development, in line with his vision to build an 'all-inclusive society' which included the relaxation of heritage and parking restrictions.[4] Then he wanted control over the OCA's email server and contact list, which worried some of the older members.

The previous OCA executive members became suspicious. They remembered all these new faces and how Abader had been determined to keep the new recruits in the meeting. They also remembered Abader at the registration table, and pulled out the list of voters. Out of the 59 registered voters, 18 had provided suspicious contact details – a number of them had used a vacant property owned by Theo Kruger as their address, for instance. Abader had also apparently ponied up membership fees for some of the new recruits.

Further investigation revealed that these recruits didn't live in the area. 'In fact, they weren't eligible to be members of the civic at all,' said London.[5] Theo Kruger himself was found to be ineligible because his business fell outside the boundaries that defined the OCA's membership. In addition, Kruger had successfully nominated his chosen candidate to head the architecture and heritage subcommittee. He had also – unsuccessfully – nominated a candidate to head the large-developments subcommittee that had questioned some of his proposed buildings. His preferred candidate's address and phone number were directly linked to his, Kruger's, business.

Paddy Chapple, the DA councillor for the area, who can often be found having a beer at Scrumpy Jack on Lower Main Road, was unhelpful. 'You can always form your own civic [association],' he allegedly advised the former OCA Chair, Tauriq Jenkins. 'The council is prepared to deal with more than one civic structure.'[6]

The former executive team decided to convene a special general meeting at which they would put the evidence to the members and let them decide what to do about the election. Himmy Abader, Theo Kruger and Tertius van Zyl threatened legal action but didn't manage to thwart the initiative.

On the evening of the meeting, the queue to get into the hall stretched around the block. The former OCA leaders were initially worried that these were Abader and Kruger's plants, intent on packing the meeting. But their fears were misplaced – word of the 'capture' had spread like wildfire throughout the community, and Obs residents had rallied around their civic association.

Confronted with the evidence of irregularities, Abader claimed that the new members and the votes he'd received reflected a marketing campaign he'd conducted ahead of the election. When Kruger was asked why he'd nominated somebody who not only worked for him but also wasn't eligible to be an OCA member, his justification was that his nominee worked in the area.

Residents who'd showed up in record numbers for the meeting unanimously overturned the election results from the annual general meeting, and reinstated the previous leadership until new elections could be held.[7] The community had rallied round and saved their civic association from being hijacked.

Cape Town's long tradition of robust civic organisation runs like a rich seam on both sides of the city's racial and class divides. Since the 19th century, the interests of property owners have been represented through suburb-based 'ratepayers' associations', whose primary concern has been to protect the value of owners' properties and lobby for their interests. While paying lip-service to broader social objectives, their parochial interests often lead ratepayers' organisations to object to lower-income developments in their neighbourhoods, a 'not in my back yard' syndrome that's so common it has its own acronym, 'nimby'.

The imposition of the Group Areas Act cast this into starker racial terms. In mobilising around basic services, security and housing, black civic organisations inevitably ran into broader political issues regarding their economic circumstances and suffrage. Organisations that stood up against the government were targeted and their members detained, and ultimately they were banned.

As the battle against apartheid intensified during the 1980s and urban townships became the primary battleground, civic organisations were thrust into a leading position in the township revolt.[8] In August 1983 the UDF, a coalition of some 400 civic, church, student, union and other organisations, was launched at the Rocklands civic centre in Mitchells Plain, and a massive crowd of about 13 000 people converged for the launch – the largest anti-apartheid gathering since the Congress Alliance campaigns of the 1950s.

As a young student and a leader of the ECC, I was swept up in this, proudly marching and singing liberation songs with black and white comrades from across the country. It was a profound moment, and I felt I finally belonged somewhere. The UDF led to a flowering of civic, youth, women's and underground ANC and South African Communist Party structures across South Africa.

In democratic South Africa, the focus of civic and ratepayers' organisations has returned to neighbourhood interests. They concentrate on municipal planning and environmental issues, and lobby the City on matters that affect their communities, which includes objecting to unwanted property development. They comment on issues such as title-deed amendments, applications to subdivide or join properties, land-use management applications, heritage applications (such as demolishing buildings with heritage value) and, once construction has begun, compliance with building regulations.

Because of these organisations' claims to represent specific communities, they're able to authoritatively comment on or object to land-use planning, property development and other decisions that affect their neighbourhoods. While larger developments are usually advertised for public comment, the smaller ones get sent to the ratepayers' or civic association for review.

Whoever ultimately gets to comment on how urban land is used has power over the final outcome. For developers, the way this power is exercised can be critical. Comments or objections at any step of the process of developing land can tie up, delay or even scupper a project, affecting timelines and profitability.

If you walk up Cape Town's Wale Street, from the city centre towards Lion's Head, you cross the busy Buitengracht Street, which used to mark the outskirts of the original Dutch town. Beyond this boundary you enter Bo-Kaap (literally, 'Upper Cape'), what used to be called the Malay quarter, and the surroundings take on a completely different character. The tarred road becomes cobblestones, and the faceless city office blocks and traffic give way to a quieter world of one- and two-storey flat-roofed houses, with simple facades painted in bright colours and elevated front balconies.

The history and unique character of Bo-Kaap make it one of the most iconic neighbourhoods of Cape Town. Pushed up against Signal Hill and bounded by busy roads, the old suburb is peopled by the descendants of slaves and political exiles, mostly from the Dutch colony of Indonesia. Their roots go back some 250 years, making Bo-Kaap the oldest surviving residential neighbourhood in the country.

On a March 2019 visit, I arrived just before noonday prayers, and passed a clutch of men wearing embroidered fez-like taqiyahs outside the Auwal Mosque – the oldest in South Africa, built in 1740 – while kids in white thobes played on the cobbled street. The scene felt timeless, rhythmed by the chant of the muezzins coming in turn from each corner of the suburb. Yet the Bo-Kaap community now feels under threat, with gentrification slowly eating away at its fabric.

I was there to meet Razeen Diedericks, a former member of the Bo-Kaap Youth Movement (BKYM) who now runs the Bo-Kaap Collective, which campaigns to preserve heritage and prevent gentrification in the Bo-Kaap area, and Seehaam Samaai, a civic activist who provides legal support to the Bo-Kaap Civic and Ratepayers' Association (Bokcra).

'The community is historically strong and very pro-poor,' Samaai explained. During the 19th century, the civil rights of freed slaves and Khoekhoe were won against colonists' attempts to impose vagrancy laws and deny coloured people the right to vote. And during apartheid, the community, led by the Bo-Kaap Action Group (Bokag),[9] had successfully resisted their eviction in terms of the Group Areas Act.

Unwanted development was what concerned Bokcra now. Being so close to the city centre, and with beautiful views of Table Mountain and Lion's Head, the suburb is an obvious target for development. Bo-Kaap was meant to have been given some protection by a heritage protection 'overlay zone', a municipal policy document setting out the heritage issues and building criteria that must be considered in approving development proposals. But despite being recommended for approval by the City's planning committee in 2014, De Lille had not allowed it to go to Council for approval.[10]

Already most of the properties that border the area along Buitengracht and Strand streets have been turned into offices, hotels and motor-sales outlets, blocking the view from Bo-Kaap across the city centre. Development is now starting to penetrate into the heart of the community. In the last few years, the city council has approved at least 15 large developments, four of which have already gone up, including a 60-storey tower that Bo-Kaap residents refer to as 'the monster building'.

Diedericks and Samaai had agreed to take me to the current flashpoint. We walked up Wale Street, past the Bo-Kaap Museum and the Atlas Trading Company, the much-loved 70-year-old family-owned spices outlet, and, after zigzagging through the streets, turned into Lion Street, a colourful rows of houses framing a beautiful view of Lion's Head at the end. Passing the old stone stairway winding up into the upper reaches of the neighbouring suburb of Schotsche Kloof, we were confronted by a vast ten-floor unfinished concrete monstrosity, completely out of keeping with the area, that blocked out the view of Lion's Head.

It towered over the old St Monica's home, once a maternity home for destitute and single mothers, for which, Samaai explained, the community felt a collective sense of ownership: 'The land was held in trust by the trustees of St Monica's, and there were reversionary rights in terms of which the land would revert to the City if it was ever sold.' But when the trustees of St Monica's decided to move the organisation, the land was sold in a silent auction involving three bidders, one of which was a developer called Blok. The City signed away its reversionary rights to the land without any public consultation.

The community was extremely suspicious about what had transpired. The law firm that had managed the transaction on behalf of St Monica's was the City's preferred attorney for evictions. Plans for a new development with 55 high-end apartments and 110 parking bays were then pushed through without public engagement. The daughter of the City official who'd signed off the plans was contracted by Blok as its communications and public relations liaison with Bokcra, which, at best, signalled a blatant conflict of interest.

The first time members of the community were able to object to the building was when the developer applied for changes to the planned parking bays and floor size. Local residents, mobilised by Bokcra, submitted some 500 objections to the development, but received no response. For almost two years nothing happened, as the developer's application for changes wasn't reviewed.

Then, in April 2019, the City informed residents that Blok had withdrawn its application for the changes. As a result, all the residents' objections fell away.

Bokcra was surprised and outraged when construction on the site began, a situation that was aggravated when trucks and cranes going to and from the site damaged the road and surrounding houses. This stirred the community into action.

Bokcra organised protests against the construction, with groups of women standing silently blocking the road. Blok countered by getting an interdict against the community, including the chair of the neighbourhood watch and various Bokcra members.

But there were also divisions within the community. Many of the Bokcra leaders had been there for more than 20 years, and younger people felt that they couldn't express themselves through the organisation. Razeen Diedericks was part of a group of young people who had decided to start a youth organisation, the BKYM, in 2017. 'Originally it was a well-intentioned movement,' he explained. 'We wanted to focus on issues that affected us as young people, such as drug abuse and unemployment. We also felt Bokcra hadn't done enough to stop developments in the area. We wanted to prevent threats to our heritage and stop property rates being pushed beyond what people can afford.'[11]

For a while, the youth and Bokcra seemed to be working together. 'But then something strange started to happen,' said Diedericks.

As the conflict between the community and Blok started to heat up, Diedericks found that decisions involving BKYM were being made and agreements signed that he didn't know about and which hadn't been discussed in the group. In June 2018 BKYM registered as a conservation organisation with Heritage Western Cape, using a consultant whom the group clearly didn't have the resources to pay.[12] It subsequently turned out the consultant was employed by another development adjoining Blok's.

Once registered, development proposals would now be sent separately to Bokcra and BKYM for comment, which meant that Bokra's objections to developments could be countered with alternative views.

On 14 July 2018 a community meeting was called at the Muslim Judicial Council to discuss the developments in the area, at which Blok's heritage and community-participation consultants pitched up. When members questioned their presence, some of the youth insisted that they would be able to assist in answering questions.

In July 2018, BKYM appointed a top legal firm, Norton Rose Fulbright, to act on its behalf in relation to the Blok development. How the organisation could afford such support was unclear at the time; later, it was revealed that the law firm had been retained by Blok.[13]

In the same month Norton Rose Fulbright purported to act as neutral facilitators in a court-mandated mediation process between community organisations and Blok mediators in seeking a resolution after Blok's first interdict against Bokcra, claiming they'd obtained all the parties' consent – a claim that Bo-Kaap organisations, apart from BKYM, said was untrue.[14]

In July 2018 a confidential cooperation agreement between BKYM and Blok was signed, in terms of which BKYM would use 'its best endeavours to ensure that all building works in respect of the developments in the Bo-Kaap continue without interruption, violence or other hindrance'.[15] The agreement also confirmed that Norton Rose Fulbright would act as 'facilitators', which, as it transpired, included investigating Bokcra, obtaining its financial statements, and interrogating the legitimacy of its nominated leadership.[16]

Blok and BKYM proceeded to discuss setting up a non-profit company to share the benefits of the development, to employ individual members and to contract with companies set up by BKYM for (unspecified) goods and services.[17]

When Blok tried to bring in a crane to resume construction work in August 2018, however, community resistance stopped the development from proceeding. It appears that opposition also became increasingly violent, with equipment vandalised and destroyed.

In November 2018, Norton Rose Fulbright, acting on behalf of BKYM, lodged a Promotion of Access to Information Act application with Bokcra, demanding that it make its books and financial records available. BKYM also called a press conference, at which they made serious allegations about Bokcra's undemocratic behaviour and its failure to perform its fiduciary duties.[18]

On 20 November Blok tried to bring the crane back to continue construction work, but the community formed a human chain to prevent access to the site. The South African Police Service were called in, and they resorted to using stun grenades on the crowd.[19] Blok brought a second interdict, citing the chair of the Bo-Kaap neighbourhood watch and some members of Bokcra, seeking to prevent them from disrupting construction work at 40 Lion Street.

In court papers answering Blok's interdict application, filed in January 2019, Bokcra went public about the way BKYM had seemingly been co-opted by Blok and Norton Rose Fulbright, and argued that it was no longer a legitimate representative of the community.

In his replying affidavit, Jacques van Emden said that the 'respondents are employing the false narrative that the applicant is seeking to stifle the right of the Bo-Kaap residents to legitimately protest the gentrification of their neighbourhood'. He denied the accusations regarding co-option of BKYM, and justified the involvement of Norton Rose Fulbright on the basis of that company's longstanding commitment to pro-bono work in the community.[20]

In response to a massive outcry from the community, the City eventually published the Bo-Kaap heritage overlay for public comment in January 2019.

At public hearings in February 2019, BKYM raised objections to it. They started by questioning the process, saying that they had not been properly informed about the proposal. 'We are concerned about the unintended consequences of the heritage overlay, which our community is oblivious to,' said a representative. 'What is the rush to implement it?'[21]

Even though a number of property projects had already been signed off without it, the overlay and the building restrictions it would impose were seen as a threat to future development opportunities in the area. But the Bo-Kaap community won the battle and secured permanent protection of its heritage when the city council finally approved the heritage overlay in March 2019.[22]

In the meantime, Bokcra had been preparing a review application to set aside the original sale of land to Blok and overturn the development approval. But they were distracted by multiple requests in accordance with the Promotion of Access to Information Act 2 of 2000, which enables people to gain access to information held by both public and private bodies), and requests for further information, including documentation that was already in the public domain. 'You know, we don't have legal resources,' Seeham Samaai told me. 'All of this is intended to stop us proceeding with the review application. It is now so difficult to be able to keep everything together. Every day the prospect for doing the review gets slimmer and slimmer.'[23]

I was shocked by what Diedericks and Samaai had told me. It showed the extent to which developers were prepared to go to block or undermine community objections. It also showed a cynical effort to manufacture what appeared to be legitimate public opinion. I wondered if there were more widespread instances of manipulation taking place.

Sea Point is an affluent coastal neighbourhood close to the city centre – and prime real estate. In the 1990s it was somewhat eclipsed by the V&A Waterfront development, and became a favourite hangout for figures from the Cape Town underworld, but in the last decade it has recovered its appeal.

In 2010, the Sea Point, Fresnaye and Bantry Bay Ratepayers' and Residents' Association (SFB), which had apparently been dysfunctional for many years,[24] managed, as part of a broader coalition, to block the development of a boutique hotel and the rezoning of public open space for commercial use next to the very popular Sea Point public swimming pool and Sea Point Pavilion.

From 2014 onwards, however, a new team of development professionals took an active interest in SFB. The online community newspaper *GroundUp*, which focuses on social-housing campaigns and urban access for the poor, claimed that developers had captured SFB: at the time of its investigation in February 2018, the secretary of SFB was none other than Jacques van Embden, Blok's managing director. Jacques' father, Marco van Embden, the chair of SFB, was Blok's chairman. At the time, Blok was driving nine major residential developments in and around Sea Point.[25]

But that wasn't all. Six of SFB's nine-person executive committee were involved in the property industry, including Paul Berman, the CEO of Berman Brothers Property, which had its head office, The Point, in Sea Point; Suzanne Kempen, director of S Kempen Property Management; and Ari Vayanos, director of Arcamp Real Estate in Sea Point. And, besides supplying personnel, the property industry had also been sponsoring SFB: in 2017, the organisation had received some R500 000 from corporate sponsors including Pam Golding, Dogon Group, Lew Geffen, Re/Max, Seeff, Durr, Knight Frank, Jawitz, Tyson, and the Real Estate Business Owners of South Africa.[26]

SFB has a planning committee whose role is to consider and comment on development and heritage applications and compliance with building regulations – all crucial steps in the property-development process. At the beginning of 2018, the planning committee was comprised largely of players in the property industry, including two architects, a town planner, a developer, a retired businessman and an attorney; and the committee regularly reviewed development applications that affected its members or their relatives and associates. Most planning-committee meetings took place in the offices of property developers – in 2017, the committee members met at The Point.

For Gavin Silber and Sarita Pillay, activists for a community-based campaign promoting social housing, this was a clear conflict of interest. 'You have a committee representing property interests responsible for vetting their own development applications', Silber pointed out, thus acting as 'both players and referees'.[27]

According to Paul Berman, however, it was standard practice for planning-committee members who were involved in a property development to recuse themselves from the discussion. Marco van Embden also rebutted accusations of impropriety: 'The planning committee is run professionally according to proper processes by individuals who give up a lot of their time on a voluntary basis,' he said. 'We get a lot of wonderful reports.'[28]

Besides SFB's leadership and processes, *GroundUp* also questioned how representative of the community's diverse interests the Sea Point civic body really was. SFB claimed to represent the 8 500 ratepayers in the area, but only 32 people were present or had a proxy at its 2017 annual general meeting. The approximately 5 000 black residents of Sea Point weren't represented by SFB at all.

SFB has consistently objected to any developments that would affect the character of the area, including efforts to build social or affordable housing. SFB secretary Jacques van Embden appeared to exemplify this aversion to social housing – in January 2017 he'd played a prominent role in evicting residents from Bromwell Street in Woodstock, which community activists had earmarked as a social-housing project.[29] However, it appeared that when it came to social housing, residents themselves sometimes put up the stiffest obstacles; some developers I spoke to pointed out that they had initially included elements of affordable housing in some of their Sea Point projects to facilitate approval from the City, only to face stiff opposition from local residents.

Janey Bell, a Sea Point resident and the former vice-chair of SFB, was one of the members of the executive committee of SFB when the sale of the Tafelberg land in the heart of Sea Point was being debated in 2014. There were conflicting proposals about what to do with the Tafelberg site, which used to be a school. Bell was a lone voice on SFB's executive arguing in

favour of social housing on the site, to which SFB strongly objected, arguing instead in favour of selling the land. 'Oh boy, was I unpopular,' Bell told
me. 'I lost all my friends in one go.'[30]

The Western Cape provincial authorities ended up selling the Tafelberg
land to a private school at a massively discounted price. SFB's opposition
to social housing may have added weight to the province's decision, but
social activists saw the hidden hand of developers behind the manoeuvring.
When I met with Gavin Silber in August 2018, he told me that having
property interests in SFB's key executive positions guaranteed that future
development proposals in Sea Point would be pushed through without
opposition from the community.[31]

Janey Bell, however, wasn't convinced that the developers needed SFB
to get their proposals through, because they already employed so many
former City employees. 'The developers' staff walk the corridors of the
City as if they own the place; they are able to get their applications through
very easily.'[32] But she conceded that their involvement in SFB gave them a
platform and standing in the community, which helped their cause.

Nevertheless, some residents were convinced that SFB had indeed been
hijacked. Lucy Graham, who in February 2018 had been living in Sea
Point for ten years, felt that the association was being controlled by a few
property developers with vested interests. On joining the association in
October 2016, Isa Jacobson felt that both the association and the planning
committee were 'not people who do this for the greater good'.[33]

Once *GroundUp*'s investigation into SFB was published in early 2018,
the negative publicity drove Paul Berman and Jacques van Embden to
resign; Marco van Embden remained as chair. Berman and Van Embden
Jnr's level of influence remained high, however, as a pattern of behaviour
had been established around an unwritten code of maximising property
values and promoting high-end developments.

Bell said she eventually resigned in July 2018 because she couldn't stand it: she felt it was simply inappropriate for developers to be so involved in a civic organisation that should ordinarily be concerned only with the interests of residents.

Similar concerns had cropped up briefly in the Maiden's Cove for All alliance. The Clifton Bungalow Owners' Association was a key member of the alliance. Mostly high-net-worth individuals, members included some prominent characters such as the high-profile divorce lawyer Billy Gundelfinger. More concerning, however, was the presence in the alliance of Mark Willcox, who'd once been Tobie Mynhardt's business partner around the original proposal for the development, before the two apparently fell out. When Willcox rocked up at a coalition meeting, Albie Sachs and his partner Vanessa wondered whether the supposed split between Mynhardt and Willcox had a more sinister intention behind it – to white-ant the coalition by infiltrating it and gathering intelligence about its fightback strategy.[34]

They were somewhat reassured when they heard Willcox's side: he felt that Mynhardt had got too big for his boots and abused their relationship to ingratiate himself with political leaders. Willcox, miffed, had extracted himself from the development deal. Ironically, he then became one of the formal applicants in the court case opposing the proposed development that he'd initially sponsored. Clearly, Willcox wasn't trying to undermine the coalition's opposition to the project – the Maiden's Cove for All alliance was ultimately successful in blocking the proposed project – but Albie Sachs wondered whether Willcox's opposition to the development was sincere, or if he'd been using the Clifton Bungalow Owners' Association to settle personal scores.

My enquiries into the dynamics behind the Observatory, Bo-Kaap and Sea Point civic associations had revealed disturbingly sinister motives. Some property developers in Cape Town were attempting to take over problematic civic organisations in order to minimise public input into the approval process and clear the way for their developments. It was also clear that the City's political leaders, who are tasked with looking after the public interest and catering for the needs of the urban poor, were playing an active role in pushing through controversial developments in spite of significant objections from the public. This felt like a blatant manipulation of civic organisations to distort and manufacture public opinion.

It reminded me of scientist-philosopher Noam Chomsky's writing about how elites manipulate and control public opinion to defend their economic, social and political agendas – what he terms 'manufacturing consent' – thereby enabling their continued domination of society, the state and the global order.[35] In itself, the hijacking of Cape Town's civic associations was hardly of global or even national significance, yet it echoed Chomsky's concept at local level.

It also reminded me of older attempts to manipulate civic associations and community movements. In the late 1980s, as the apartheid government made its last desperate efforts to keep control, state infiltration and co-option of civic organisations became a common tactic. Some civic leaders had links to the security branch, which used these networks to identify underground activists, as well as tying up civic organisations in internal conflict so as to neutralise them.

Particularly in the Western Cape, the authorities managed to exploit ideological and racial divisions among coloured and African civic organisations.[36] The consequences were sometimes devastating; for example, violence among rival groups in the Crossroads informal settlement in the 1980s left hundreds dead and at least 60 000 homeless. And in 1991 an open struggle for political control of informal settlements broke out between rival civic associations in Khayelitsha, Lwandle township and Waterkloof in Somerset West, with similar tragic results.[37]

I realised that the attempted hijacking of civic organisations by property interests was perhaps the most recent incarnation of an entrenched
and enduring pattern. Its manifestation was different, of course. It was
meant not to foment violence or sustain an undemocratic system, but to
advance financial interests. Its weapons were bank accounts, public relations and bylaws, rather than violent coercion. Yet the same strings were
being pulled to weaken community organisations and protect entrenched
interests, even if the puppeteers and their motivations had changed.

I wasn't yet fully clear, however, on how these financial interests inter-
faced with the City administration. Was there some other game in play, a
hand of cards I couldn't see?

11

The riddle of the sphinx

$\wedge\!\wedge\!\wedge$

'**A**re the officials and politicians in Cape Town on the take?'
I asked this of the chair of the WCPDF, Deon van Zyl, as we sipped our cappuccinos in a trendy coffee shop on Buitenkant Street, which used to mark the southern boundary of the early Dutch town, beyond which lay the grim quadrangle where executions took place.

Usually loquacious, Van Zyl was stumped by my question. 'Not in my experience,' he said, after a moment's reflection. In fact, he explained, the terror of clean audit and compliance was so great that officials tended to the other extreme: not taking any decisions at all for fear of making a mistake.[1]

Van Zyl is affable and passionate about his job, which is to represent the interests of the property-development industry in the Western Cape. He knows the industry intimately. His background is in town planning, and for many years he worked for AECI, unlocking the chemical company's vast land holdings in Somerset West, and in Modderfontein in Johannesburg.

I'd posed this question in different ways to various property developers around Cape Town. Some property deals in Cape Town, and the behaviour of officials and politicians around them, had raised enough red flags to make me suspicious. Having worked in a large number of dysfunctional municipalities where corruption was rife, I'd learnt to look out for consistent patterns of behaviour that aren't easily explained by available evidence or don't otherwise make sense. So I'd set out to search for the hidden hand, the under-the-table transactions that might explain the oddities I'd picked up.

My line of enquiry took me in two directions. First, I wanted to find out whether some officials or politicians were taking bribes for pushing development applications through the system. These could be either in the form of payments to politicians and officials for their personal benefit, or donations to political parties in exchange for influence and favours.

Of course, none of the developers I interviewed, even those who seemed dodgy, ever admitted to bribing any official or politician. On the contrary – the former CEO of a listed property company, who'd leased 70 000 square metres of office space to provincial and national government, told me that they were routinely asked for bribes by tenants, who wanted kickbacks for both signing the lease and paying rent every month. 'I constantly had to draw the line,' he told me.[2]

He belonged to a group of property developers in Cape Town who seemed like genuinely good people, with integrity and solid reputations, and who convinced me that much of the property-development industry runs according to sound business practices. Even though it takes longer, they said, they operate without having to grease palms. On the whole, I was told, the City's planning bureaucracy operated efficiently and cleanly, although there were some areas, such as Athlone and Khayelitsha, where the officials in charge didn't return calls, and applications were endlessly delayed.

Quite a few of the developers I talked to admitted, however, that they'd hired planners who'd previously worked in the City and used them to wield influence back in the metro administration. This was standard practice, I was told.

Yet 'influence' didn't stop there. In fact, there was a whole industry in 'development facilitation', which extended into ever-greyer areas of passing on information, invitations to dinners, entertainment, giving gifts and exchanging favours.

'How do the guys go about capturing the officials and politicians?' one of the developers said, and went on to describe the steady way in which these relationships developed. 'You start off with a rugby match or a soccer match. You then elevate it to a dinner. You then elevate it to a hunting weekend. You then elevate it to a grand [R1 000] for the kid, or a bursary loan. You then elevate it to something else. And, eventually, this snowballs to the extent that you've actually got the business. That's what they did with the [former] president [Jacob Zuma].' Referring to my previous book, he added, 'You should know. How do you steal a city? Bit by bit. How do you develop? Bit by bit.'[3]

These cosy arrangements seemed to be changing, however. One of the planning officials still working for the City told me that the flow of annual 'gifts' to which they were accustomed had dried up in the last three years. These weren't bribes, I was told, but 'retrospective acknowledgement' for jobs well done – but no official dared to accept them any more, and the developers didn't dare to openly proffer them either.

At the same time, Barbara Southwood, a former city planner who runs a successful urban-design business, told me that deals between developers and officials had been going on for years, and that there were officials who were prepared to bend the rules and grant applications in return for kickbacks. These officials often went on expensive overseas holidays and seemed to be living beyond their means.[4]

My overall impression was that, while the odd official may still be willing to be involved in irregular deals, Cape Town's administration seems generally well run and clean – particularly when compared to those of other cities. By most statistics, the Cape Town metro is doing well. The City administration has received clean audits for years, and its level of irregular and unauthorised expenditure is the lowest of any metro. Citizen satisfaction and trust is the highest among the eight metropolitan municipalities in South Africa (65,2% in 2018, albeit 3,3% down on 2017).[5]

In 2018, only 6% of the corruption reports submitted to Corruption Watch, an NGO that monitors bribery in government agencies, related to the Cape Town metro. Although higher than five smaller cities around South Africa, the proportion of corruption complaints about Cape Town was much lower than in the economic hub of Johannesburg (20% of reports) or the capital city, Tshwane (10%).[6] While these are allegations, not proven wrongdoing – Corruption Watch doesn't have the capacity to investigate the reports it receives – it nonetheless does suggest that there are indeed instances of corruption in Cape Town, even if not as many as in other South African cities of similar size.

If administrators and politicians were, on the whole, not lining their own pockets, what of political corruption? Was there any link between deals being pushed through and party funding? This was a question that organisations such as the OCA had been asking.[7]

While political parties do serve a public interest, financing them through state contracts and property deals is nevertheless corrupt. In my experience, these deals usually take place around election campaigns, when desperate politicians make promises about transactions they will approve once in power in exchange for campaign contributions.

Unfortunately, from the dawn of democracy, we'd had a largely unregulated system of party funding, and it was almost entirely hidden from the public's view. Until very recently, political parties weren't required to disclose who funded them and how much money they raised. There were no restrictions on cash donations or anonymous donations – particular favourites among the less scrupulous operators. Donations from overseas weren't limited either. This made South Africa an international laggard in terms of party-finance transparency.[8] It also made research into whether and how party finance influences decision-making within the state extremely difficult.

An NGO based in Observatory, My Vote Counts, has done ground-breaking work on party funding in South Africa. I spoke to Janine Ogle, the national coordinator at the time, in the organisation's cramped offices above Lower Main Road, not far from where I lived as a student. It's achieved remarkable things on a shoestring budget. For one, it was a driver behind the new legislation that seeks to make all party funding transparent.

In June 2018, My Vote Counts won an important Constitutional Court judgment that the public had a right to know where political parties got their funding.[9] On the back of this, Ogle wrote to all political parties asking for a list of their financial contributors. None of the parties was willing to divulge their funders, although the DA indicated that they were waiting for the new legislation to be implemented.

In August 2018, along with other civil-rights organisations includ-ing AmaBhungane, the Dullah Omar Institute at the University of the Western Cape, the Open Democracy Advice Centre, Corruption Watch and Right2Know, My Vote Counts wrote to Cyril Ramaphosa to ask him to expedite the legislation 'in the interest of upholding democracy and improving our political system through greater transparency'. The lack of disclosure posed a danger to the stability of the political and electoral sys-tem, the letter argued, and the public was being 'robbed of and denied their constitutional right to be informed of the nature of relationships between political parties and their private funders'.[10]

Ogle had been amazed that, during the Parliamentary hearings on this legislation, the DA had steadfastly opposed any moves to disclose party funding to the public. Their argument, which was echoed by some of the DA leaders I interviewed, was that the ANC, which was in power nation-ally and in eight of the nine provinces, would use sensitive information to victimise and intimidate the DA's funders.

Ogle, however, wasn't convinced. 'We're trying to fix gaps in the law which should have been done at the start of democracy,' she told me. 'Surely the benefits of disclosure outweigh any individual party concerns? If everyone takes the DA's line, then there will never be change in the system, and the politicians will just continue doing what they want.'[11]

Ramaphosa took an inordinately long time to sign the bill into law, and the Political Party Funding Act 6 of 2018, which regulates disclosure of donations, among other things, was only finally enacted in January 2019 – too late to cover the 2019 election. And, unfortunately, the legislation isn't retroactive, so we'll never get access to past information, and it will take some time before the reporting now required by law is systematised.

Even if I couldn't get access to information on actual political donations, I wanted to know how the DA funding machine worked. I spoke with Grant Pascoe, a former DA leader and mayoral committee member in the City of Cape Town who defected to the ANC in 2014. In the circumstances, I wasn't going to be able to take at face value whatever Pascoe told me but his story did seem to tie up some loose ends.

Pascoe said that the genesis of the DA fundraising model dated back to around 2004. Back then, he'd been recruited into the office of then DA leader Tony Leon, right when the party's internal management was being corporatised. This included a data-driven, scientific approach to canvassing, a performance-management system for party leaders, and a centralised fundraising operation supported by a call centre.[12]

James Selfe, the chairman of the DA's federal executive, told me that the streamlined fundraising system came into effect in 2006, partly in response to scandals linked to donations from German fugitive from justice Jurgen Harksen and corrupt mining magnate Brett Kebble.[13] [14] Ryan Coetzee, the DA's main political strategist, brought in by Tony Leon in 1999, who became CEO in 2005, completely modernised the party's fundraising system and turned it into a tight operation run from the DA's head office. He did this with very direct encouragement from Helen Zille, who was party leader at the time; Zille promoted the fundraising model that had been used at UCT, where she'd been director of development and public affairs in the mid-1990s.[15] David Maynier, a smart young man with a master's degree from Harvard, was recruited as the first director of fundraising.

According to Pascoe, DA leaders weren't allowed to raise funds on their own initiative, and instead were selectively pulled in to play particular roles. Pascoe explained to me how he, for instance, was assigned specific potential donors to meet, from whom he was tasked to raise a target amount of contributions. 'I would get an information sheet with all the funders' details, what they had donated last year and what amount I should be pushing for. The funder would already know why I was coming to see them, so I didn't have to do a hard sell. I would seal the deal, complete the form and submit it, all in the same day.'[16]

Immediately after his report was in, someone from the call centre would follow up to arrange the actual deposit. Having the person collecting separate from the person sealing the commitment provided not only checks and balances but also meant that no party activist actually handled any cash. 'The DA may have many flaws, but they are very diligent about proper management and accounting for their own resources,' Pascoe said me. 'The systems need to be implemented 100%.'[17]

Pascoe and I laughed about the contrast between this efficient operation and our experience of the ANC's chaotic fundraising efforts, in which we both had first-hand experience. I'd been involved in ANC fundraising campaigns in Nelson Mandela Bay, and had found the system highly opaque and disorganised. Every ANC leader seemed engaged in farming their particular pool of donors, and a large proportion of funds raised in the ANC's name funded factional campaigns and battles inside the party or was creamed off as 'commissions' for personal benefit.

'It's just a free for all,' Pascoe concurred. 'Everybody just goes and collects money. You don't know what has happened to it. Mostly the organisation never sees the money. You hear there's money been collected, or somebody has given so much, but you never get to see it.'[18]

In the DA, party leaders' annual performance was determined in part according to the amount of funds they'd raised, and there was a strong competitive element. Every year at the DA's federal congress, the leader who'd raised the most money received an award.

Pascoe was irritated that the award for top fundraiser of the year went to James Selfe – as the person at the centre of the DA's organisational machinery, Selfe was responsible for liaising with the most important donors. 'He controlled the system; it was his system. He would deal with the big guns that would give the big cheques,' Pascoe said, 'so he was basically giving himself an award because he was in charge of the system.'[19]

When I asked Selfe about this, he said he'd only ever won the award once, in 2010, for his efforts in the 2007/8 financial year. He was miffed at Pascoe's barb. 'It was much more difficult to raise money then, and I had to work really hard to raise what I raised.'[20]

I know from practical experience that political fundraising may in many respects be a slippery slope. No potential donor is purely philanthropic – they're all seeking some sort of influence or advantage, and for the unwitting party activist, procuring what had initially seemed innocent favours could rapidly turn into administrative interference.

To illustrate his point, Pascoe mentioned the case of auction house Auction Alliance, a generous donor to the DA that had been managed directly by James Selfe, the party's federal-executive chair. In 2011 Auction Alliance had wanted to put up an advertising billboard and was told by City officials to first submit a visual-impact assessment and traffic study. According to Pascoe, Selfe asked him (Pascoe) to see if he could assist them and 'make the problem go away'. Pascoe apparently pointed out to Selfe that the officials were following the rules set out by a bylaw, but he duly spoke to the officials, and the approval for the Auction Alliance sign was expedited.[21]

Selfe said that Pascoe's account about Auction Alliance was inaccurate. While he confirmed that Auction Alliance had asked him to intervene in a dispute they had with the City regarding signage, Selfe said he simply escalated the matter to the mayoral committee, of which Grant was a member at the time, but was told that there was nothing that could be done. Selfe said he informed Auction Alliance accordingly.[22]

The Auction Alliance donations to the DA and the subsequent intervention on the company's behalf reveals the ease with which seemingly innocent requests from donors, once raised with decision-makers in government, transform into political interference in the administration. This is the slippery slope of party funding, in which political influence is exchanged for party donations, sometimes from donors whose business practices turn out to be questionable.

But Pascoe went further – he alleged that the DA leveraged its power in the City to support its funding operation. Once the DA took the reins at City Hall in 2006, and mayoral-committee positions were being allocated among coalition partners, the party made sure that it controlled the finance and planning portfolios. 'That's when the DA really fell into the money, when Helen became mayor, and she put Ian Neilson in charge of finances and property,' Pascoe said. 'Between those two, and James Selfe and Alan Winde [who at the time were DA caucus leaders in the national and provincial parliaments], they controlled the party's fundraising.'[23]

Through the City's finance portfolio, which included property management, Neilson supposedly had access to the municipal property and billing database, which contained details of every land-holding and property owner in the city. This allowed him to extract data – ordinarily confidential

– on both ratepayers and developers, which was fed to the fundraising team. If true, using such information for political fundraising was highly questionable.

Selfe rubbished Pascoe's allegations. 'There is absolutely no truth in the imputation that we "leveraged" control of the City of Cape Town for fundraising purposes. We are at pains not to do that, and for good self-interest: any scandal involving fundraising damages us and makes it impossible for us to raise any money at all. Harksen and Kebble taught us that.'[24]

Selfe said that every fundraiser was carefully briefed to tell donors that the DA could offer them only what they were entitled to receive as citizens and taxpayers. 'Many citizens have problems with government services in all spheres, and the duty of elected representatives is to assist those citizens to receive those services.'[25]

Nevertheless, Pascoe was emphatic that donors called the shots in the DA. The party's funding heartland in the city was the Atlantic Seaboard, as well as the areas around Durbanville and the South Peninsula that used to be controlled by the NNP. According to Pascoe, these traditional donors to the party benefited from preferential treatment in their business with the City: their objections were taken seriously, and their development applications signed off expeditiously.[26]

'It is the funders that really control the DA's policies, that's why the party is so supportive of the private sector,' Pascoe explained. 'I don't have a problem with being pro-business, but there's no counter-balance to what the party is trying to achieve. The donors control the party so much that the DA can't move into a more progressive, social-democratic space.'[27]

Businesses can secure political influence in many ways, some perfectly legal, and not all influence-peddling flows into party coffers. For instance, in September 2014 Sun GrandWest, a casino in Goodwood, Cape Town, owned by Sun International, sponsored the Mayor's Golf Day at the Rondebosch Golf Club to raise money for Patricia de Lille's charity. They continued to sponsor mayoral golf days with De Lille for the next three years. This apparently generous gesture was part of Sun International's commitment to 'have a positive impact on the communities in which we work'.[28]

Yet the Sun GrandWest casino's noble motivation gets muddled when considering that its period of exclusivity (it was the only casino allowed to operate in Cape Town) had expired in 2013 and that it had every interest in making sure a second casino licence wouldn't be awarded for Cape Town – a decision that the Western Cape province had been considering, and which would have taken business away from Sun GrandWest. De Lille was DA Western Cape party leader at the time. It may seem churlish to portray this as influence peddling, but the supposedly philanthropic efforts of Sun GrandWest seemed to have another objective.

De Lille's personal links to property developers and businessmen such as Mark Willcox, who reportedly contributed to her charities, had also come under scrutiny during the controversy over the Maiden Cove proposed development.[29]

At that stage, beyond a few anecdotes, it wasn't clear how I was going to be able to look into the links between party funding and influence over the City administration.

Beyond Selfe's candid response, my efforts to verify what Grant Pascoe had alleged hit a brick wall. David Maynier declined to meet with me. And when I had lunch with Deputy Mayor Ian Neilson, he was pretty forthright and engaging about De Lille and her failings, but the minute I started asking questions about party funding or the property industry, he clammed up. He outright denied that he was involved in any party fundraising activities, as this would conflict with his fiduciary responsibilities as head of the City's finances.

I also had tea with Helen Zille, who told me that she'd never engaged with property developers in the Western Cape 'because it is a slippery slope, and I don't want to be exposed to what they will ask for'.[30] But her response begged the question: if Zille wasn't meeting with the developers, who in the DA had been handling them for the purposes of fundraising?

Nevertheless, Zille exhorted me to read her autobiography, in which she wrote of the ongoing tensions between the NNP and DP wings of the DA following their merger in 1998.[31] She described a war waged for the soul of the DA in the period between 2000 and 2007. According to her, the NNP had joined the DA with a whole lot of baggage inherited from its apartheid past, including shady practices such as falsifying membership numbers, manipulating organisational processes, creating secret decision-making structures, and offering financial inducements.[32] This caused Zille to worry about a 'reverse takeover' of the DA by the NNP, which would create 'a new patronage-driven party in which they would be the dominant force, controlled by ethnic nationalism and racial mobilisation, cronyism and corruption.'[33]

Her autobiography describes the unrelenting campaign she waged against these practices, a debilitating fight that she narrowly survived, leaving her battle scarred and hardened – and even if corrupt practices were progressively weeded out, some of them persisted for some time.

Zille's description of the conflict with the NNP echoed what Grant Pascoe had told me about tensions in the DA's funding approach. Under Tony Leon's centralised system, every ward or constituency would have a budget allocated by party headquarters: the party wanted to minimise expenditure on fixed costs such as constituency offices and focus instead on capable grassroots organisers. The more affluent constituencies would be expected to fund themselves, while priority areas such as Mitchells Plain were subsidised.

This didn't sit well with the NNP wing of the DA, who wanted to control their own constituency and ward-based funding system, as well their party funding machinery. 'In fact, the NNP team under Marthinus van Schalkwyk never really loosened their grip on their own funders,' Grant Pascoe told me. 'When [the NNP] left the DA to join the ANC, they took their whole funding machinery with them. That's why you can see [former NNP MP] Daryl Swanepoel is still there, running the ANC's Progressive Business Forum.'[34]

Even the normally candid Brett Herron went quiet when I asked about DA funding and property deals. Judging by the silence that met my questions, I seemed to have hit a nerve.

But in early 2019, a few months after he'd left the City administration, Herron gave an address to the Cape Town Press Club, which he kindly forwarded to me. In his address, he described the influence of party funding over property development. He revealed that, while still working for the City, he'd been asked by a DA MP to join him at a fundraising meeting with property developers who were donors to the party. Most of Cape Town's main property developers were there.

During the meeting, Herron had become very uncomfortable when questioned about his plans for social housing in Woodstock and Salt River – he felt that a party funding meeting was encroaching on City policy issues when the developers questioned him about what kind of developments they could expect to see. 'I was asked if I was planning a 'tent city' on one of the sites – as if the proposal was to build some kind of refugee camp.'

After he'd answered the property developers' questions, Herron was politely asked to excuse himself from the meeting before the discussion on party contributions, to avoid even the appearance of a conflict of interest.[35]

As he explained when I met with him, Herron didn't think the DA's old guard sufficiently trusted the former ID members in the party with fundraising. Herron wasn't privy to the party-funding discussion that took place after he left, 'but, clearly, there was some pushback from some donors against the idea of addressing our affordable-housing crisis and our plans to do so,' he said.[36]

Brett's social-housing programme formed part of a larger Woodstock and Salt River Precinct, in which the City was making available 11 sites it owned for housing development. Five of the sites were earmarked for affordable housing, with an emphasis on social housing. Early in 2018 the City had asked developers and social-housing companies to come forward with innovative proposals for the sites.

Not long afterwards, the DA caucus blocked the disposal of the Salt River Market and Woodstock sites that had been identified for the development of affordable inner-city housing. Herron thought that a group of white DA councillors, led by ward councillor Dave Bryant, and egged on by developers in the area, had lobbied for the project to be overturned.[37] 'This all goes to show the relationship between political power and land – and how this relationship is perpetuating exclusion and entrenching apartheid spatial structuring of our country,' he concluded. 'I think it comes down to party political funding.'[38]

I wondered whether this went both ways. Patricia de Lille had refused to subject herself to the DA's strict performance and fundraising system that Grant Pascoe had described. Did her resistance suggest that she wanted to keep her own fundraising out of the DA's central control?

James Selfe, the chair of the DA's federal executive, seemed to think that De Lille had been building up independent means to fund her own political initiative for some time even though he'd never been able to substantiate this.[39]

'Not at all,' Brett Herron said when I put it to him. According to Herron, De Lille was the worst fundraiser. 'She can't ask for money. She could make the pitch, but she always took someone with her to actually ask for the cheque,' he said. 'She starts fidgeting in her handbag and she just can't ask for money.'[40]

If I couldn't go any further looking at the equation between party fund-ing and the property industry from the DA angle, was there any other way I could find out about political influence? Perhaps looking at the property developers themselves would be more enlightening.

12

The gilded calf

~~~

A journalist and outspoken DA critic, Lester September, wrote a scurrilous blog in March 2016 alleging that the WCPDF was an integral
part of what he called Helen Zille's 'from red tape to red carpet' political
strategy.[1]

According to September, Zille's campaign against bureaucratic inertia
had morphed into special treatment for select developers. He claimed that
developers who signed up as members of the WCPDF would get access to
the DA's decision-makers in the City and the Western Cape province, and
that membership fees for the WCPDF were being used to fund the DA.

According to the WCPDF website, its purpose is to 'actively engage
with politicians and government representatives to provide detailed input
and feedback on draft legislation and policy'.[2] Its business plan trumpets
that it 'interacts with high-ranking politicians and officials within the City
and provincial administrations to ensure its effectiveness'.

Even though there's no overt political link, the setup sounds similar to
that of the ANC's Progressive Business Forum, which has been used to
raise business donations for the party and which for many years has mar-
keted access to politicians in exchange for party funding. The Progressive

Business Forum website advertises as 'participants' benefits' 'interaction with ANC policy-makers at ministerial, MEC and metro executive levels' and promises participants that they will be able to network and exchange ideas, information and contacts with ANC-elected representatives.[3]

It was clear that the WCPDF did have access to key decision-makers: the provincial minister for Economic Opportunities attended its 2018 conference, along with Deputy Mayor Ian Neilson and Brett Herron, who back then was in charge of the TDA; the year before, Patricia de Lille and Brett Herron had attended that same event. But while the WCPDF certainly seemed to have excellent access to provincial and local politicians, this could simply be a reflection of the DA's commitment to support the private sector.

Lester September had worried that 'the ear that the city council gives the WCPDF appears to be part of a takeover of planning and development of our city by developers and building companies, which hold massive power through their non-transparent funding of political parties. Does this non-transparent funding of political parties and the cosy relationship between [the Western Cape] provincial government and the WCPDF, in effect not amount to corporate capture of the State?'[4]

I'd heard a similar complaint from one of the campaigners battling against developments in the PHA, who alleged that the WCPDF was a funding front for the DA, and that any developer who wanted to get their proposals approved had to join the WCPDF and make financial donations to the party.[5]

I was curious enough to apply to join the WCPDF through my consulting company and was quite easily admitted as a small business involved in the environmental sector. The membership fees were reasonable, and I wondered whether there would be a phonecall at some stage, making an additional funding request. I never received one but I did arrange to meet the chair of the WCPDF, Deon van Zyl, and that was when I asked him point-blank whether the City's officials were on the take.

Although his initial answer about the City's clean audit obsession had been straightforward, the perspective he then shared on the challenges faced by the industry painted a more nuanced picture. Van Zyl patiently mapped out the process involved in developing land. First, developers had to acquire the land, or get legal right to it through an option or leasehold. Then they had to obtain development rights, which consisted of multiple regulatory decisions that could include changing the urban edge, precinct plans, zoning, heritage approval, environmental-impact assessment, subdivision and building-plan approval. Last, they had to get the bulk infrastructure in place – roads, stormwater drainage, electricity, sewerage and water. Only then could they start building.[6]

'A best-case scenario for a medium-sized retail development is that it will take you three years before a spade hits the ground,' Van Zyl concluded. 'In complex cases it could easily take a decade. That just pushes the costs up. Just for the regulatory approvals, you'll need to spend between R2 million and R10 million. But the biggest challenge is the uncertainty. The banks won't touch it until you've got the rights in place. All that time, the development has to be financed on risk.'[7]

The situation had become so bad that many of the traditional mid-sized development companies had decided that they wouldn't buy land that still required regulatory approvals. Instead, they would pay a high premium for land that came with development rights already in place.

Van Zyl had recently spoken to a Cape Town property financier. 'Don't come to us unless you have a tenant, the land is secured, and your development rights are in place,' he was told bluntly.[8]

In Van Zyl's view, this was a crisis, as no one wanted to undertake the first part of the land-development process. 'Next time you drive past a construction site, you've got to wave at those construction workers, because that building ran the full suite of regulatory approvals,' he said he'd told

De Lille at the last WCPDF conference. 'It's a miracle that that building is coming out of the ground.'[9]

Van Zyl was concerned that the byzantine bureaucracy and the complexity involved in property development were stretching timeframes to the point where developments were no longer viable, resulting in bankruptcies. He didn't know of anyone who'd paid a bribe, he said, but administrative logjams and mounting financial pressure could drive people to seek unsavoury solutions. 'It just creates an incentive for the developers to start doing silly things, and a breeding ground for corrupt politicians to operate in. What would you do under those circumstances, if you thought a politician might be able to push something through?'[10]

The remarkable feature of regulatory approvals for property development is that they create enormous value for the developer without any financial transfer from the City. Value is created at a distance, and because there is no direct financial transfer, auditors don't easily pick this up.

At the same time, Van Zyl pointed out, the string of regulatory approvals involved different departments. It would be extremely costly and time-consuming to pass a brown envelope across each of them, he mused. No, I thought you'd need to curry favour and win influence right at the top in order to ensure success in each step of the process.[11]

He made this remark casually, but it was a revealing insight. Cutting through the regulatory obstacles would need to be driven at the centre of the City administration.

After talking to Deon van Zyl, I set out to look more closely into business practices within the property industry. If financial pressures might lead to desperate measures, I wondered what was considered accepted or even standard practice among property developers to drive a project through the system.

To understand its ethical underpinnings, I had to learn how the property industry was structured. First came speculative land 'beneficiators' (a term used by Van Zyl to describe those 'beneficiating' raw land by enabling it with rights), with a higher risk appetite, who were typically involved in the earlier stage of the development process – securing development rights and bulk infrastructure. In Cape Town, the economic environment, regulatory hurdles and costs had squeezed the bulk of the small-scale first-tier beneficiators out of the market.

The second-tier operators then put complex deals together, usually with multiple partners or divisions within one company handling different aspects of development projects. And last came the asset managers, with a much lower risk appetite and a preference for predictable income flows and liquid assets that they could buy and sell.

In addition to developers, estate agents buy and sell properties, which managing agents lease and maintain, while financiers and banks back particular developments. Sometimes, some or all these functions are clustered within an integrated property group.

I realised that the property industry is highly driven by transactions: very few people in the industry earn a monthly salary. Professionals such as architects, planners, quantity surveyors, and environmental and heritage consultants earn fees on work delivered, but often they go on risk for some or all of the job, becoming increasingly invested in the transactions' going through to get paid. Brokers earn commission only once they've secured a tenant and the lease is signed. The same goes for investment brokers. The long lead times without income are painful, and when the money does come in, it's usually quite a large cheque. This can seriously blur notions of right and wrong.

You'd think that the listed property sector, which is subject to considerable oversight from the Johannesburg Stock Exchange and public investors, would be the segment of the industry that best sticks to the straight and narrow. High-profile scandals have highlighted that this isn't the case, however.

In early 2018, a dramatic share sell-off in the listed real-estate investment sector, specifically the Resilient group of companies, including Resilient, Fortress, Nepi Rockcastle and Lighthouse Capital, triggered an investigation for insider trading and market manipulation that spanned more than a year. A number of asset managers and research firms accused the companies and their executives of trading large volumes to artificially boost share prices. The companies were also suspected of using their cross-holdings in each other, through questionable accounting policies and 'accelerated bookbuilds' (rapid expansion of their investment portfolio), to boost profits, dividend payments and net asset values.[12]

Although the Financial Sector Conduct Authority (FSCA) announced in March 2019 that the insider-trading investigation into three of the companies had been 'closed' due to insufficient evidence, a separate market manipulation probe is ongoing.[13]

More recently, in March 2019, accounting fraud at agri-processing business Tongaat Hulett, responsible for large property developments north of Durban, led to a collapse of its share price and criminal charges against an executive. At the end of May 2019 the board of Tongaat Hulett announced that the 2018 financial statements could not be trusted, and trading in the company's shares was suspended.[14]

It seems clear that some of the largest listed property companies have been sailing pretty close to the wind, suggesting a lack of business scruples.

Property transactions seemed to lend themselves to corporate malfeasance in other sectors too.

Nestled among beautiful vineyards on the outskirts of the quaint town of Stellenbosch, next to the Rupert Museum and the Remgro head office, sits the headquarters of Steinhoff, a global furniture and household-goods retail business operating in 30 countries, with 6 500 outlets and 90 000 staff. In late 2017, the auditors' refusal to sign off the financial statements due to irregularities led to the exposure of systematic accounting frauds, insider trading and fronting (obscuring the people behind a deal by using another entity to do the transaction), and the inflation of the company value by some US$12 billion (equivalent to roughly R150 billion at the time). Steinhoff's CEO Markus Jooste resigned, while the Steinhoff share price lost 96% of its value.

The investigations by regulatory authorities exposed how Jooste and his inner circle had woven 'an intricate web of opaque deals hidden from shareholders to covertly enrich themselves'.[15] Among the irregularities were various property deals in which Jooste, members of the Steinhoff family and a UK property developer, Malcolm King, had interests. It appeared that they'd set up offshore entities in which their ownership was carefully hidden, then used these entities to purchase property from Steinhoff and lease it back to the company. Known as 'pre-letting', the acquisitions were externally financed on the back of Steinhoff's promise to lease the properties.[16]

While the practice is fairly common in the industry, these particular deals were highly dubious because the Steinhoff top brass were secretly in on both sides of the deal, pulling the strings and filling their pockets. As they got greedier, Jooste and his team started flipping properties, buying them at discounts and selling them back to Steinhoff at inflated prices. Put simply, Steinhoff had sold properties to someone's friends and then overpaid to buy those properties back. Sources inside the company agreed that the outcome was that the 'friends' got rich and Steinhoff's balance sheet was artificially inflated.[17]

We can speculate about Jooste's moral justifications for his behaviour, but the corporate culture in which it was incubated is what's most concerning. An essential part of doing business in the property industry is that the dealmakers get a cut, and everyone is aligned around the pursuit of the next elusive deal. In the Steinhoff case, this was enclosed within a code of silence in which trust was the glue that held the company together across its different jurisdictions.[18] Clearly, 'trust' included lying about the hollowing-out of the company's assets, and covering up the true nature of the transactions.

What the Steinhoff saga did reveal was that the very heart of corporate culture in Stellenbosch was infected with a deep-seated disregard for accountability, which led to the creation of a 'web of deception' bordering on criminality. But how far did it extend? And if in Stellenbosch, why not elsewhere, in Cape Town, or the satellite nodes of Tygerberg or Century City? Were there other mini-Steinhoffs, buried like time bombs within Cape Town's property sector, waiting their turn to explode?

I had a list of potential suspects to consider, but Uvest, the company that had been churning up the PHA, seemed a promising place to start.

Uvest, which grew out of its forerunner, MSP, is a classic example of a vertically integrated property company, with various divisions covering each step of the property-development value chain. It had branched out from property development into construction, finance, asset management and facilities management. It's an established player with big developments under its belt, including Helderberg Gateway in Somerset West, Big Bay and Eden on the Bay in Blouberg, Madison Square in Tyger Waterfront, Stonehurst in Constantia, and Avonwood Square in Elsies River.

I tried in vain to find out who the financiers were behind the Uvest group of companies. Its website is mysteriously silent on this, although it does indicate that Old Mutual is a partner in some of the housing funds.

In October 2018 I was granted an interview with John Coetzee, Uvest's head of development projects, at Uvest's head office in an office block in Tygerberg that lacked character but offered a breathtaking view over the Tygerberg hills. Coetzee, his signature thick gold chain around his neck, was affable. He told me that he'd been working in property development for 18 years and loved it. Catherine Stone, he said, was being driven by a 'personal agenda' – what that agenda might be, however, he did not say – and was protecting the PHA despite all the evidence that it was doomed. 'The land is degraded, squatters are moving in and stealing from the farmers, those farms aren't profitable. Mark my word, in ten years Nazeer [Sonday] and that lot will have moved on.'[19]

Coetzee found Japie Hugo, Stone's boss, arrogant, but he thought highly of De Lille: she'd been the one person willing to meet Uvest and deal with the obstacles that they faced, he explained.

I felt it was time to ask my question: had Uvest ever been asked to pay a bribe to get a decision through?

Coetzee's response was to tell me a story about a development they had tried to do in Khayelitsha in 2012. He'd been invited to a community meeting on a Sunday morning, and after going through the plans for the development, was asked by the community leaders, 'What legacy are you going to leave behind? In Coetzee's view, this was a request for a pay-off.

'Legacy?' he'd said. 'The legacy I'm going to leave behind is a beautiful development inside of Khayelitsha. That is my legacy. I don't know what else you want.'[20]

That was seven years ago, and the development, Coetzee noted wryly, had still not materialised. 'I don't pay bribes,' he said, 'but there are a lot of people out there who are looking for bribes.'

Coetzee told me about a group who operated in Tygerberg, via the Tygerberg Forum, who made it their fulltime occupation to object to any development. According to Coetzee, the property industry was beset by such people, who positioned themselves so that they could reach a 'settlement' with developers who were desperate to get their projects signed off. He said that he didn't consider Nazeer Sonday and groups like the NGO Ndifuna Ukwazi to have genuine motivations.[21]

Apart from confirming the way that Uvest aligned itself within the City's politics (against the planners and for De Lille), and a claim that the company didn't bribe anyone, it was clear that our conversation wasn't going to reveal anything more – especially about the funders behind Uvest.

The *Daily Maverick*, in reporting on developments in Philippi, had indicated that Uvest and MSP were associated with Tokyo Sexwale, the founder of empowerment juggernaut Mvelaphanda, Mark Willcox, the former CEO of Mvelaphanda, and Walter Hennig, a notorious South African businessman based in London.[22 23]

In 2008, investment vehicle Palladino Holdings, of which Hennig was the CEO, entered into a joint venture with a US-based hedge fund and Mvelaphanda to build up a portfolio of 'natural resources' deals in Africa. Mvelaphanda eventually pulled out of the joint venture, called Africa Management, due to Reserve Bank restrictions, but Mark Willcox stayed on as CEO of Africa Management until 2012. The extent of the bribery was revealed in 2016 when US authorities arrested Samuel Mebiame, the son of a former Gabonese prime minister, who'd been hired to secure mining rights for the joint venture. Mebiane had 'routinely' paid bribes to government officials in order to secure deals, and admitted to a conspiracy to 'provide improper benefits to government officials in multiple countries in Africa'. He was sentenced to 24 months in prison.[24]

In September 2016 the US hedge fund Och-Ziff admitted to one charge of conspiracy and paid a US$41-million fine as part of a deferred-prosecution agreement to settle the criminal and civil charges.[25]

At the time neither Willcox nor Uvest was willing to comment on the link between Uvest and Palladino, but an examination of the directorships showed extensive links between Uvest, Palladina and Mvelaphanda.[26] It's a

169

veritable web of connections but the underpinning financial relationships are obscure.

Hennig and Wilcox were also sinister when crossed. An old friend, Pearlie Joubert, recounted an investigation she'd conducted in 2014 as a *Sunday Times* journalist. At the time, she was looking into Walter Hennig's business dealings with Mark Lifman, an alleged kingpin in the Cape Town mafia, through Cape Town's trendiest restaurant and nightclub, the Shimmy Beach Club, located in the Waterfront.[27] The original lease agreement between the Waterfront and Shimmy Beach Club was signed with Mark Lifman.

The *Sunday Times* received a series of threatening emails from Hennig's attorneys before any publication took place, and Joubert was convinced that someone linked to the investigation had been illegally monitoring her emails and movements. Joubert was also investigating the close relations between Willcox, Hennig and Sexwale. Willcox, who had no overt connection to the Shimmy Beach Club, openly threatened to give Joubert a lesson she would never forget and said he was going to make her 'kak'. When she subsequently bumped into him in a carpark, he told her that she 'had to stop this war'.[28]

Another journalist who'd been investigating Lifman, Marianne Thamm, gave me a chilling account of how the criminal underworld in Cape Town hooked its wagons to the modern economy – and how property provided an interface.[29]

The forced removals of families onto the Cape Flats in the 1960s and 1970s, with the breakup of established social networks and family resources, had created the ideal conditions for disaffected youth to be drawn into a life of organised crime. Large criminal syndicates operated in the city, controlling gangs on the Cape Flats and the trade in drugs, prostitution, guns, stolen goods and abalone. This vast criminal underworld was constantly trying to launder its cash, and one of the easiest ways it could store value was through property investments. These criminals' property interests are extensive and double up with the protection rackets they run.

Rival groups battle over control of the city's nightlife, restaurant and entertainment business – the world in which the shady Mark Lifman operates.

Lifman, who's suspected to be linked to the leader of the Sexy Boys gang, also did business with ANC Western Cape leader Marius Fransman, and they had supposedly channelled cash into the Seven Sirs property development group. And a South African Revenue Service audit revealed that Lifman had at one stage been linked to Auction Alliance, the company that, according to Grant Pascoe, had made generous financial contributions to the DA.[30]

My exploration of the property industry had introduced me to many of its players. Suave, image conscious, persuasive, relentless, they cultivated their networks carefully. As one developer wryly remarked, 'Every dodgy guy is in the property industry' – although he also pointed out that 'not everyone in the property industry is a dodgy guy'.[31]

I'd learnt that the transactional nature of business in the industry, the way that the development process was structured so that people relentlessly chased the deals through to conclusion, meant that the incentives to procure political influence, and influence or control community objections at critical stages, were very high. This was expressed in the innumerable instances of corporate malfeasance. And, more worryingly, elements of the property industry seem to blur with organised crime. Given the highly suspect financial dealings behind the property developments I was investigating, I was sure that some of this funding was finding its way into City politics.

I might not have discovered the silver bullet, but I knew enough to draw

171

some conclusions. It seemed that most property developers operating in Cape Town were (and likely are) making donations to the DA – and often to other parties as well. Rabie Properties, for example, defended its funding to the NNP over the Big Bay development because, it said, it donated to all political parties.[32]

As in other cities, developers were invited to party fundraisers, or to meet one-on-one with senior leaders. In these discussions, they raised particular issues that they would have liked to see addressed. These issues were duly passed on to the City administration, often innocently along the lines of 'Can you sort this out?' but subservient officials treated the referral as an injunction, subverting the usual way of doing things.

Among the really big deals that a mayor has to navigate, property development always involves some big trade-offs – splitting costs for bulk infrastructure, exchanging planning permissions with adjacent developments, pushing developers to take on less-profitable social objectives. This is what the exercise of power in the City is about. As the public, we aren't privy to the precise nature of these deals, but it's not unreasonable to expect that politicians will inject party-political interests into the transactions. At the very least, relationships between party funders, developers and political leaders can become incestuous.

We may not know whether or not the deals are irregular, but the operative question is whether the public interest is being served. What happens when implicit obligations are created, and City leaders get people within the administration to cut their funders some slack? Do these deals with funders create an undue hold over party direction and policy, and limit attempts to create a more racially inclusive and progressive party? And how was this enormously complex brokering affected by the fall-out between Patricia de Lille and the DA in 2017?

In earlier moments during her first term, De Lille and the party appeared to be acting in concert around property deals. In her second term, her interventions around catalytic developments made the party uncomfort-able. A much broader factional battle had unfolded, which might at least in part have been linked to battles over funding.

Did the DA suspect De Lille was cutting funding deals with developers on her own? The nature and extent of this factional split seemed to hold the next clue to understanding Cape Town.

13

The road forks

〰〰

'Those in the support of the mayor's proposal stand on this side,' shouted Suzette Little, the caucus chair, over the hubbub that had broken out in the DA gathering, 'and everyone against it stand on that side.'

It was April 2017, and 150 DA councillors were crammed into a committee room on the spacious mayoral floor of the civic centre. There was a temporary pause in the acrimonious shouting, and the DA's councillors looked shocked, unsure whether to believe this was happening. Usually, disagreements in the caucus were resolved through debate and consensus; sometimes, decisions went to a vote.

In this instance the assistant whip, Rose Rau, had been unable to count the hands in the cramped space, and called for a division. Never before had there been a physical division between those for or against a particular position. To make matters worse, Suzette Little presented the matter as those for the mayor and those against her.

As the city councillors slowly moved to different sides of the room, councillor Malusi Booi led the singing of *Senzeni Na?* – 'What have we done?' – a well-known struggle song, by the group opposing the motion.

Mayor De Lille threatened them with disciplinary action. This was becoming tense.[1]

The issue dividing the caucus was a payment of R9 million to the V&A Waterfront for the 'maintenance of public open space'.[2] A late memo had been circulated just before the city council convened, signed by De Lille, requesting authorisation for the extraordinary expenditure.

The DA councillors were uneasy about it: the contract with the Waterfront was outdated, such extra payments had not been made before, and the supporting annexures were missing, as were the necessary signatures from officials. A flimsy legal opinion was attached, which indicated that a payment could be made but didn't clarify why this particular payment was due.

During the council's lunch break, the DA caucus had been hastily convened, and clear dividing lines had formed. De Lille had argued that the City was obliged to honour the contract with the Waterfront, even though it was an old agreement that needed to be reviewed. She claimed it was urgent and needed to go through immediately.[3]

But Ian Neilson, the deputy mayor, had put his hand up and said bluntly that the sum being requested didn't have a sufficient justification. Other councillors had joined in, arguing that they hadn't been given sufficient information or supporting documents to decide the merits of the matter.

De Lille had become visibly frustrated, lambasting caucus members for their failure to comply. She'd then threatened to use her recess powers to push the payment through while council was no longer sitting.[4] The meeting had become unruly.

When Little, the chair, had asked for a show of hands, it was difficult to see the people at the rear, and Rau proposed that councillors physically separate.

They did so, and for a long moment, it wasn't clear which of the two groups was the larger, with a number of councillors hesitating in the middle of the room before making their move. Then the group around Malusi

175

Booi seemed to swell: they held the majority, and the payment request was rejected.[5]

The DA councillors opposing the request questioned the true nature of the payment, particularly when De Lille threatened to take legal action to force the council's hand. In a meeting with senior officials after the council meeting, De Lille said that she would approach the courts for a declaratory order to compel the payment to be made. Caucus members were worried that if the V&A Waterfront took the City to court, De Lille would ensure that the City administration didn't defend the case.[6] (A subsequent investigation by the DA noted there was probably no justification for any payment, since the matter was never brought back to council.)[7]

The DA's leadership subsequently lambasted the decision by the caucus chair to call for a physical division as a fractious move that had intimidated members of the caucus, escalated tensions and sown further divisions in an already acrimonious environment. But the die had been cast, and it was as if a poison bomb had exploded inside the caucus. The damage to the party was irrevocable.

By the time I'd looked into the City's administrative meltdown, as well as the internal and external pressures to ram some property deals through, I wondered whether these dynamics were in any way connected to the acrimonious divisions pitting Patricia de Lille against part of the DA, which were in full swing by then. Were the property deals and planning decisions somehow caught up in the conflict? How had De Lille's centralisation of power played out with the rest of the DA councillors? And was there any truth to De Lille's claims that her pro-transformation agenda was being blocked by the DA old guard?

When I directly approached the politicians involved in the drama – in spite of the City administration's refusal to grant me official access – I was surprised when most made themselves available.

It had all started out so well. In early 2010, Helen Zille and Patricia de Lille sat down to one of their regular early breakfast meetings on the top floor of a downtown hotel. Zille described the city slowly waking up as the two of them took some momentous decisions.[8]

The two politicians had been political adversaries since Zille's days as mayor of Cape Town, but she was seeking to bring opposition parties together to fight the ANC as a united front.

Up until that fateful breakfast, De Lille had spurned any suggestion of joining the DA. But in spite of her high public profile and charisma, she'd done quite badly in the 2009 general elections, as a new party, the Congress of the People (Cope), ate into her party's traditional base: the ID had garnered only 2,9% of the vote in Cape Town, and 4,7% for the province as a whole – significantly down from the previous elections.

The DA, on the other hand, had done well, securing a slender majority in the province (51,5%) and a slightly higher majority in the city (53,8%).[9]

Zille was desperately trying to get the DA to expand its voting base by making its leadership and membership more representative, and when she became premier of the Western Cape in 2009, she cannily offered De Lille a position in her cabinet as provincial minister for Social Development. (De Lille had immediately implemented a major restructuring of the department under Gerhard Ras, who was subsequently to become her axeman in the City as executive director for corporate services.)

For Zille, the deal with De Lille wasn't really about the numbers. As a former trade unionist and struggle leader of the PAC, De Lille offered enormous brand value. A much-feted veteran politician, she'd been a vocal member of the National Assembly, respected for her fiery and dogged push to investigate the infamous arms deal brokered by the ANC government and expose corruption. Her reputation and standing on South Africa's political landscape vastly outsized the electoral performance of the ID she'd launched in 2003, and her values seemed aligned with the squeaky-clean image that the DA was projecting. On the face of it, this was a match made in heaven.

According to Zille, 'Patricia agreed with my argument that there was no point in remaining separate parties, but she did not want to take the step alone. She was clearly concerned about the reaction to her merging with a party that the ANC had branded racist.'[10]

As part of the deal, Zille promised to support De Lille for the position of Cape Town mayor. For the DA, this was a big concession. The party considered the City of Cape Town to be its flagship, the genesis of its good-governance model, which gave them a platform to contest political power elsewhere. The DA's track record in the City was the basis on which it had fought and won the Western Cape province, as well as a string of municipalities around the country.

But there was a small hurdle to overcome: to become mayor, De Lille had to subject herself to the party's selection process.

Zille was particularly proud of the DA's candidate-selection process, which was 'structured to prevent it from degenerating into a manipulative patronage scheme, where leaders reward friends and penalise opponents'. She added the rider that 'we don't always succeed, but we come closer than any other party I know of'.[11]

Still reeling from the impact of the disastrous merger with the NNP on the DA, Zille had no intention of compromising the organisational machinery she'd painstakingly built to preserve what she saw as the party's values and integrity. As she noted in her autobiography, 'All political parties have their factions, internal battles and leadership contests, which at times become bitterly divisive, but comparatively few have built the internal institutions that are necessary to manage the tensions that arise across these faultlines'.[12]

In light of the bitter battle that would later unfold, her words now seem ironic, of course. But back then, Zille was still able to firmly hang on to that belief, so, for her, 'merging' with De Lille's party meant that the ID would be subjected to the DA's organisational processes.

Zille told her DA colleagues in the City that she was talking to De Lille about joining forces. Having been badly burnt by the NNP amalgamation, they had mixed feelings. Also of concern was De Lille's electoral showing.[13] But Zille won the argument, and the ID and DA announced they were merging in August 2010.

Local-government elections were scheduled to take place the following year, and the DA started selecting its candidates almost immediately after the announcement. Four candidates were in the running for mayor: Dan Plato, who'd taken over as mayor from Zille when she'd become premier, DA councillors Shehaam Sims and Grant Pascoe, and De Lille.

The candidates were interviewed one by one by the DA's electoral college, consisting of party leaders from the region and nationally. As a newcomer to the DA, De Lille didn't have strong support within the party, and the candidate who did best in the interviews, Shehaam Sims, was a forthright, no-nonsense grassroots activist who had strong appeal in the coloured community.

Zille spent four hours arguing De Lille's case with the electoral college – De Lille ran a political party, she said; she also had an established brand and had been tested in the community, whereas Sims had not – and she was eventually able to convince them to back De Lille as the candidate.

It had been a nail-biting process, and it cost Zille a fair amount of political capital. 'Most decisions are not a choice between the best and the worst options; nor even between good and bad,' she wrote prophetically in her autobiography. 'The most common decisions in politics are between varying shades of bad. And it is often impossible to predict the impact of different choices without the wisdom of hindsight.'[14]

Yet her strategy with De Lille and the ID seemed vindicated when the DA won the municipal election in Cape Town with a whopping 61%

of the vote – more than the combined shares of the DA and ID votes in 2009. Part of the success was due to clever branding of the party, with Helen Zille, Patricia de Lille and Lindiwe Mazibuko, the party's national spokeswoman, all appearing on the election poster. Three strong women leaders, representing the diversity of South Africa, presented a powerful and inspiring alternative to the ANC's more race-based campaigning.

Zille had built up a successful team in the metro administration, people she trusted to keep the City on an even keel and to give her early warnings if matters started to go awry. This included some DA old-timers who had their own networks of power and influence – and a direct line to Zille – such as Deputy Mayor Ian Neilson, who was also in charge of finance, as well as Anthea Serritslev and Belinda Walker. They all thought that De Lille would continue with Zille's largely collegial system. According to Walker, De Lille was initially 'very meek and mild, she started off very gingerly and gently'.[15]

De Lille seemed to quickly get a feel of the decision-making process. The caucus was where party positions were developed, and it was the key to effective power. Initially charming and persuasive, she very quickly got the large DA caucus on her side, adding to the support of former ID officials like Brett Herron and Shaun August, who were close to her. When faced with a contentious decision, she would come to caucus, present the problem, then express her preferred solution. Although the approach didn't always work in her favour, she often swayed the caucus to support her.

On the face of it, there appeared to be some ideological and political differences between the former ID and DA members of the caucus, however. De Lille came from a more social-democratic background, while the majority of the DA were firmly rooted in a liberal tradition. De Lille was also pragmatic in the way she approached issues, and Herron maintains that in her first term as mayor, she implemented most of her policy agenda without the DA even realising it.[16]

She seemed to bring a much greater focus on transformation, both within the City administration and in terms of service delivery to black communities. Seth Maqetuka, the executive director in charge of housing who was later pushed out by De Lille, at first welcomed her transformation agenda, which complemented the existing focus on good governance and clean audit. He remembered being exhorted to upgrade informal settlements and target the poorest of the poor in terms of service delivery. The focus on transformation was also reflected in the renaming of streets in the city after struggle icons such as Nelson Mandela, Steve Biko and Robert Sobukwe, as well as prominent civic leaders such as Bishop Tutu. There was a palpable feeling of change, which initially gave Maqetuka great hope for the future.[17]

Brett Herron felt that a more social-democratic approach suited Helen Zille's political agenda at the time, even though it felt somewhat at odds with the party's liberal ideology.

I asked Zille whether there were differences over De Lille's agenda of social inclusion and integration. 'Of course not; it's my agenda as well,' she replied, without missing a beat. To back her words, she pointed to a string of properties she wanted developed to fundamentally remake the city of Cape Town. 'I've been pushing this for some time through the province and will continue to do so until I leave office.'[18]

Herron nevertheless felt that this didn't reflect the prevalent sentiment within the DA caucus, and that diverging policy agendas were never truly brought together.[19]

A look at the City administration during De Lille's time as mayor partly – but not entirely – reflects this narrative. By 2018, the proportion of non-white staff in skilled, professional and managerial positions had steadily increased.[20] But at the same time, De Lille had presided over the neutering of that very administration in favour of the overwhelmingly white 'laptop boys' of the SPU that she'd created in the mayor's office.

Officials in the planning department also felt that the mayor's transformation agenda was quite superficial, and the way that old money and business interests held sway in planning decisions continued. The focus of the planning policy was to foster high-value properties that expanded the municipal tax base.

The poor weren't part of this, and were instead accommodated through the programmes of the human-settlements department. For lower-income areas, it became housing delivery at any cost. 'Essentially it was planning for the rich, and human settlements for the poor,' explained one City official.[21]

Many officials also described to me how De Lille castigated them for putting too many constraints on private developers, which seems far more aligned with the DA's traditional liberal approach than with a social-democratic sensibility.

None of the six major human-settlements projects listed in the IDP towards the end of De Lille's first term was anywhere near the city centre.[22] Annandale in Diepriver was 18 kilometres from the city centre, Delft Symphony Way was 24 kilometres distant, Blueberry Hill in Durbanville was 32 kilometres away, Pelican Park phase 2 near Philippi was a 23-kilometre trip, Vlakteplaas on the N2 near Strand was 51 kilometres away, and Wolwerivier inland from Melkbosstrand was 32 kilometres from the CBD.

Maqetuka also told me how, when he was still in charge of human settlements during De Lille's first term, her transformation agenda had stopped short of supporting his efforts to develop social housing near more affluent areas, leaving him disillusioned.[23]

After the 2016 election, however, the City's housing strategy shifted towards the densification of the city centre along designated transport nodes and corridors. The new strategy also involved a 'precinct development approach' to affordable housing, described as 'more economically integrated neighbourhoods, leveraging government investment, helping to stabilise areas, and encouraging greater private investment in regeneration'.

The first precinct was to be in Woodstock/Salt River, with a second one planned in Parow.[24]

In spite of these good intentions, however, the administration's restructuring had by then severely dented its ability to deliver on housing and other investment, resulting in capital underspending and a marked downturn in service delivery.[25] In addition, even though some of the catalytic property-development projects that the mayor had pushed so relentlessly appeared to include some affordable housing, that component was minimal at best.

Looking beyond rhetoric, I wondered whether the ideological differences between the DA's old guard and the ID grafts within the DA were as profound as De Lille and her supporters claimed them to be. When I asked Shehaam Sims, who was initially the mayoral committee member for utility services after De Lille first became mayor, about these differences, she argued that it was primarily a cultural and communication problem, rather than an ideological one. By way of example, she described an interaction she'd had with Belinda Walker, one of the veteran DA councillors in the city. When they were discussing the housing strategy, Walker had bluntly asked Sims, 'Why do you want to give houses to poor people?'[26]

Sims said she couldn't believe that Walker would ask such a question, but nevertheless tried to understand her logic. Walker's concern was that putting people with no income into houses when they couldn't pay for the associated services or upkeep would be disastrous. 'What do you expect that person to do with the house if they haven't got an income?' Walker had asked.

Sims realised that Belinda was concerned about affordability and sustainability, but her initial questions could easily have been misinterpreted.[27]

When I spoke to Belinda Walker about this, she acknowledged that spatial integration was incredibly complicated, partly because of the way Cape Town is configured. Walker had fought against what she called foolish strategies to get business to relocate to Khayelitsha and other townships, saying that business couldn't be forced to move to particular areas. 'You have to take people to the jobs, not the other way round.' In Walker's view, De Lille understood this simple equation, and became its champion.[28]

Although she didn't believe there were ideological differences between them, Walker felt an antagonism of a different nature. She believed De Lille harboured a deep-seated resentment and mistrust towards white middle-class housewives like herself, who she thought were judging her – a feeling that, according to Walker, was misplaced.[29] Of course, one of the characteristics of the white middle class is that we have little insight into the subtle racism and unconscious bias that often permeate our outlook.

According to Suzette Little, however, the differences ran deeper. 'I had to fight for years about social development in the city,' she told me when we met at a café in Rondebosch. 'The DA just doesn't believe in it.'[30]

Little, who'd planted her flag firmly in De Lille's camp, had not been part of the ID graft: she'd started out as an ANC activist before joining the City administration as a secretary when Helen Zille was mayor. Climbing through the ranks, she'd become a DA city councillor in 2010, before the merger between the DA and the ID.

She remembers how, when she became part of the mayoral committee in charge of social development, Belinda Walker had invited her for coffee and asked what her plans were for the portfolio. Little candidly pointed out that she had a skeleton staff and a budget that would only cover biscuits. She was shocked when, at the next mayoral-committee meeting, Walker announced that Little and she had agreed that social services should be shut down.[31]

Little was furious at the misrepresentation of their discussion, and was convinced that the DP veterans within the DA didn't support what she saw as De Lille's more progressive agenda. Little felt that a core group of conservatives from the DP days had been fighting De Lille from the day she became mayor and was now controlling the party. 'If the DA could be honest with themselves and get off their high horse, they would admit that it's this small group that's the problem, not the DA as a whole,' she told me. 'The DA is a private club; it's only for certain members. Life members come from certain families; they must have certain connections,' she explained. 'If you're black or coloured, you will never become a life member. They will make you this or they will make you that, but you will never be a life member.'[32]

Chief whip Shaun August concurred. 'The DA under Helen Zille is not the DA under Mmusi Maimane. There used to be procedure and processes. But those aren't being followed any more,' he said. 'We didn't sign up for this white cabal that's running the DA now'.[33]

Besides some unresolved ideological disagreements, organisational differences clearly created friction and mistrust on both sides. For instance, the ID newcomers rankled at the DA's tight system of control of party activists, and in particular the performance-management system, which measured job performance but also fundraising, and was much hated among the former ID activists. De Lille simply refused to subject herself to it, and her refusal irritated the DA head-office team and raised questions about her motives.[34]

As I already knew from talking to many City officials, De Lille's leadership style and her efforts to centralise power in her office also sowed unhappiness and growing concern. Sims found that she wasn't able to debate with her because she'd already made up her mind. 'It didn't matter what you said, you weren't going to convince her. In the end, her stubbornness counted against her.'[35]

De Lille's primary weakness, said Sims, was that she wouldn't listen to the officials when they tried to guide her.

In her defence, Sims said she felt De Lille was trying to get things done as fast as possible, 'which is the right thing for her to do as the mayor, because she must deliver'.[36]

This reminded me of my own days as a director-general in national government, trying to run a vast bureaucracy that had ossified to the extent that I felt I could get nothing done. After trying all the softer team-building stuff, I had in the end resorted to increasingly disciplinarian measures, at times even threatening and bullying incompetent staff. 'There's going to be blood on the floor' was a phrase I used frequently in front of staff.

Towards the end of my management stint in government, I felt that the job had irrevocably hardened me, turning me into a monster I no longer recognised. So I had some sympathy for De Lille, and I wondered how much her growing frustration towards the bureaucracy and political processes accounted for her outbursts and bullying of staff, as well as the push to centralise power in her office.

'She wanted it done, and even if she had to bend the rules to do it, then you must do it,' Sims explained.[37]

Perhaps De Lille's determination to cut through red tape to speed up delivery and transformation had led her to cut corners instead.

Deputy Mayor Ian Neilson felt that De Lille's struggle background gave her a particularly autocratic style, which didn't sit well within the DA's liberal outlook and deliberative approach. 'Her instinct isn't liberal; she isn't fundamentally a democrat,' he said.[38]

If De Lille displayed autocratic tendencies, I don't buy the view that it has anything to do with her struggle background: having spent what probably amounts to years of my life sitting in political meetings, I can attest that the DA doesn't have a monopoly on inner deliberation and compromise.

De Lille's struggle background might, however, have influenced her stark approach to loyalty and trust. Andrew Boraine, who had set up and run the Cape Town Partnership, a partnership between the City and multiple stakeholders to address urban decay in the CBD, found that if you got on the right side of her, and she liked your projects and programme, then she would back you to the hilt. However, if you fell out with her for any reason, she could be very judgemental, not being able to steer a middle ground. She also took things very personally, and disagreement voiced by officials or councillors was often interpreted as a sign of disloyalty. Boraine recited part of the Henry Wadsworth Longfellow poem, 'When she was good, she was very, very good, but when she was bad, she was horrid.'[39]

Over time, more and more casualties built up as De Lille cast her opponents into oblivion. 'You can't run a big city with too many enemies. You've got to hold your enemies inside the tent, you've got to keep the caucus going. But she fell out with more and more people,' said Boraine.[40]

Belinda Walker felt that De Lille never trusted her – nor, she thought, anyone she didn't have a hold over. 'Patricia doesn't trust anyone who isn't frightened of her. She doesn't understand that you can be a loyal and principled supporter and still argue with her,' she said.[41]

Walker contrasted this with Helen Zille, who didn't think you were disloyal if you disagreed with her; she just thought that you hadn't understood properly.[42]

Shehaam Sims got to the point where she appealed to De Lille to change her attitude. 'You've got to learn to trust us,' she blurted out during a mayoral committee pre-meeting. Sims felt that she could talk frankly in the caucus, where the politicians were supposedly on a more equal footing. 'I'm asking you, please, can you trust us, because we're going to be your support going forward.'[43]

Yet, according to Sims, De Lille harshly criticised senior officials in a way that she felt was unfair and ill informed.[44]

For Sims, it was the last straw. Not long afterwards, in January 2013, she resigned from the mayoral committee and took up a post in Seth Maqetuka's housing department.

14

Walking on broken glass

~~~

The gradual centralisation of power during Patricia de Lille's administration made the DA's old guard increasingly uneasy.

The appointment of mayoral-committee members was the prerogative of the mayor, but inevitably, the different factions within the party had to be reflected in its composition, and the party leadership took a close interest in how it was appointed – the mayoral committee was still, after all, where most of the controversial decisions were hammered out. During her first term, De Lille tried to give strategic portfolios to her close allies, but veterans such as Ian Neilson retained control of finance, Belinda Walker retained corporate services, and Anthea Serritslev was party whip. The faultlines within the mayoral committee were evident even to the senior officials sitting in on the discussions.

Quite early on, De Lille started tackling mayoral-committee members on the way the City was being run. She would argue that they hadn't fully understood the executive-mayor model and weren't applying the law properly when insisting on decisions being made through an executive-committee system. From her point of view, executive decision-making vested in the mayor, and the mayoral committee was merely an advisory structure.

De Lille started to chip away at the mayoral committee's powers. The system of delegations was reviewed, and De Lille took more and more decisions away from the city council's committees and the mayoral committee, and centralised power in her own office. This started out as an effort to reduce the extremely long mayoral-committee agendas, which meant that the mayor alone would take the more administrative decisions (eg, planning departures, zoning and subdivision of land, disposal of assets, approval of overseas travel, approval of leave for executive directors). Ian Neilson commented that De Lille would offhandedly say, 'Oh well, the staff in my office can deal with it.'[1]

Decision-making steadily shifted from the mayoral committee to the SPU in the mayor's office.

During her first term, De Lille was patient. If she couldn't get her way, she would wait and then try again, and the centralisation was progressive. But members of the mayoral committee started to get worried and insisted that they all had to be involved in decisions.[2]

Their brewing unease coincided with broader political events, which solidified De Lille's position within the DA and triggered a new phase in her behaviour.

In 2015, Zille started implementing her succession plan, which was to usher in strong black leaders to head the DA, while she would stay on as provincial premier in the Western Cape until the end of her term in 2019.

Zille first stepped down as the DA's national leader, passing the baton to Mmusi Maimane, the DA's articulate leader of the opposition in the national Parliament, in May 2015.

De Lille was elected provincial leader of the DA in the Western Cape, while one of her key allies, Shaun August, was elected party chair in the Cape Town metro. This put De Lille at the height of her power within the DA, controlling the party machinery at both provincial and City level.

The sudden role reversal between De Lille and Zille was noticeable.

Provincial cabinet members felt uncomfortable with the way De Lille demanded things of them, which they found brusque and demeaning. Some of the DA old-timers felt that the party was being hijacked, and that something had to be done.

Ian Neilson commented that De Lille was 'well managed' in her first term, when Zille was still party leader: checks and balances were in place, and the administrative machinery that Zille had left continued to operate largely unchanged. 'When Helen ceased to be party leader, and Patricia took over the province, she thought she could do what she wanted and no one could stop her,' he said. 'Everything changed suddenly, and if you were a white liberal, you were targeted.'[3]

Neilson said that in the early stages he'd made a considerable effort to be close to De Lille and support her, but he felt that she never fully trusted him. He nevertheless tried to calm his colleagues, who were becoming increasingly unhappy with the situation.

JP Smith, a longstanding DA councillor in charge of safety and security, said that he too had started out on a solid footing with De Lille and made a big effort to get along with her. But he felt that the way De Lille behaved with councillors and staff was unacceptable: 'She went from a reasonable colleague to a petty despot. In caucus meetings, Patricia would treat DA councillors like little children and chop their heads off. She's a bully.'[4] De Lille's bullying behaviour triggered something deep inside JP Smith, who himself was bullied as a child, and evoked in him strong feelings of outrage.

It's quite likely that Smith triggered similar feelings in De Lille, however. Direct and intense in his communications, he's known for driving issues relentlessly and for being assertive. Even his most ardent supporters concede that he sometimes goes too far when dealing with matters that exercise him. A senior official described him as 'very forceful, in fact a bully. It is either his way or the highway'.[5]

JP Smith became a thorn in De Lille's side, often leading the attack against her in caucus meetings, which escalated into a catastrophic and irreparable fallout.

The DA's old guard didn't view De Lille's close allies on the mayoral committee kindly, which couldn't have helped the growing tension. De Lille had given the strategically important portfolio of planning to Johan van der Merwe, whom Belinda Walker regarded as 'a well-trained old man who runs up and down to Patricia's office and does whatever madam says'. According to Walker, he was known around the City as 'Noddy', because he simply agreed with anything that was said to him, nodding while mumbling 'yes, yes, yes'.[6]

Brett Herron, meanwhile, was in charge of transport on the mayoral committee. Both Ian Neilson and Belinda Walker found Herron difficult to read. 'He never reached out to anyone,' said Neilson. 'It was very difficult to engage with him; he would only ever deal with Patricia.'[7]

Walker also struggled to engage Herron. 'He arrived, we liked him, I've never had a cross word with him, but he never opened his mouth, just sat and kept quiet in [mayoral committee] meetings. He's a doormat, insubstantial; it's like grasping a cloud.'[8]

De Lille's once-subtle moves to assert her authority over the mayoral committee became far blunter in 2015. When she saw that the debate in mayoral-committee meetings wasn't going in the direction she wanted, she would tell members that they were merely an advisory body and that she could choose to ignore their advice. Legally speaking, she was correct, of course: the mayoral committee reported to her and was meant to advise her; it didn't have independent executive powers. 'The end result is that [the mayoral committee] itself had been rendered irrelevant,' Neilson concluded.[9]

Besides De Lille becoming DA leader in the province, the 2016 local government election was another watershed moment in the brewing tensions within the DA. Not only was De Lille perceived as a key architect of the DA securing a two-thirds majority in the metro, but old-timers like Belinda Walker and Anthea Seritslev were no longer on the council, leaving only Ian Neilson and JP Smith in key leadership positions. This strengthened De Lille's hand.

Many of the DA's councillors were new, and they didn't have the confidence to stand up to De Lille. Previously, such new councillors would have been mentored by more experienced ones.

Walker thought that Patricia had been 'accelerating for some time, but with the handbrake on. Then the handbrake was lifted.'[10]

Soon after the elections on 16 August 2016, a caucus meeting was held to elect a new leadership. As mayor, De Lille was already ex-officio leader of the caucus, so the crucial position in contest was that of deputy caucus leader.

In the run-up to the meeting, De Lille's allies lobbied caucus members with a 'slate' (list) of candidates to be elected to the caucus's executive committee (which was important because it discussed the issues to be put to caucus and prepared the agenda for caucus meetings), with Brett Herron as deputy caucus leader and Shaun August as chief whip.

The slate caused a fair amount of discomfort within the DA councillors' ranks, since ordinarily each position would be competitively contested and slates were frowned on. As an alternative, JP Smith was put forward to contest the position of deputy caucus leader.

De Lille's supporters alleged Smith made calls to caucus members in which he referred to them as 'ID people' – supposedly a euphemism for coloured people – which added a racial dimension to the already fraught divisions in the caucus.[11]

When the votes were tallied, Smith had won. There was massive consternation in the De Lille camp.

Throwing her arms wide and shouting, De Lille was reported to have said that she alone had won the elections and that all the caucus members were there because of her and her popularity – adding as an afterthought that the electoral success was also due to Brett Herron and Shaun August's hard work.[12] This outraged many of the DA councillors, who felt that the entire caucus, the DA campaign strategy and the national DA leadership had also played a decisive role.[13]

At the first caucus meeting after Smith's election, De Lille said that she wouldn't work with him under any circumstances. In fact, she said, a new caucus election was needed.[14]

From that point on, the mayor didn't attend any meetings of the caucus executive. Instead, she started running her own side meetings, where her team of loyalists would discuss what positions and decisions to push through caucus and caucus executive meetings.

Smith complained that, during full caucus meetings, De Lille would stand up and raise her own issues, ignoring the caucus agenda, which he argued caused tension and disruption within the caucus. He also felt she was openly hostile to him during these meetings, which spread further tension and mistrust.[15]

A Facebook page titled 'Hands off Alderman JP Smith' was created. Smith denied knowing who was behind the page and drove its content, which appeared to be curated by someone who had detailed insight into City and caucus issues.[16] The page contained regular attacks on De Lille and her allies, and perturbed the caucus, deepening divisions.

When De Lille started putting together her new mayoral committee following the 2016 elections, she was determined to keep JP Smith out of it. Rumours swirled around the caucus and made their way to the party leadership, who weren't happy with the prospect of his exclusion.

A furious period of bargaining began. De Lille insisted she couldn't work with Smith, while the DA's leadership worried about the looming factional split. Neither side was willing to relent. Complicating the debate was De Lille's insistence on reorganising portfolios on the mayoral committee in line with what was laid out in the ODTP to restructure the administration.

For a five-month period, from August 2016 to January 2017, the City was without a mayoral committee or heads of portfolios. During the political standoff, none of the officials dared to take any decisions, wary of being caught in the crossfire. In any case, the ongoing administrative reorganisation meant that many of the executive directors were acting appointments, and managers were anxious that they wouldn't be appointed in the new structure.

In the absence of a functioning mayoral committee, the only person who could make decisions was the mayor, and it was simply impossible to process all the City's multitude of complex decisions through De Lille. Senior officials told me that the City just stopped functioning – right when the water crisis was starting to unfold.

In the middle of January 2017, the mayoral committee was finally announced. Even though JP Smith was on it, there were other big changes. Brett Herron was in charge of the crucial transport and urban-development portfolio, which included the TDA. Xanthea Limberg, a soft-spoken former ID member, was given the large portfolio of informal settlements, utilities and energy, which included managing the response to the water crisis.

De Lille presented the reshuffle as a way to accelerate spatial integration. 'The City of Cape Town has not done enough to get rid of the remnants of apartheid planning. I refuse to build far out of the city any more,' she said.[17] Large tracts of land had been identified for low-income housing, which she wanted to bring closer to the CBD.

Although De Lille had significantly strengthened her hold on the executive, she hadn't been able to make a clean sweep. Neilson remained deputy mayor, although he lost the finance portfolio to the ever-compliant Johan van der Merwe. And on the DA leadership's insistence, Smith was given the combined portfolio of social services and safety, which must have rankled with De Lille.

Two weeks after the new mayoral committee was appointed, De Lille announced that she was resigning as DA leader of the Western Cape. She said she wanted to focus on her role as mayor and the roll-out of the ODTP.[18]

This caught everyone by surprise. James Selfe felt that De Lille wasn't interested in doing the hard work of party leader, such as sitting through interminable party executive meetings. 'She wasn't interested in the job,' he remarked.[19] Also, internal party elections were scheduled for later in 2017, and the speculation had been that De Lille was likely to lose the contest.

Shaun August, a De Lille ally, was nominated in her place, but he lost to Bonginkosi Madikizela, the provincial minister for Human Settlements and the deputy leader of the DA in the Western Cape province. For the DA old guard, this was the first indication that De Lille's grip on power in the City could be broken. 'Up to that point, it had seemed as if she was untouchable, that she had the power, the party supported her, she could determine things,' Neilson remarked.[20]

From then on, he felt that De Lille retreated to her power base within the City and increasingly distanced herself from party activities.

In the meantime, the appointment of the mayoral committee did nothing to lessen the tensions within the caucus. According to JP Smith, in the debate on delegations, councillors were told by De Lille to shut up and were called 'stupid' and 'useless'.[21]

The chief whip, Shaun August, sided with the mayor and didn't call her to order, especially when she made inappropriate comments, outside the bounds of normal caucus discussions.[22] August would frequently indicate that there would be 'consequences' if caucus members raised viewpoints or positions different to those of the mayor and her team, saying that such views were deemed 'career limiting' and could block their advancement. Councillors opposed to De Lille were referred to as 'die liberales' – the liberals – a reference to the ideological position of the older members of the DA.[23]

When De Lille was asked about her behaviour by the DA leadership, she said that caucus debates may become 'heated' and that 'strong words may be spoken between councillors' but that this was 'part of the political arena'.[24]

And De Lille's centralisation programme continued to fuel increasing consternation and alarm. The portfolio committees that provided oversight over different functional areas of the city council's work were emasculated. Councillors, who conducted the bulk of their work by being members of portfolio committees, were unhappy. While some committees suffered from poor quality of debate and weren't very effective, this was nevertheless the lifeblood of council.[25] In the process, De Lille further alienated her own DA councillors and party members, who already had limited access to her.

The ANC picked up on the divisions within the DA and fanned the flames. In August 2017 ANC councillors argued in council that the mayor was being 'undermined' or 'sabotaged' by forces within the DA while she was trying to build a 'transformed' city.[26]

A war of accusations and counter-accusations started within the DA over who was leaking information to the ANC. As part of his portfolio, JP Smith had set up a special investigations unit to tackle gang related crime on the Cape Flats, and the speaker, Dirk Smit, accused Smith of using the unit to illegally spy on councillors. De Lille said that, according to the restructuring plan adopted in August 2016, the special investigations unit was exceeding its mandate, and she ordered that it be shut down. Smith was enraged.[27]

Then accusations by anonymous officials emerged about supposedly excessive security upgrades to De Lille's home.

Smith accused De Lille of irregular appointments of political staff, including councillors' children and spouses. There was some substance to these accusations: the mayor's sister, Veronica Paulse, had been employed in Brett Herron's office as an executive support officer, and there were questions around the appointment of one of the mayor's friends to the board of the city's stadium.[28]

A former ANC activist, Loyiso Nkohla, who'd been hired by De Lille, started to throw his weight around. His precise role was unclear, but he was linked into national housing contracts and worked closely with 'landlords' (community leaders who control the allocation of sites, usually in return for allocation fees) in informal settlements such as Imizamo Yethu. 'I act with the mandate of the mayor,' he often said in public meetings and with officials. When questions were raised about him, Nkohla was moved to Xanthea Limberg's office as a 'community liaison officer'. Limberg later said she was 'most uneasy' about this arrangement, as she had no control over Nkohla or what he did.[29]

New concerns surfaced about the mayor's relationship with the CEO of an outdoor advertising company, Brent Dyssel. Dyssel had unfettered access to senior councillors and officials in the City, and in his correspondence with them, intimated that he had personal interactions with the mayor and other City leaders. Among other things, Dyssel had erected an illegal billboard at the end of Long Street; the City needed to obtain a court order to get it removed. De Lille had centralised decisions over legal action, however, and she initially blocked the City from going to court. Because bylaw enforcement fell under JP Smith, the City's officials went to him and asked what they should do. Smith went into De Lille's office, and suggested that she'd been advised poorly, and that the enforcement should go ahead. Smith felt that she knew exactly what was going on.[30]

Dyssel was also engaged in trying to amend the outdoor advertising and signage bylaw to retrospectively legalise his signs. The City experts who should have drafted the bylaw were marginalised, and the SPU under Craig Kesson took it over. There was email correspondence between Kesson and Dyssel regarding the bylaw, which even the mild-mannered Brett Herron was suspicious about.[31]

By the middle of 2017, De Lille's staff were alarmed by her increasingly mercurial behaviour, which fuelled more unhappiness and division. The security staff who used to drive her around said that they never knew whether 'sweet Auntie Pat' or 'dreadful Auntie Pat' would get into the car in the morning.[32] The staff in her office could never predict how things were going to go in a meeting.

By this stage, the City administration was operating in a climate of fear. Senior managers claimed that they were routinely abused, not just by De Lille but by her allies in the administration as well. Procedures went out the window and rules were broken. 'The mayor trades on fear,' Frank Cumming said. 'Accountability was thrown out the window and power was abused in order to get a narrow outcome, not one that was consistent with policy.'[33]

Staff in the planning and property-management divisions complained that there were frequent issues relating to planning approval that they knew were problematic. 'We advised her that we shouldn't be doing this because this is not right,' Cumming said. 'Instead, she leans on the city manager, who leans on Melissa [Whitehead], who then says to the officials, "Get it done!" I thought, do I want to lose my job over this or am I just going to stamp this thing? And I stamped it.'[34]

Suzette Little, however, dismissed complaints about De Lille's behaviour as part of a drive to bring her down. 'Patricia is driven, feisty; I just love her.'[35]

The media picked up on the vicious internal fight, casting it as a battle between Patricia de Lille and JP Smith. It appeared as if the reports were being stoked by insiders, either councillors in the caucus or those in the City administration.[36]

For months the battle raged, and the media criticised the DA leader-ship for not adequately seeing the warning lights and taking timely action. Eventually the DA federal-executive leadership stepped in, placing both De Lille and Smith on 'special leave'[37] during which they were forbid-den from dealing with the media, but continued to exercise their functions in the City.[38] It was an ambiguous decision, a placeholder, while they appointed the affable John Steenhuisen, the DA's chief whip in the national Parliament, to lead a team to investigate the factional split.

The media interpreted the factional battles in the DA as driven by a personality clash, and therefore focused on the prominent characters in the drama. While this certainly was a factor, I wondered about broader forces shaping the divide and the battle for power within the City. Had Patricia de Lille grown increasingly frustrated with administrative inertia, vested interests and old patterns of influence as she took control of the City and attempted to carve out a new course? Had she read that invisible power as a conspiracy to block her and her agenda? Perhaps she felt that, in order to disrupt the status quo, she'd had to take the reins by force.

I wondered how John Steenhuisen had interpreted the clash, and I went to ask him about his findings in his wood-panelled office in Parliament. When I suggested that he'd been handed a poisoned chalice, he laughed. The assignment had been difficult, he said, but these kinds of jobs are part of being a leader. The fracas had cast the party in an extremely poor light, and he thought that it continued to significantly damage the DA brand.[39]

The situation he confronted was highly conflictual, with entrenched factions clustered around De Lille and the rest of the caucus. There clear-ly were old ID/DP allegiances at play in the split, although there were councillors from the old ID and DP who had crossed over. For instance, Xanthea Limberg, who had come from the ID, had made accusations that De Lille had meddled in the appointment of the city manager.

Steenhuisen had also stumbled on evidence of a 'black caucus' of DA councillors representing African constituencies, which he thought was an extremely unhealthy development.[40]

He said that the divisions within the caucus were centred around two main personalities: JP Smith and Patricia de Lille. 'The relationship between these two individuals within the caucus has broken down irretrievably, and it's unlikely that it can be repaired,' was his glum assessment.[41]

Steenhuisen considered De Lille's leadership style since the 2016 election as 'extremely problematic', and was of the opinion that it had paralysed the City administration and the DA caucus. In his investigation, he'd also been surprised at De Lille's response to many of the submissions made to the subcommittee established to enquire into the tensions in the City of Cape Town. She'd been irritated and impatient, dismissing concerns or denying complaints, instead of attempting to understand why there were such deep divisions and unhappy members in her caucus – and considering what responsibility she held for this.[42]

From what I could tell, there were many fracture lines in evidence – personality clashes, a failed integration of the ID into the DA, newcomers versus old-timers, and some policy differences. For all of De Lille's glaring faults, the old DA was far from blameless.

Central to the fallout was a failed political merger – the second one for the party. From the old guard's point of view, this was never a merger but a takeover. The party's existing systems and policies were meant to stay intact, while it gained a charismatic figurehead to broaden its appeal. Brett Herron felt that, unlike the 'life members' in the DA old guard, the former ID members were merely 'visitors' and were never fully trusted.[43]

Surely this wasn't the type of 'merger' the ID had in mind? What did it say about the DA's ability to work across party lines, as South Africa contemplated a political future in which coalitions were likely to become far more common?

There were certainly some real issues at stake, real debates over the

200

future direction of Cape Town and the extent and pace of its transformation. If the DA suffered from divergent ideologies about development and the place of the private sector, I felt that these could have been navigated, even resolved, if properly managed. If the DA really did want to break out of its old white liberal straightjacket and become the majority party in the country, it had to dig deep and find a convincing way to create an inclusive economy that benefited everyone. Business as usual wouldn't resolve the structural inequalities we'd inherited from our past; it could only perpetuate them. Was the DA ready to embrace that reality?

And what of Patricia de Lille? It was possible that her rhetoric genuinely reflected convictions over transformation that were somewhat at odds with the DA's. It was possible that during her first term she adopted the DA's outlook and position to establish her standing within the party, before pushing her own agenda much more forcefully once her position was stronger. Yet she didn't help her case by letting her frustrations translate into a divisive and overbearing leadership style that led to questionable decisions and left her isolated.

She also had a case to answer over her ill-conceived reorganisation of the City administration. Rather than accelerate delivery, she achieved the exact opposite, undermining her own power by cutting off at the knees the very troops supposed to help her formulate and carry out a more inclusive vision.

De Lille's promise, her vision of an inclusive, racially transformed city, had been sidetracked. The stickiness and inertia generated by established power structures and business influence over politics may not always equate with active conspiracy, but they are enduring.

The final stages of the Cape Town drama were to reveal in graphic terms how these interests played out.

15

Things fall apart

$\wedge\wedge\wedge$

By the winter of 2017, while Capetonians were praying for rain, the forces on both sides of the divide in the City were in full combat mode.

JP Smith's stand against Patricia de Lille had put out a clarion call that reverberated across the DA ranks, and the more traditional forces within the DA viewed this conflict as a battle for the liberal soul and the integrity of the party.

Arrayed against them were De Lille and her supporters in the party and the City. She still had considerable support in the caucus, and she controlled the administration through her key officials – city manager Achmat Ebrahim, head of the SPU Craig Kesson, head of corporate services Gerhard Ras, and the all-powerful head of the now expanded TDA Melissa Whitehead. Supporting De Lille's camp in the background was a hodgepodge of economic interests – union pension funds and empowerment players such as Mvelaphanda, property developers she'd assisted, and businessmen such as Mark Willcox.

The sides were highly polarised; there was no middle ground. Everyone had to take a side.

It feels ironically appropriate that the final act in this political drama was to unfold over a highly symbolic part of the city. In the middle of the busy Heerengracht – 'gentleman's canal' – that runs down the centre of old Cape Town stands a statue of a grandiloquent Jan van Riebeeck, the first coloniser of South Africa. He forever occupies the spot where he suppos- edly made landfall when the VOC dispatched him to set up a victualling station in the Cape.

Apart from the painful reminder of conquest that the statue represents, what is striking is that today Van Riebeeck would have to sail through a kilometre of concrete to land at that spot, which now sits far from the coastline. The land between the statue and the harbour is known as the Foreshore, reclaimed from the sea when the new Duncan Dock was built in the 1930s and 1940s.

The apartheid planners had a field day with this new space. The head- quarters of Nasionale Pers (now called Naspers), the apartheid-era private media empire that played a crucial propaganda role in propping up the regime, were built on the Foreshore in the 1960s. An ambitious freeway system was designed in the same decade, linking arterials from the east and south into the city and the suburbs on the other side. In the 1970s, work was started on the new civic centre, a vast and ugly rectangle of concrete plonked down next to the railway station – a statement of bureaucratic authority.

The Foreshore freeways were planned in two stages, with phase two meant to commence when traffic reached a certain density, which it didn't do until the 2000s, by which time there were competing demands for capital expenditure. This left a pair of incomplete flyovers suspended in mid-air, nicknamed 'Solly's folly' after Solly Morris, the city engineer who'd designed the freeways.

In the post-apartheid era, the land on the Foreshore was reconfigured and carved up into developable sites, which were then provided with bulk infrastructure. This created massive value both for Naspers (which owned the land on which the Cape Town International Convention Centre, or

CTICC, extension was built, plus some other sites) and the City.

In a joint venture between the province and the City, the modernistic CTICC converted the otherwise drab Foreshore into a designer space, and linked it via canals to the tourist mecca of the V&A Waterfront. From a dreary place of apartheid hubris, the Foreshore now had a new identity, substantially lifting its investment value.

The value of the land and the rights that the City could dispense attracted the interest of private developers such as George Georgiou, who started buying up buildings on the Foreshore and getting government departments to sign long-term leases for the sites.

In July 2016, the City issued a somewhat vaguely worded request for proposals for the development of the 'Foreshore Freeway precinct' and rushed to get the tender out. According to a National Treasury official who looked into this deal in 2017, there had been inadequate planning for such a large procurement and the announcement had come out of nowhere. The official said that the City didn't have detailed criteria against which to assess the bids that came in. 'The moment you're inventing criteria on the go, you're exposing your process to subjectivity – which is exactly what happened.'[1]

In their book, however, De Lille and Kesson boasted about the City's Foreshore development project as one of the major urban-development projects fostered by the City administration – it was considered a catalytic project, an opportunity to get the private sector to invigorate the area by building a mix of residential, office and retail spaces – including some social housing – while solving the problem of the incomplete freeways.[2]

The bids were complex to put together – they required innovative and ambitious urban design, detailed engineering solutions and viable commercial financing proposals. But the City had sweetened the deal with the offer of six hectares of public land on the Foreshore.

It was like a flare had been shot. All the big players in the property industry started mobilising around this opportunity. Consortia formed, with different investors lining up behind them.

The costs of putting bids together ended up being high, anything between R10 and R20 million, which caused many players to drop out, and by the closing date of 9 February 2017 proposals had been received from seven consortia, which were publicly exhibited in the civic centre. Proposals included demolishing the existing freeways, completing them, and replacing them with tunnels.

For a moment it seemed like this catalytic project might proceed. A multidisciplinary bid-evaluation committee was duly convened, and, as she was in charge of the TDA, Melissa Whitehead insisted that she should participate on the committee along with her key staff. The involvement of someone so senior in the tender review was unusual, but no one challenged it at the time.

Whitehead's involvement was the spark that was to unleash the political firestorm.

In the meantime, Craig Kesson was carefully watching the unfolding factional dispute and wondering how to position himself within the City's increasingly fractious politics. He might also have still been smarting from the way Melissa Whitehead had hijacked his ambitious restructuring of the City, which was by now coming apart at the seams.

As part of the restructuring, Kesson had given himself responsibility for 'probity', which included overseeing forensic investigations in the City. One of the investigations involved the MyCiti bus-stations tender contract – a contract for which Whitehead had been responsible.

Cape Town had been the first metro to set up a bus rapid-transit system linking different parts of the metropolitan area. The system had then been rolled out to other metros, where the transport planning and bus procurement had been subject to widespread fraud. In Nelson Mandela Bay, for example, some R2 billion had been spent without any buses actually running.[3]

In Cape Town, however, the MyCiti system appeared to have been implemented extremely well. It was lauded as one of Whitehead's big achievements in the city, which was partly why she'd ended up in such a powerful position as head of the TDA.

The forensic report that Kesson commissioned into the MyCiti bus-stations tender contract, however, found a massive loss, estimated at R43 million, due to fraud by the cashiers responsible for fare collection. It appeared that Whitehead and other City officials had been aware of this loss for some time, but had chosen to do nothing about it.[4]

Kesson reported the matter to De Lille in July 2017. According to Kesson, the mayor told him bluntly that she didn't want to know about the report, and that he needed to make the issue 'go away'.[5] He was dumbstruck.

Kesson went on leave for the remainder of that month, and when he returned to the office, he discovered that the city manager was about to strip him of his authority over forensic investigations. This threatened Kesson's power and authority in the City administration, and he immediately complained in writing to De Lille. She didn't respond to his letter, but the city manager's move was (temporarily) halted.

Then, on 31 August 2018, Frank Cumming, who was leading the work on the Foreshore Freeway project, laid a complaint against Melissa Whitehead for undue interference in the bid evaluation committee.[6] Cumming alleged that Whitehead had been improperly favouring the Circle of Good Hope consortium led by Urban Dynamics, one of the two frontrunner bidders.[7]

Whitehead had also attacked the other frontrunner, Mitchell Du Plessis Associates (MDA), whose proposal included completing the freeways, building 11 giant tower blocks between them along Nelson Mandela Boulevard, and sticking social housing on the bottom floors. Whitehead apparently said that she was worried about the 'political acceptability' of the location of the affordable-housing component, and claimed that Brett Herron and Patricia de Lille didn't support MDA's proposal.[8]

When I asked Herron whether he or De Lille had had a predetermined view on the bids, 'Not at all,' he replied. 'We didn't discuss it. I was excited about all the bids and amazed that we got so many. The one that came out at the end wasn't my favourite, but I never leant on anyone about it.'[9]

Whitehead was accused of pressing members of the committee assessing the bids to support the Circle of Good Hope consortium's proposed affordable-housing location – curiously, not specified in the tender documents – which was supposedly favoured by the mayor. But because the tender documents weren't specific about where the affordable-housing component should be located, some committee members worried that they were unable to score this element at all.

Accounting firm Moore Stephens also looked into the matter and their findings were scathing, concluding that Whitehead had indeed unduly favoured the Urban Dynamics consortium and improperly pressured other members of the committee who worked under her.[10]

When it came to the commercial assessment, Cumming thought that the Urban Dynamics proposal was 'fanciful' and 'unfundable', and that it created an unacceptable level of financial risk for the City.[11]

Whitehead dismissed his concerns. The financial assessment was part of a later phase, she argued, and many issues could be sorted out in the contractual negotiations.[12]

In her response to the accusations against her, Whitehead explained that she was adamantly opposed to the MDA proposal because she felt it reproduced apartheid spatial planning.[13]

When Kesson became aware of the Moore Stephens report's conclusions at the end of August 2017, he met with De Lille to voice his concern that the mayor's name had been mentioned in the context of a tender adjudication.[14] De Lille instructed the city manager, Achmat Ebrahim, to convene a meeting including, among others, Melissa Whitehead, Brett Herron and herself, to discuss the Foreshore matter early in the morning of 5 September 2017. Kesson thought this was a bad idea, in light of the accusations against them; but, he suggested, if the meeting were to go ahead, Deputy Mayor Ian Neilson should also be invited.

Neilson was a vocal critic of the project and the tender process, which he said was open to corruption. Besides the poorly drafted call for proposals, he felt that the project concept of bundling freeway and social-housing components was fundamentally flawed and 'a quick fix to a difficult issue'. 'A solution to resolve both the transport needs of the city and to address the needs of inner-city social housing was never going to work by requiring a developer to achieve both ends with the limited resources of disparate pieces of land,' he declared. Neilson concluded that there must therefore have been ulterior reasons for doing so.[15]

Kesson's advice and objections were ignored, which fuelled his suspicions.[16] The meeting went ahead without the presence of Neilson, but it was difficult and tense. There seemed to be fundamentally different views on how to respond to the situation, with Kesson and the CFO, Kevin Jacoby, in a minority.

Kesson wanted the accusations over the Foreshore project tender reported to council and a full investigation of the allegations undertaken. Ebrahim countered that corrective action had already been taken: he'd obtained a legal opinion, and the evaluation process would be restarted with a new committee. Kesson had asked his probity division for an opinion on whether Whitehead should be serving on the bid evaluation committee, for which he was attacked by De Lille; she seemed convinced that Frank Cumming was to blame for this, and she instructed that his employment be summarily terminated. Herron, meanwhile, argued that Kesson was misusing his authority and should be relieved of his probity responsibilities.[17]

Kesson, who was meant to travel to the USA on official council business, cancelled his trip in light of the situation; he was also acutely aware that the last time he'd been absent from the office, Ebrahim had tried to take some his responsibilities away.

Kesson went back to De Lille the next day, 6 September 2017, to make the case for an investigation into both Whitehead and Ebrahim, who he felt had enabled Whitehead's behaviour. According to Kesson, however, De Lille felt that Whitehead was being unfairly picked on. In addition, she charged that forensic reports that had fingered other executive directors for wrongdoing had been suppressed. This was an extraordinary accusation, and Kesson offered to look into the matter immediately and personally.[18] Perhaps this was an off-hand remark, but De Lille did not immediately grasp the full import of what Kesson was suggesting.

Kesson instructed his staff to pull out all the forensic investigations from the last five years, supposedly to check for any possible inconsistencies and preferential treatment. He also decided to scrutinise the reports himself, supposedly 'so as to provide an additional, management perspective'.[19]

Given the context, he might very well have been on a hunt for other ammunition to be used in the unfolding internal battle – Ebrahim and De Lille certainly thought so. When he got wind of this exercise a week later, Ebrahim summoned Kesson to his office and told him that all probity functions were removed forthwith from his authority.

Kesson was furious, and the two of them marched off to the mayor for an urgent meeting, which became highly acrimonious. An argument developed over where the responsibility for probity lay.[20]

When Ebrahim reported that another official on the bid committee, David Marais, was suing Whitehead in her private capacity, De Lille repeated that Whitehead was the victim of an orchestrated political campaign, this time pointing a finger at Ian Neilson, Kevin Jacoby, Frank Cumming and David Marais, as well as a host of other officials. According to Kesson, she instructed Ebrahim to terminate Frank Cumming's and David Marais' contracts with immediate effect.[21] De Lille later denied she had done this, and accused Kesson of trying to tarnish her reputation and integrity.[22]

Despite the disastrous meeting, Kesson had won a reprieve of sorts, as Ebrahim backed off trying to remove probity from his management.

Kesson's review of the forensic investigations continued, but dark clouds were swirling around him. He found out that members of his forensics team were briefing senior officials and political office-holders about the review without his knowledge.[23]

Kesson and his team went through 1 100 forensic reports, and while Kesson found no evidence supporting De Lille's claims, he did come up with one particularly useful nugget: Melissa Whitehead was the only executive director against whom allegations had been made that had not been reported to council. This involved a 2015 investigation into tranche payments made to Volvo for 29 bus chassis for the bus rapid-transit system, in spite of the buses' delivery having been delayed. (In the end the buses were delivered, so there was no net loss.) At the time, the forensic report had found the expenditure to be irregular and recommended that the matter be reported to council – which never happened.[24]

Back in 2015, De Lille had convened a meeting involving Herron, Ebrahim, Whitehead, Jacoby and Ras to discuss the forensic report. According to Jacoby, Herron had challenged whether the part payment for the chassis was indeed irregular, while De Lille had questioned the recommendation to report the matter to council and said Whitehead was being unfairly targeted. If Ebrahim proceeded to investigate Whitehead's conduct, De Lille was alleged to have said, she would have him investigated.[25] This appeared to suggest that De Lille and Ebrahim had buried the forensic report, choosing to ignore its recommendations.

News of Kesson's discovery must have leaked out, because on 3 November 2017, De Lille summoned the head of probity, Lindiwe Ndaba, who reported to Kesson, and allegedly threatened to have her investigated. She also asked for all five years of forensic reports.[26]

Kesson himself was called in to see De Lille a few days later. According to him, she ranted about the political attacks she was facing from various quarters. She felt there was an agenda to stop the spatial transformation of the city and to remove her, Brett Herron and Melissa Whitehead, and found it a strange coincidence that Kesson's reports had emerged at such a difficult political time. By going into the forensic reports, Kesson and Ndaba had investigated the city manager without authorisation from council, she said. They had also investigated the behaviour of councillors, which wasn't their duty, and De Lille said she had reported this transgression to the speaker. She intended to report the matter to council, and to get council to formally investigate Kesson and Ndaba, along with Ebrahim and Whitehead. They would all be placed on special leave while they were investigated.[27]

The rift between De Lille and her right hand was now irrevocable, and matters were rapidly coming to a head.

Kesson agonised over how to respond to the situation and decided to put down everything he knew in an affidavit. This involved sifting through the available evidence and frequent consultations with his own legal advisers, and, given the meticulous detail of the final document, it appeared that he had been documenting his every encounter with De Lille and Ebrahim for a while.

In pushing back against the mayor, Kesson's position suddenly aligned with the stand adopted by councillors such as JP Smith and Deputy Mayor Ian Neilson. He'd chosen his camp in the political battle, and there was no going back.

Meanwhile, the unfolding political crisis was distracting from the water crisis engulfing Cape Town, which by rights required the City leadership's full attention.

A high-powered technical team of local and international experts had been mobilised by National Treasury to assist the metro in thinking through the complex water-infrastructure investments that were required. Given that policy on the water strategy had been centralised in Craig Kesson's office, this was a critical moment for him to show some leadership. Yet right when the Treasury team arrived in Cape Town, Kesson disappeared for a few weeks to prepare his affidavit. Treasury officials reported being unable to contact him at critical moments, and there were some difficult meetings during which the external experts found him to be a little insulting.[28]

In a pivotal meeting on the Treasury team's findings, which were critical of the City's plans to address the water crisis, Kesson was extremely uncomfortable, at one moment sitting sullenly silent, then pushing his chair back and throwing up his hands, exclaiming in frustration with their findings. As one of the officials noted afterwards, Kesson looked completely at sea and distracted.[29]

As the head of the SPU, he was, after all, largely responsible for crafting the strategy whose wisdom was being questioned by Treasury. But, having until then played a key policy-coordination role, he'd now lost the political cover that he was accustomed to, as his rift with the mayor widened. And he couldn't just abrogate his responsibility: the structure that he'd helped create didn't work like that.

Eventually, retired Spanish expert Manuel Marino, one of the members of National Treasury's high-powered team, and a man with a vast depth of technical knowledge that Kesson couldn't challenge, shook him up. 'Craig, this is a leadership moment, don't get lost,' he blurted out. 'The City does not have an option on whether it responds or not. You have the power to make the situation a lot worse or a lot better. You're in a leadership role now.'[30]

While Kesson seemed jabbed out of his torpor by Marino's intervention, the ensuing political crisis quickly took centre stage. Kesson signed his affidavit in front of a Commissioner of Oaths on 9 November 2017. The affidavit excoriated De Lille's conduct as incompatible with her legal and ethical obligations. According to Kesson, she'd failed to ensure due process in dealing with Melissa Whitehead's alleged misconduct and irregularities around the bus-chassis payments, the bus-fare fraud and the Foreshore bid evaluations, and had pressured the city manager to do the same. This had resulted in 'condonation of systemic governance failures'. Investigations into serious issues had been suppressed, Kesson claimed, and officials who'd brought these matter to the mayor's attention had themselves been threatened.[31]

Because the allegations implicated both the mayor and the city manager, Kesson addressed the affidavit to the deputy mayor, Ian Neilson. He provided a copy to De Lille, 'so that she will not be taken by surprise or feel ambushed unfairly'.[32]

The affidavit was made according to the Protected Disclosures Act – meant to provide protection to whistleblowers against corruption. That Kesson had become a whistleblower was an irony perhaps lost on him: he had himself aided and abetted De Lille in massively centralising power and sidelining officials who didn't agree with her.

De Lille later challenged the legal basis for Kesson's disclosures – because his claims were false and defamatory, she argued, he was not a whistleblower but a criminal offender.[33]

Besides preparing his affidavit, Kesson had also written two memoranda to council, making the case for both Achmat Ebrahim and Melissa Whitehead to be suspended and investigated pending a disciplinary process. On De Lille's instruction, Ebrahim then prepared a similar memo on Kesson, seeking his suspension and investigation for insubordination.

These memos and counter-memos sailed like juggernauts towards their final denouement in council. The DA caucus called for a special council meeting to discuss the tender irregularities, the shutdown of Smith's special investigations unit and proposed disciplinary actions. The councillors also said they wanted investigations into irregularities relating to Whitehead to be reopened.

The council meeting, scheduled to take place the following Tuesday, promised to be a major showdown.

Kesson's move against De Lille coincided with a broader offensive against her within the DA. The Steenhuisen investigation, which would culminate in the December 2019 *Report of the Subcommittee Established to Enquire into the Tensions in the City of Cape Town*, was already underway, and various members of the DA's caucus were being interviewed. In the course of the DA's enquiry into the caucus and ways to resolve the tensions that had developed there, De Lille had lawyered up and launched a counter-offensive. This was clearly turning into a war.

In the middle of the unfolding drama, the DA's Cape Town metro region held new elections for its leadership. Shaun August, De Lille's ally, lost out to Grant Twigg, a councillor who'd served as Cape Town metro region leader before, and who was definitely not in De Lille's faction.

The special council meeting that took place on 21 November was, as expected, highly charged. The DA's councillors were evidently divided about which versions of the memoranda to believe, and it took some time before they agreed to appoint an independent investigator to probe allegations against Kesson, Ebrahim and Whitehead. The City's audit committee, a supposedly independent structure, was to oversee this investigation. For the time being, no one was suspended.

Nothing was said about the mayor herself, but everyone knew that she would also be a target of the probe.

Immediately after the meeting, the affidavits and memoranda containing the allegations, supposed to be confidential, were uploaded onto the City's website by persons unknown. Ironically, Achmat Ebrahim's complaints against Craig Kesson included allegations that he had 'leaked and/or caused to be leaked confidential information of the City'.[34] Previously a political appointee in Kesson's SPU had been fingered for leaks from the administration, but he had since left, while the leaks had continued.[35]

De Lille stated that Kesson's affidavit, which among other things claimed that the mayor had attempted to bury allegations against Melissa Whitehead, was a malicious attempt to attack her integrity and reputation as a corruption fighter. 'I challenge those who seek to attack my track record to bring any proof that I benefited personally from any corruption or tenders,' she said.[36]

On 10 December 2017, Steenhuisen handed his report to the DA's federal executive, although a supposedly confidential copy also made its way to *News24*. 'The City of Cape Town is in a state of crisis and turmoil, both politically and administratively,' the report found. 'Open warfare has broken out amongst councillors in the DA caucus, with some even threatening to move motions of no confidence against the Mayor. There is also division and conflict which now exists between key [mayoral committee] members. Additionally, senior staff members within the administration have turned on each other with accusations and counter-accusations. This is a completely unsustainable situation and unless actions are taken urgently to resolve these, the negative fallout and effects will continue to manifest themselves both internally and in the public arena.'[37]

It was a damning indictment for a party that had only recently been at the zenith of its power in the City. The report laid much of the blame at De Lille's feet, arguing, among other things, that she'd facilitated improper appointments and adopted an abusive leadership style within the caucus. 'The Mayor clearly believes that she holds all the power in the city and does not need to take the views and opinions of certain [mayoral committee] members, officials or indeed members of her own caucus, seriously,' the report noted.[38]

Councillors attacked 'the command culture' De Lille and leadership team had established, and complained of being belittled and humiliated when questioning the mayor. In the report, Steenhuisen referred to the DA caucus as 'an arena of massive contestation, acrimony and abuse' and said that 'many Councillors do not feel that they should raise their heads above the parapet for fear of being cut down to size by either the Mayor or the Chairperson [of the caucus, Suzette Little]'.[39]

As for JP Smith, the report pointed out that he might have been in charge of the safety and security portfolio for too long, becoming 'virtually indistinguishable from his portfolio'. The recommendation? That he be sent to the National Assembly or provincial legislature, a sideways 'promotion' that would remove him from the City.[40]

While the report accused De Lille of bullying and divisive behaviour, nepotistic appointments, and interference in decisions, it contained no allegation of corruption or financial wrongdoing.

It did conclude, however, that, apart from trying to get a friend's daughter appointed at the stadium-management company and bringing Loyiso Nkohla into the administration, De Lille had also interfered in the selection of a new city manager at the end of Achmat Ebrahim's fixed five-year term, allegedly instructing one of the interview panel members, Xanthea Limberg, to score Ebrahim the highest so he would be reappointed.[41] Both Brett Herron and Suzette Little subsequently disputed this allegation, saying that none of the other panel members, including themselves, had received such instructions. They also pointed out that Xanthea Limberg was in a relationship with JP Smith.[42]

The following week, in mid-December 2017, the DA federal executive announced that Patricia de Lille would be recalled as mayor. According to James Selfe, there were four issues that informed the DA position – suspicion that De Lille was involved in corruption, her mismanagement of the water crisis, her involvement in transport contracts under Whitehead, and her persistent lack of accountability to the party. The federal executive were almost unanimous that De Lille had to be got rid of, and that there was no accommodation to be had with her. Selfe said he knew at the time that this would be extremely costly in terms of electoral support, but did not think there was another way to manage the situation.[43] But, inexplicably, the axe didn't fall immediately.

De Lille was infuriated by the DA announcement and said that the party didn't have valid grounds to suspend her, and she threatened legal action if the DA tried to remove her through a vote of no confidence.

Some of De Lille's key allies in the council, including speaker Dirk Smit and chief whip Shaun August, also seemed to be in the firing line, and were asked by the DA's national leadership to respond to the allegations levelled against them in the so-called Steenhuisen report. Given that August had only just been campaigning to become leader of the DA in the Western Cape, the shift in his fortunes was particularly dramatic.[44]

Early in January 2018, an independent report by Bowman Gilfillan attorneys, which had been commissioned by the council to look into whether De Lille had failed in her duty to report to council the various irregularities relating to the Foreshore Freeway project, as well as the earlier bus-chassis and bus-fare forensic reports, was tabled to the council. It was almost immediately leaked to the media, giving the public a comprehensive picture of the alleged wrongdoing and cover-ups involving top City officials and politicians.[45]

In the report, city manager Achmat Ebrahim laid the blame for not reporting Melissa Whitehead's alleged transgressions over the bus chassis contract at De Lille's door. He claimed that, together with former executive director for corporate services Gerhard Ras,[46] the mayor had blocked him from taking action against Whitehead and from reporting the matter to council. This was disingenuous, as Ebrahim had an obligation as city manager to inform the city council that wasn't conditional on the mayor's approval. But it was clear that Ebrahim had also now shifted position and was leaving the sinking ship.

The council meeting reviewing the Bowman Gilfillan report went on for three hours.[47] Council decided to follow the report's recommendation that disciplinary action be taken against Whitehead and Ebrahim, and the mayor investigated in a separate probe. Whitehead and Ebrahim were nonetheless given a week to justify why they shouldn't be suspended. Kesson, on the other hand, escaped without so much as a rap on the knuckles.

A week later, Achmat Ebrahim resigned, after a 40-year career in local government. He maintained his innocence, but his position had become intolerable, as neither side in the factional battle trusted him any more.

None of the City officials I spoke to felt sorry for Ebrahim. They felt that he'd failed to stand up and protect his staff against political interference and bullying by politicians; he hadn't done the right thing by the City administration and its officials during the restructuring, instead going along with it. Ultimately, he was largely perceived as a weak, compliant administrator without a real backbone.[48]

Despite various attempts I was unable to get Ebrahim to meet me so I could hear his side of the story.

In a meeting on Friday 19 January 2018 the city council revoked the system through which its executive powers were delegated to the mayor and which had given Patricia de Lille her unfettered powers. This dismantling of the hugely centralised political machine centred around the mayor's office meant that De Lille's powers to manage the water crisis were removed.

De Lille contested the decision on procedural grounds.[49]

In the same meeting, Melissa Whitehead's arguments why she should not be suspended were dismissed, she was suspended from her position and a disciplinary process was started against her. There were mixed feelings about Whitehead's actions, however. One of the National Treasury officials I interviewed thought that she was 'collateral damage' in the political war. While there had been irregularities, Whitehead had certainly not personally benefited from the payments for the bus chassis, and there had been no net loss to the City. 'It's non-compliance, but it's not technically illegal. It doesn't seem to me like the most major contravention,' said the official.[50]

Regarding the Foreshore Freeway project, at fault were the tender's vague specifications, particularly in the social-housing component, due to the way the project had been rushed through the system. Nevertheless, the official remarked that Whitehead was no innocent bystander: she herself had seen to the eviction of many officials considered problematic. 'If you live by the sword, you'd better be prepared to eventually die by it,' the official concluded.[51]

The scorched-earth tactics of the political war were now laid bare. Despite the DA's intention to recall her, De Lille had no intention of resigning.

At the end of January 2018, the DA federal council announced that it would table a motion of no confidence against De Lille. Then, on 4 February, the DA announced that it was laying criminal charges against her for corruption, based on an affidavit received from businessman Anthony Faul.

Faul alleged that De Lille had solicited a bribe of R5 million from him in 2013 in exchange for a contract with the City to supply fire extinguishers. It wasn't clear why Faul had waited so long to report this alleged transgression, and De Lille rejected the claims 'with contempt'. 'Why did he go to the DA first instead of going to the police? Why did he wait almost five years to make these allegations?' she said. 'It is becoming increasingly obvious that the concerted efforts to damage my reputation and the haste to get rid of me is reaching desperate heights each day.'[52]

Meanwhile, the motion of no confidence was delayed. De Lille insisted on a secret ballot, which the speaker, Dirk Smit, who by then had switched factional sides, initially refused. De Lille took the matter to court. The court ruled that the decision was up to the speaker, but it also ordered the DA to tell its members that they were free to vote in line with their consciences.[53]

When the vote finally took place on 15 February 2018, the speaker opted for an open ballot. De Lille stormed out of the meeting and went to her office to begin packing. But 39 of the 154 DA councillors voted against the no-confidence motion, tipping the scales, and the motion was defeated by 110 votes to 109.

'The reason I support Patricia is that she has done nothing wrong,' DA councillor Suzette Little later explained to me. 'I'm not asking anyone to marry her, but what has she done?'[54]

Suddenly, De Lille was back in the game. Her supporters streamed into her office, singing hymns.

It was a joyful moment of victory for the mayor's camp but the fight was a long way from over.

In mid-February 2018 – in the middle of the all-out factional war – the City had announced the outcome of the Foreshore Freeway tender that had set political fire to the DA's internal powder keg.

The bid committee had reconvened without Melissa Whitehead, but they hadn't interviewed any of the bidders. Instead, they'd watched videos of the bids with poor sound quality. On the basis of this imperfect evaluation, MDA – the bid that Whitehead had so bitterly opposed – was selected as the qualifying bidder.

Ironically, Brett Herron, who himself didn't favour that bid, made the announcement, welcoming the news as a 'historical moment' and the first building block of an inclusive inner city. 'Reversing the legacy of apartheid spatial planning is a key priority of this government,' he said. 'This means

220

that everything we do in the housing realm should be aimed at providing affordable housing opportunities that are located on land with easy access to public transport and jobs.'[55]

Poor Herron. The announcement was immediately attacked by planning academics, social-housing activists and *GroundUp* journalists – a large part of his own constituency.[56] MDA's proposal was the least innovative or creative of the bids submitted, they said, and perpetuated the freeway-dominated vision of the 1960s transport planners; the proposal ran against the City's own transport policy, which sought to de-emphasise motor vehicles in favour of public and non-motorised transport. Vanessa Watson, a veteran urban-planning professor at UCT, called it 'a wall of towers between the city and the sea'. The 450 affordable-housing units were ridiculed as 'minuscule' compared to the 3 200 market-related residential units, making little impact on the spatial segregation of the city. It also transpired that the City would have to make a financial contribution for the affordable-housing units, on top of the six hectares of land and additional development rights it was already providing.[57]

Having lost the February vote of no confidence in the mayor, the DA national leadership became aware that De Lille was going to fight them on every technicality she could. So they launched formal disciplinary proceedings against her, adding a hodgepodge of unrelated allegations to accusations already contained in the Steenhuisen report.

MP Glynnis Breytenbach, who used to work in the National Prosecuting Authority, was appointed to lead the charge. In April 2018, an amendment to the DA's constitution was adopted at the party's national congress, allowing for the recall of a publicly elected representative in executive office. The media dubbed it 'the De Lille clause'.[58]

And the factional battle seemed to keep rearing its head elsewhere, albeit on a smaller scale. Neilson and De Lille found themselves once again lock-ing horns in a dispute over 400 parking bays due to be handed over by the CTICC to Naspers – this was part of a deal in which Naspers sold land to the CTICC, with two big sweeteners – the parking bays, and a height restriction so that Naspers's panoramic 360-degree view over the city would never be blocked. When the deputy mayor tried to insist on the bays being delivered, De Lille removed him as the liaison person with the CTICC. Allegations were made that Neilson's interventions were benefiting Naspers and George Georgiou because they were longstanding DA funders.[59]

There were other weird things going on too. The building plans for the CTICC extension had been rushed through – they were approved in a record five hours. The project was R120 million over the original budget of R832 million. Strange things had been going on for some time with the CTICC extension project, which was seemingly being held up by cer-tain councillors and officials unless the CTICC did an unfavourable deal with a private developer, George Georgiou, on an adjacent property.[60] An anonymous source sent me the notes of a meeting about the extension that involved De Lille, Herron, Ebrahim, the CTICC chair and CEO, and vari-ous officials, dated April 2017. The notes said that the city manager was tasked to 'remove anyone that's an obstacle' through the administration restructuring.[61] An obstacle to what? I wondered. My efforts to meet with the CTICC CEO went nowhere.

De Lille then presented the DA with an opportunity to exercise its new powers. On 26 April, in a radio interview with 702 talk-show host Eusebius McKaiser, she argued that she only wanted to clear her name. McKaiser asked her whether she would resign from the DA if she proved her inno-cence in the disciplinary proceedings and any subsequent court case. 'I will walk away,' she replied. 'Because really it is not about hanging on … I'm serving there at the behest of the DA.'[62]

The DA's federal council summarily terminated her party membership, saying that she'd publicly announced her intention to resign. Reading the transcript of the interview, I wasn't so sure.

Ian Neilson immediately called a press conference and announced that since De Lille's membership had ceased, she had lost her seat as a councillor and her position as mayor of Cape Town.[63] He announced that, as deputy mayor, he automatically became acting mayor.

In the four days in May during which Neilson occupied the position, the proposals to construct affordable housing in Woodstock and Salt River, which Brett Herron had been pushing, got torpedoed.

Still De Lille didn't give up – this had turned into a no-holds-barred fight to the finish. She once again went to court and, four days later, succeeded in overturning her dismissal as a DA member and mayor on procedural grounds. The DA had bungled it again, tripping over its own rules and regulations.

As internal negotiations were taking place, a second no-confidence motion was withdrawn at the last minute in late July – a deal with De Lille was apparently being brokered by the DA national leadership.

De Lille was still facing the party's internal disciplinary charges, however, and she wanted the hearings to be open to the public. Asserting that the DA's charges were trumped up, she wanted the party leaders to be exposed for the factional campaign she claimed they were running, and advanced that the DA was opposing her efforts to integrate black people into the city and build affordable housing. The DA leadership had badly bungled most of its moves against De Lille, and by attacking them for racial bias, she was turning the fight on its head.

In preliminary discussions, the DA leadership agreed to open hearings, although it was going to be very difficult to manage their case with every statement broadcast to the nation. De Lille was a far better fighter in open public debate than any of the DA leaders.

In the final build-up to the hearings, however, Mmusi Maimane had some frank discussions with De Lille. He was deeply concerned about the severe damage the factional battles in Cape Town were wreaking on the DA's support: opinion polls showed that the fight was losing the party support by bringing into question its proclaimed good-governance model.[64] The DA's selling point that where it governed, it governed best, looked increasingly hollow as the accusations and conflict escalated. It didn't help that the DA's coalitions in other metros, particularly Tshwane and Nelson Mandela Bay, were imploding.

The party still believed there was a case for De Lille to answer, but Maimane had to balance this against the political damage it would cause. He also had serious doubts about whether the DA's federal executive would win the public-opinion battle against De Lille.

Without involving the federal executive, Maimane took the initiative and reached a 'mutual agreement' with De Lille: she would step down as mayor, and there would be no disciplinary hearing.

This made me wonder whether there was dirty laundry that neither side wanted aired. While the DA claimed to have evidence of what they alleged was criminal wrongdoing, De Lille was ready to challenge them on procedural grounds, where the DA had repeatedly been proven inept. She also claimed to have evidence of DA wrongdoing. While De Lille appeared to be linked to controversial property developments, she had for many years been toeing the party line in opening doors for developers. The open hearings promised to turn into an ugly showdown, and both sides might have realised that they would destroy each other in the process.

Maimane had to sell the deal with De Lille to the federal executive and the DA caucus. On the evening of Saturday 4 August, he met with key DA leaders and told them that De Lille had tendered her resignation – she didn't want to go through with the disciplinary hearing, he claimed. The De Lille camp, however, trumpeted a completely different version: the DA had 'withdrawn the charges' against her because they 'feared an open disciplinary committee'.[65]

The next day De Lille and Maimane announced the resolution in a stiffly polite press conference. De Lille would resign as mayor at the end of October. All party disciplinary charges were dropped in what Maimane described as 'an opportunity to close a difficult chapter in our history'. It was also an opportunity for the DA caucus in the City 'to take stock, to regroup and to unite'. The media called De Lille 'the Teflon politician'.[66]

In September 2018, a few weeks after Maimane and De Lille had announced their truce, and a month before De Lille was due to step down, a scandal broke about another Foreshore site, again involving Ian Neilson.

The housing-activist organisation Ndifuna Ukwazi, which had been monitoring property sales by the City, alleged that a piece of land on the Foreshore had been sold to Growthpoint properties for R140 million below its market value. The sale had been authorised in September 2016 when Neilson still headed the finance portfolio.[67] Although well-founded questions were raised around the Growthpoint deal, the timing of the revelations – two years after the transaction – made me wonder whether this was yet another episode in the political battle within the DA. Neilson denied that there was anything untoward about the sale, while other developers that had bid on the site felt that Growthpoint had paid a market-related price.

Nevertheless, a month before she was due to leave office, De Lille requested a full forensic investigation of the transaction – a decision that she wasn't shy to share publicly. The forensic report, released in July 2019, didn't pick up any irregularities, but Brett Herron wasn't satisfied with the findings and the Good party referred the matter to the Public Protector.[68]

De Lille kept everyone guessing right up until the date set for her resignation as mayor at the end of October 2018. When a journalist asked if she really was leaving, she said, 'I am taking it one day at a time. I have now consulted my lawyers and I'm going back to court because of all of these procedural errors and things that they have done.'[69]

Despite the deal she'd struck with Maimane, the DA caucus in Cape Town was still troubled, and some councillors hadn't finished with De Lille yet. The forensic reports into the Foreshore Freeway project and into De Lille herself were tabled to council and again immediately leaked to the media.

De Lille exploded and withdrew her resignation as mayor, saying she wanted to clear her name. More worrying for the DA, she wanted them to disclose who had been interviewed for the Steenhuisen report – City officials, who should not have been engaging in a political process, had obviously been involved.

De Lille finally did resign, at the very last moment, on 31 October 2018, saying that her relationship with the DA had become 'abusive', and telling 'those idiots that continued to smear my name in public' that she would clear her name. 'After 18 months, I am free. Free from oppression. Amandla!'[70]

She continued to fight in court to have the DA abandon the Steenhuisen and Bowman reports – a fight she would eventually win in November of that year.[71] By that stage, however, the public had lost interest. A *Business Day* headline seemed to sum it up – 'De Lille saga vents record blast of hot air'.[72]

16

The almond hedge

∿∿∿

In July 2019, as I prepared to leave Cape Town to return home to Johannesburg, I reflected on what I'd learnt from my months of research. I'd started out on my quest at the height of the City's water crisis, wondering how a City, together with the other spheres of government, could so monumentally mismanage a situation they'd known about for years. My enquiry had led me to look into questionable property-development projects, and the dynamics between the property sector, the City administration, political funding and local communities.

I'd also ended up looking into the roots, unfolding and denouement of a devastating factional battle within the DA. What did all this reveal about political power not only in the City, but more generally? What did this mean for the DA and South African politics? And where did this leave the City of Cape Town and its residents?

The City's management of the water crisis had been an administrative, political and leadership failure. Despite being warned a decade earlier that the city would run out of water, the necessary water-augmentation projects weren't initiated until June 2017. At the time the tenders were finally published, the City had announced that the first plants would be able to start producing a month later, by August 2017 – a preposterous prediction.

As the water crisis accelerated in late 2017, and panic peaked in January 2018, Capetonians became increasingly irritated with Auntie Pat's constant stern admonishments and finger-pointing for the water crisis. It was the local equivalent of the national blame game when South Africans were told by Eskom chairman Jabu Mabuza that the Eskom crisis and rolling blackouts were the fault and responsibility of 'all South Africans'.[1] It was also enormously frustrating to watch the petty infighting unfold when a real crisis needed attention – for a prolonged moment the adults had left the room while the children squabbled. It meant that Capetonians had a double whammy – let down by the national ANC government on energy security, and let down by the DA for not properly handling either the water crisis or the conflict with De Lille. It was a failure of leadership that affected Capetonians at a deep level.

At the height of the crisis Capetonians did make a huge effort to reduce their water use, eventually cutting total consumption by half. The City can claim some credit for this achievement, through ramping up water restrictions and its crisis communications.

But the DA then created more confusion. In March 2018, without any change in rainfall or water outlook, Mmusi Maimane started backpedalling on the scare story and announced that Day Zero would probably not arrive.

Not everyone was happy with the news. The Western Cape farmers, for example, who'd been forced to drastically reduce irrigation of their crops, felt 'let down and betrayed by government' and said that Day Zero had been a hoax. 'Nothing much has changed in the City. The prevailing drought continues unabated. None of the City's augmentation schemes are up and running yet … There is no guarantee of the coming winter season's rainfall being sufficient to break the drought.' The City appeared 'to have cried wolf too soon and now needs to backtrack on its expedient Day Zero predictions'.[2]

In the winter of 2018 strong squalls of cold weather moved across the Cape Peninsula, flooding the Cape Flats informal settlements, and the City had to call out its disaster response teams. By July 2018 the dams were 60% full, and by the end of winter they were at 80% capacity.

The worst had been avoided but water restrictions remained in place,[3] and Cape Town's residents had to absorb hefty tariff increases starting in July 2018. This included a fixed charge each month in addition to the consumptive charge, a version of the 'drought tariff' that De Lille had originally proposed and which had contributed to her downfall.

These measures are unlikely to ever go away completely. Cape Town will evermore face water scarcity and will need to manage its remaining resources, even if augmented, very carefully.

I'm still somewhat mystified as to why nothing had been done earlier; I can only chalk up the lack of long-term planning to leadership myopia – not just in City of Cape Town, but in the national Department of Water and Sanitation as well.

Looking back at the water crisis and what was revealed in the process of my research, however, I now understand why, even as the prospect of the drought became far more real, the City was so incapable of properly responding.

For several years, it had been progressively wounded by a massive, ill-conceived organisational restructuring, laid on top of many previous restructurings whose vestiges remained unresolved. As a result, most staff didn't know if their jobs were secure. Policy and strategic leadership functions had been taken away from senior managers, and experts within line departments were often ignored. There was a five-month period, between the end of 2016 and early 2017, while the DA haggled with De Lille over her mayoral committee, when the City was rudderless, deprived of the leadership a mayoral committee could and should provide. Unable to read the political tea leaves, no one wanted to take any significant decisions.

At the same time, a massive factional contest had erupted within the City. Towards the end of 2017, as accusations swirled around De Lille and her key allies and staff, everyone was fighting for their lives. In hindsight, it was a miracle that anything had been done about the water crisis at all. But for the citizens of Cape Town, it was an injustice, as public interest had suffered.

In many ways, the water crisis had been the proverbial canary in the coalmine – a stark symptom of a far deeper disease. The City's administration had been neutered, rendered pliant to the whims of the mayor's office. This highlighted a systemic problem in the way that government in South Africa is positioned in relation to politics. In the immediate post-apartheid period, the imperative had been to transform an apartheid state bureaucracy, and the vehicle for that transformation was seen as political control. The legal framework for public administration put executive power in the hands of politicians and didn't sufficiently protect senior civil servants from political interference.

All of our senior civil servants, including at municipal level, are on fixed-term contracts of not longer than five years, and when their term of office is up, politicians can easily not re-employ them.

In municipalities, there's a constant churn of senior officials coinciding with the five-year electoral cycle. Frequently managers aren't retained by the incoming political team, even from the same party. This has made senior municipal officials highly vulnerable.

If politicians lack integrity, the blurring of that line creates fertile grounds for a patronage-based system to take root. In municipalities such as Nelson Mandela Bay, I'd seen how these powers to intimidate senior managers were used to enable the capture of the City administration and rampant looting. But even in 'clean' administrations, it often creates undue influence from business interests, who maintain ties to political leaders via political funding and even social interactions. This influence then gets transmitted down through the echelons of the administration.

This may not strictly be state capture in the way we've come to define it in South Africa, but it creates an uneven playing field (of which politicians themselves are not always fully aware) between business interests and other public constituencies that don't benefit from the same level of access to and influence on politicians.

In addition, in response to a period of ANC rule in the Cape Town metro, the DA adopted an overbearing political stance towards the administration. This created an unhealthy interface between the political and administrative spheres, which unnecessarily politicised the upper layers of the City administration and made it vulnerable to political whims.

Jens Kuhn, one of the Cape Town officials who was fired through the restructuring, had told me about the vastly different worlds of politics and public administration, and how they operated according to different sets of rules.[4] It was a profound point, which made me reflect on how incompatible the political and administrative domains are.

Politics is about the constantly shifting terrain of public opinion and the memes politicians trade in to cultivate it. The currency of politics is loyalty – who's with you and who's against you, and whether your actions gain you political leverage or not.

The administrative world has a different set of imperatives – it's hierarchical, rules-based, and focused on defined outputs, and on the budget and staff needed to achieve them.

These two worlds intersect in the state, and we tend to take for granted that they can easily coexist. In cities, the interface is the city manager and executive directors. They have to hold the line against irrational politi-cal decisions, because further down the hierarchical line, officials just take instructions. And yet the way we appoint these senior managers and the way we support them make them extremely vulnerable to political pressure.

Patricia de Lille and Craig Kesson's motivation for their devastating re-engineering remains an unanswered question in my mind. Was De Lille motivated by a misplaced belief that ruling by fiat was the best and fastest way to reshape the City and deliver for residents, particularly when it came to housing pressures? Or was it collateral damage due to accommodating new economic interests, dislodging the DA's traditional funding base?

Regardless, the consequences are plain to see. The degree of centralisa-tion was jaw-dropping, unparalleled in any municipality I know.

Combining this with her initial standing within the DA, De Lille amassed an enormous amount of political and executive power during her first term in office. She was in charge of a well-run city with a healthy bal-ance sheet, and she had the technical, financial and political resources to be ambitious and remodel the metro to create a living example of an integrated post-apartheid 'opportunity city' that worked for everyone.

How did she use the power she amassed, and what did she achieve?

More than any other initiative, De Lille's signature property developments defined her mercurial legacy. She had staked a lot on them, willing to incur enormous risk and to wreak enormous damage to advance them.

Some of the so-called catalytic projects have survived, at least on paper – the Two Rivers Urban Park, the redevelopment of Conradie Hospital, the repurposing of the old Athlone power station, and the Bellville CBD trans-port node. Ironically, the City showed the least interest in the first two of these, and, given the Western Cape province's support for them, there may well have been broader support for these developments that transcended factions in the City. Yet other catalytic projects fell by the wayside.

As I write this, the Foreshore Freeway project, the ambitious attempt to create an iconic development at the gate of Cape Town's city centre, is in deep trouble. A few months after the City had announced the winning bidder, it cancelled the project.[5] According to the acting city manager, Lungelo Mbandazayo, this was based on legal considerations, after some of the losing bidders challenged the outcome. The legal opinion indicated that the vague evaluation criteria in the tender created an irredeemable problem with the procurement process.[6] The City's statement invoked the economic conditions in the country and 'the additional burdens that the City, its ratepayers, and residents are facing at the moment'.[7]

When I asked Ian Neilson whether they would re-tender the Foreshore project, he equivocated. The developers involved in the bidding process were also not sure whether they'd be willing to trust a fair rerun of the process or incur the high costs of bidding again. So the project seems dead, at least for now.

I wonder whether the economic interests clustered around the Foreshore – the CTICC, the V&A Waterfront, Naspers, George Georgiou – have already repositioned themselves and are reverting to the status quo.

Other development projects that De Lille had championed also unravelled. In October 2018, the sale of public land in Maiden's Cove was overturned after the Clifton Bungalow Owners' Association went to court to object to the lack of substantive consultation around the project. The massive cash injection that the City was to receive from privatising the coastal reserve in Camps Bay evaporated.

Wescape had already ground to a halt because of financial difficulties, but the tide seems to have turned against all the PHA developments too. There were already signs that the council's attitude to the PHA was shifting when they announced in March 2018 that there would be no further development in the PHA.[8] According to Nazeer Sonday, both Heritage Western Cape and the municipal planning tribunal seem to take a far more balanced view of competing land uses in the area. Sonday has now gone to court seeking to overturn all the planning decisions in the PHA, including the Oakland City and Uvest developments, the outcome of which will be decided later this year (2019). For the time being, his review application is still being contested by the City.

As for Paardevlei, I've heard from City officials that the mayoral committee are looking for a way to exit the ill-considered acquisition of land.

De Lille has alleged that conservative members of the DA caucus in the City 'used a cocktail of rich ratepayers, environmentalists, and heritage and planning regulations to prevent the development of public spaces for public good – in Clifton, the city centre, Woodstock, Salt River, Hout Bay, Rondebosch, Plumstead. The conservatives in the party will tell you that there is virtually no available land in Cape Town suitable to accommodate poorer people ... Unpalatable as it is, the truth is that the DA-led City of Cape Town does not believe that integration is a priority. If it did, it would begin to bring coloured and black Capetonians who were forcefully removed under apartheid back into the city and its suburbs.'[9]

I'm not so sure. Even if conservative elements within the DA did oppose her ambitions, the mayor was far from blameless. De Lille broke the power of the administration and ran the City by executive fiat. She targeted 'obstructive' spatial planners and cast aside 'constraining' planning instruments such as the urban edge and the CTSDF, yet planners and their tools were precisely what she needed to deracialise the city and drive spatial integration – initiatives like the social-housing project in Salt River were initially the brainchild of City planners. And the City's housing programme seems to have collapsed after the liquidation of the housing department, setting back housing delivery in the city by years.

In addition, I couldn't discern an obvious or credible element of spatial integration in most of the catalytic projects that De Lille tried so hard to ram through. The clearest effort was in the Foreshore project, yet that intention was ultimately undone by very poor tender execution – another symptom of the administrative weakness to which she had contributed. And even though a portion of the proceeds from Maiden's Cove were to be earmarked for affordable housing, it was unclear where it would be developed.

De Lille's administration did take steps towards formalising an inclusive housing policy involving consultations with industry and civic organisations that would mandate property developments to include some affordable housing and provide incentives to do so. Yet it did so only late into her second term: the mayoral committee adopted a concept document on inclusionary housing[10] in September 2018[11] – the month before she resigned. In any case, Mayor Dan Plato and his administration seem to have picked up where she left off, which contradicts her claim that the pushback against her was all about stopping spatial integration.

Once created, political factions have a way of self-perpetuating by cloaking themselves in justifications that often have little to do with the initial rift. Was the conflict within the DA perhaps less about policy itself and more about which economic interests would benefit from it? I'd been hoping to find out but was unable to pierce that veil, and this remains an open question. I don't know what deals were being done behind the scenes, what charities or political programmes were being supported, what rights were being traded or granted elsewhere in the city. But, on the face of it, the catalytic projects appeared to be more about developers' interests.

What is clear is that in the process, political capital was squandered, opportunities missed and, ultimately, public interest suffered. Patricia de Lille and her office were unwilling or unable to perform the function leaders are supposed to: bring conflicting constituencies around the table and find a way to align, or at the very least balance, their interests. For example, some developers told me that, desperate to find a resolution to the standoff with Reclaim the City and Ndifuna Ukwazi, they had been ready to strike an agreement around an inclusionary housing policy, but the City never stepped up to the plate and played a brokering role.

Successful leaders inspire, convince and build coalitions around a common vision, rather than try to impose their will. This is a difficult and frustrating task, which requires patience. But it's a task that's essential to generate sound initiatives, advance them and make sure that they endure – and not only because of the mayor's or any other leader's strength of will, which only goes so far and lasts for so long, but because a broad constituency supporting them has been created. Most of the catalytic projects were left in tatters, mainly as a result of flawed conception, political interventions and hubris.

In a democracy, wielding executive power alone ultimately generates an equal amount of pushback, regardless of how much authority the law provides. For Patricia de Lille, the pushback came from within her own party and her own administration, as well as from civic organisations that felt ignored.

You can choose to lament that pushback and believe in conspiracies: this is the road that Patricia de Lille seems to have chosen. The alternative is to reframe zero-sum games to align interests, and work towards finding common ground; and, in so doing, unleash collective power.

In the end, De Lille's efforts to push for social and spatial integration failed. But neither side in the ugly spat that unfolded within the DA covered themselves in glory. What role had the party played in this sorry rift, and what share of responsibility did it carry? Regardless of De Lille's shortcomings, the DA was not blameless, which raised questions about the party's own future – and by extension, the future of South African politics.

South Africa needs a competitive democracy in which the party in power is held in check by strong opposition parties. Even though I've never supported the DA, I feel sad for where they've ended up.

Under Helen Zille, the party made a really good attempt to build a different political model. For well over a decade, they ran the City of Cape Town along fairly solid lines, even if they at times fumbled matters. And for a moment under De Lille and Maimane, it looked as if the party was at last becoming more racially inclusive and would genuinely be able to put the different parts of Cape Town together in a way that worked for everyone.

But that vision came adrift. The unification project failed to find a middle ground, and more conservative elements in the DA weren't forced to accept a strategic compromise that would build a truly integrated city. They considered the merger between the DA and the ID as a takeover, one that would see the newcomers adopt their views, their values and their internal systems. Convinced of their righteousness, they seemed unable to make space for some element of osmosis. They certainly weren't prepared for a feisty and independent Patricia de Lille, who ultimately refused to toe their line.

Caught up in their own internal battles, the DA leaders in the City failed to properly manage the water crisis, faltering on the very ground they claimed as their own: administrative efficiency. In spite of the DA's desire to pitch itself high on the good-governance totem pole, I found that the administration of Cape Town, while largely corruption free, had been left wanting. The 'growth coalition' between City and business leaders, while preferable to the 'rent-seeking coalition' that I encountered in Nelson Mandela Bay, is unlikely in itself to resolve gaping socioeconomic inequality and redress spatial exclusion. It's also unlikely to expand the party's electoral base much further.

Both in Nelson Mandela Bay and in Cape Town, the losers were the poor.

In Cape Town, the DA's conservative funding base still seemed to call the shots. Maybe this is simply the way that power works, a cosy relationship between money and public office, part of the grubby transactional nature of politics. As Stephen Watson prophetically wrote in the conclusion to his collection of stories, *A City Imagined*, 'metropolitan politics will doubtless persist, here as elsewhere in South Africa, as the public domain (though lately privatised) of the seven deadly sins, avarice chief amongst them'.

The bruising political battle in Cape Town echoed the factional warfare I'd observed within the ANC. Perhaps the 'high risk' that the City administration had feared when rejecting my research application was the discovery that, in the end, the DA has not entirely escaped the challenges that blight the ruling party. Yet the high risk materialised on its own, as the DA's dirty laundry was ultimately aired in public, severely denting the squeaky-clean image it had been trying so hard to project. And once that dirty laundry was out, the party leaders weren't above fighting a public-opinion battle by pushing their narrative through media leaks or feeding me information that had been hitherto inaccessible. I can't exclude the possibility that, just as the clean-up operation in Nelson Mandela Bay became part of factional battles, my research became in a small way a potential tool in the DA's internal battle.

What does this mean for our national politics? The DA's alliance with Patricia de Lille's ID in 2010 was the party's second attempt to widen its political base through a merger. And just like the first, short-lived one with the NNP, it ended in a divorce. This raises questions over the DA's ability to expand beyond its current relatively narrow base.

To inch the ANC out of power at the local level, the party has entered into marriages of convenience in several metros around the country. These opportunistic alliances have at times been with partners that have little in common with the DA's platform and outlook, making for odd bedfellows. Some of these coalitions have unravelled, including in Nelson Mandela Bay.

Yet the ebb and flow of coalition politics is most likely what awaits South Africa, as the ANC loses ground and faces the loss of its absolute majority.

The challenge isn't whether one or another party gains power, but whether the fractious world of City coalitions can overcome the insidious influence of old and new money, and still advance the social agenda that the country so badly needs to bridge its devastating faultlines.

In the last week of October, just before De Lille was scheduled to resign, five councillors who were loyal to her, including the chief whip and two mayoral-committee members, themselves resigned, citing the DA's 'bullying tactics, racism and abuse' against the mayor. Another two councillors resigned on the day De Lille stepped down.[12]

Brett Heron resigned the next day, saying that the DA was a 'lost cause'.[13] The last straw for him, he said, was when the DA blocked the Salt River market and housing project, the social-housing programme that he'd championed.[14] (Ironically, Catherine Stone, the former city planner who'd been pushed out, had originally developed the social-housing proposals for Salt River and Woodstock.)

Herron said that there'd been many events within the DA that had made him feel 'uncomfortable' and he realised that 'the organisation is not what it claims to be and it has been hijacked by the wrong people. The DA is not committed to the transformation or change that this country needs. They pander [to] and pacify privilege.'[15]

Herron may have been correct in his judgement, but neither he nor De Lille explained why they'd spent so much effort on large property deals that seemed to do little to advance their own stated agenda.

On the day Brett Herron resigned, I met Helen Zille at her provincial government headquarters. As she graciously poured tea for me in her wood-panelled office, I asked her about the breakdown in relations in the

City. 'It's simply terrible,' she said. 'The resignation of Brett Heron is a disaster, and I don't believe that he's corrupt in any way. I've been feeling depressed all day about it.'[16]

We talked more broadly about the breakdown in relationships in the City, and the way the DA had fumbled it. Although by this stage Zille had fallen out with the DA's leadership and was politically very isolated, it couldn't have been easy for her to watch from the sidelines as the political marriage she'd arranged unravelled. She was unhappy with the charges against De Lille, who she believed was well intentioned and principled, as well as the unprocedural way in which De Lille had been hounded and her allies charged.

'The DA's approach has exacerbated the split and fanned the accusation that it's ideological [a policy difference between liberals and social democrats],' Zille said frankly.

In April 2019 De Lille talked about the humiliation she'd felt towards the end of her mayoral term. She'd spent two years untangling herself from 'a web of scurrilous and false allegations of impropriety levelled against me by conservative members of the DA caucus', she said. 'I have been forced to seek the assistance of the courts to defend myself, and the courts have found in my favour every time.'[17]

The DA was a divided party, she said, split between liberals and former NP members. She felt she was fronting for a conservative cabal intent on using their numerical advantage in the caucus to outvote her and like-minded colleagues, and block all efforts to transform a city still fundamentally constructed on apartheid lines. 'To have continued smiling in my DA T-shirt, while drawing a handsome salary, would have been dishonest to the people with whom I have worked since my trade union days, and to myself. I am a social democrat who believes that a capitalist system skewed towards social justice is the only sustainable solution to fixing the ravages of our apartheid past. I had to return to something I can believe in.'[18]

Patricia de Lille may no longer have been mayor, but the apparent victory of her detractors within the DA was to prove short-lived and hollow. Soon after leaving office, in December 2018, De Lille launched a new political party with the remains of her faction pried away from the DA's ranks. The new party was called Good, with loud orange branding around a genial picture of 'Auntie Patty', which stood in contrast to the overbearing bully most of the City officials remembered. Her new party's name reminded me of the Longfellow poem Andrew Boraine had quoted to me – 'When she was good, she was very, very good ...'

Brett Herron was appointed as the party's secretary general and Shaun August was its national organiser. The Good party platform was a mix of market and social-democratic measures, with a focus on using land for both historical redress and growth. It wanted cities to have a bigger say in what happened to the land they own, and for land-restitution cases to be handled within five years. There were plans to develop higher-density housing in urban areas, moving away from the costly low-cost housing on cities' outskirts. This was what De Lille had been championing all along, even if she'd failed in large part to achieve it as mayor of Cape Town.

Good, which signed up 60 000 members in the space of a few months, sustained a national campaign ahead of the 2019 election, and I wondered how it had managed to amass such an electoral war chest so quickly.

The national election proved to be a tough one for the DA. The bruising political battle, and the allegations of shady deals, ideological rifts and racial fractures that had been wielded in the process, had dented the image the party had been trying so hard to project, and this ended up costing them at the polls. The Western Cape, the only province governed by the DA, was on a knife edge, at times rumoured to be headed to below 50%, according to polling data. In the end, the DA took 55,4% of the votes and held on to the province. But from a two-thirds majority in Cape Town in the 2016 local-government elections, the DA's percentage of the vote in the city in 2019 fell to 53%, a dramatic drop of 13 percentage points.[19]

And Cape Town wasn't the only embarrassment for the DA. In the capital city of Tshwane, where the DA had governed through an unstable coalition with EFF support, DA support dropped by an eye-watering 17,7 percentage points. Although the less significant losses in other cities meant that the DA lost only 1,5 percentage points overall compared to the 2014 election, it was still a sobering result for a party that had been gaining electoral ground in every election in the preceding two decades.

The DA was by no means the only loser, however, suggesting that the very public factional battle in Cape Town might not have been the only reason for the party's electoral setback. Even though the ANC maintained a comfortable majority with 57,5% of the national vote, it dropped 4,6 percentage points nationally, its worst electoral performance ever, and the first time the party had dropped below the psychologically significant 60% threshold. Extremes on both sides of the political landscape, on the other hand, gained ground: the populist left-wing ECC obtained a whopping 10,8% of the vote nationally, while the right-wing Freedom Front Plus garnered an unprecedented 2,4%.

And what happened to Patricia de Lille's Good? She had anticipated that she would carve out a huge chunk of DA supporters, enough to be the kingmaker in the Western Cape and possibly form a governing coalition, but the party obtained only 3% in the Western Cape and 2,4% in Cape Town.[20] It produced its best result in Beaufort West, a Karoo town on the N1 highway, where it received 7,5% of the vote. So clearly not all the votes lost by the DA went to Good – it appears that DA supporters were also haemorrhaging to smaller right-wing parties such as the African Christian Democratic Party and the Freedom Front Plus. Politics was realigning itself in interesting ways.

While the DA's base had clearly been turned off by the ongoing factional dispute, conservative white voters were embracing far-right, even racist parties. What did this mean for the conservatives who'd reasserted control within the DA? Was their base shifting underneath them, and did they need to move left or right?

Ultimately, Patricia de Lille was to punch much higher than her party's electoral weight. She and her longstanding ally Brett Heron took up Good's two seats in the national Parliament, and the country waited anxiously for the new president, Cyril Ramaphosa, to appoint his Cabinet. There were rumours that De Lille would be offered the strategically important chair of the Parliamentary oversight committee on public accounts, which traditionally went to one of the smaller opposition parties.

On the afternoon of Wednesday 29 May, De Lille received a call from the president's office, asking her to go to Pretoria.[21] This could only mean one thing: even though the ANC had won the national elections with a solid majority, it was following a tradition, extending back to Nelson Mandela's time, of appointing some opposition MPs to the Cabinet.

De Lille phoned Brett Herron and asked him if he was sitting down. She was busy packing a bag, she told him, and on her way to the capital.[22]

On arriving at the Union Buildings, her cellphone was taken away from her, so Herron heard nothing further until just before the president's announcement that De Lille was to be appointed as minister of Public Works and Infrastructure in the national Cabinet. This was an extremely strategic portfolio, responsible for all the property holdings and large-scale infrastructure investments of government.

There was no doubt that De Lille had scored a huge coup, and that her delicate repositioning after the fallout with the DA had paid off. It nevertheless set tongues wagging. She was the only opposition MP to be appointed to the Cabinet, yet Good was among the smallest parties. The DA questioned whether this was part of a strategy to undermine the DA in the Western Cape. It's a 'well-executed ANC plan', said Mmusi Maimane, referring to De Lille as 'part of the ANC's infrastructure'.[23]

But Helen Zille, who'd supported De Lille throughout her fight with the DA, welcomed the appointment. 'Patricia de Lille as Minister of Public Works opens real opportunities, especially for Cape Town. For years, she and I tried in vain to secure the release of department of public works land in well-located areas to build affordable housing to overcome the spatial legacy of apartheid. Here is a real chance!'[24]

So, ironically, De Lille's appointment could indeed offer another opportunity to reshape Cape Town, with vast government land holdings close to the city centre, such as Culemborg, Wingfield and Youngsfield, now in her portfolio. Yet would she be able to mend bridges and work with the City administration ruled by the party that had so unceremoniously ousted her? If so, I wondered whether these would go the way of previous hubristic interventions, or if a 'new dawn' could indeed be in the offing. I also wondered whether the notoriously inefficient and corrupt national Department of Public Works knew what was coming for them.

Where did this leave the City of Cape Town?

Although the City never formally revoked its denial of my research request and Craig Kesson steadfastly refused to meet with me, in November 2018 I was granted an audience with the newly appointed city manager for Cape Town, Lungelo Mbandazayo. It was near the end of my research, but I was extremely grateful.

We met at the imposing and modern Cullinan Hotel, appropriately situated on the Foreshore opposite the CTICC. A lawyer, Mbandazayo had previously been in charge of the City's legal department and its corporate services. Tall and elegant, with a chiselled face and a kindly expression, he talked in a way that reminded me of Nelson Mandela – considered, principled, firm, and infusing his moral outlook into whatever he said.

I wanted to know about the fate of the administrative restructuring, and whether it would be overturned. He replied cautiously, saying that these weren't official views and he was 'just talking generally'. 'We started to tweak elements of the ODTP, because we could see what was working and what was not working. The only thing we haven't tweaked was the macro-structure,' he said.[25]

Some of Mbandazayo's bugbears appeared to be the way that the housing and planning functions had been liquidated and dissipated across the organisation. 'When I took over, it was the first thing I said: irrespective of where you put it, human settlements as a function must be in one place.' He also seemed to be uncomfortable with the bloated size of the mayor's office and the centralisation of policy under the SPU.[26]

The big elephant in the room, he said, was the TDA. He found the assignment of four mayoral-committee members to oversee the TDA to be a disaster, because they ended up competing among themselves, and ultimately no one was in charge or coordinating. There did, however, seem to be political support for unwinding the massive coalescence of functions under the TDA.[27]

These seemed to be wise insights, and even though I shuddered at the thought of another restructuring, Mbandazayo had to pick up the pieces of the vast re-engineering experiment that Patricia de Lille and Craig Kesson had unleashed.

My meeting with Mbandazayo gave me other reasons to hope. He seemed determined to redraw the line between the political and administrative spheres in the organisation. His emphasis was on the integrity of officials, who he said had to develop a backbone and stand up for sound administrative practice. 'You know, I don't blame Patricia and the politicians around her for what happened. Politicians will always test you, to see what sort of person you are. They will push you to do things. Once you say, "I will see what I can do for you," you've started on a slippery slope. If you try and massage things in response to their request, you'll compromise your principles. There's one thing I say to my officials: they can take everything away from you except your integrity; integrity, you can only give away yourself. That is my advice: don't do it.'[28]

I was left somewhat unresolved by my research into Cape Town. While the City remains the best-run metro in the country, outranking all others on a number of key criteria, we all seem to have been impoverished by the outcome of a political drama in which there were no victors, and neither side held the moral high ground. Also, I found no easy answers to the difficult questions about fractious identities in a divided society.

Maybe that's why I started to turn back to myself, back to my own failings and sense of loss, to the uncomfortable silences that seemed to black out parts of my own history. There's a lot of damage that can't be undone, but perhaps I could start with small steps.

I wondered about my boyhood friend Gammie: how had his life unfolded after his family's devastating relocation? Where in the world might he be? And was it possible to reach out over distance and time and touch that friend that he once was?

I spoke to my mother about what had happened to Gammie's family. Based on her recollections, I was able to locate the street where they'd lived in Manenberg. It's a rough neighbourhood, plagued by gang violence, so it was with some trepidation that I drove along the street to see if I could recognise their semi-detached house with the cement wall around it. The area was very run down, and graffiti proclaimed the turfs of rival gangs – the Americans, the Hard Livings, the Clever Kidz. Refuse was piled on the side of the road, and there was a long stretch of polluted water from a Consol sand-mining operation. As I travelled through this wasteland, the factional

246

battle I'd spent so much time dissecting felt small and inconsequential.

The DA's ward councillor is a devout young Muslim by the name of Aslam Cassiem. His status as a religious teacher allows him to walk freely in the community, and the gangs seem to respect his role. He spends most of his time trying to help with problems of domestic violence, missing people and gang fights. Everyone comes to him asking for assistance with housing, education, health or social workers – problems for which the municipality is often unable to offer help. Many of Cassiem's own relatives and friends have died in gang wars, or from drugs or violence.

Cassiem was 'unaligned' in the fallout with De Lille and had abstained during the no-confidence debate; he hadn't wanted to get involved in a fight about which he didn't know enough and felt that neither side was completely blameless.[29]

As I drove around looking for Gammie's old house, I stopped next to a group of youths on a vacant corner lot, and I spoke to a pimply boy wearing running shoes, a baseball cap and bling. He was disappointed that I wasn't there to buy drugs, and was no help in remembering a family who'd lived in the area 40 years before.

I enquired at the Primrose Park Mosque, hoping that someone would remember the family, but I was greeted by shakes of the head. It was just after Eid, and one of the religious teachers told me about their efforts to bring the violence-racked community together after the fast was broken.

The epicentre of the gang battles is a notorious road called Die Laan, and community leaders had arranged to close the road to traffic and put out long trestle tables with a variety of delicious food donated by the mosque and other organisations. Aslam Cassiem was integrally involved in brokering the ceasefire with the gangs in order to get everyone to put down their guns for the night and attend the celebration. The gangs had declared a temporary truce, and the normally anxious Manenberg residents had joined in the fun. I took solace in this hopeful story, a small moment of reconciliation, as I left Manenberg without answers about Gammie.

I haven't given up, though. Aslam Cassiem has offered to help. He'll take me to the next community event he'll organise and we'll talk to some of the old people in the area, and perhaps someone will remember the young boy who was once my friend.

On my last day in Cape Town, my friend Miriam, who'd kindly put me up while I was in town, took me walking on the slopes of Table Mountain near Kirstenbosch, and we wandered along the line of the old almond hedge that once constituted a boundary around the early Cape settlement. The hedge had been planted in 1660 on the instructions of Jan van Riebeeck as a vain attempt to keep the Khoi herders from crossing into what had been their ancestral grazing lands, and to protect Dutch settlers on VOC-'owned' land from attacks by the Khoi, who had refused to move as the settlers had spread out from the castle along the line of the mountains. Van Riebeeck had envisaged that 'the belt will be so densely overgrown that it will be impossible for cattle and sheep to be driven through and it will take the form of a protective fence.'[30]

Ultimately, the barrier was ineffective – the creation of a boundary as a way of excluding the Khoi was foreign to them, and the Dutch settlement rapidly expanded beyond it anyway – but by delineating where the Khoi could graze or build their huts, the Dutch had created both physical and 'imagined' boundaries.[31]

Now overgrown and hard to follow, the almond hedge was not just once written on the landscape but also a mental barrier, the ultimate dividing line between insiders and outsiders. It was this frontier that had shaped the South African history that came after it, as the frontier moved, to the railway lines set by the Group Areas Act, to the townships where the insurrection against apartheid was fought, and ultimately inward to the mental spaces that we occupy.

The beauty of the view across the flats to the distant Hottentots Holland was breathtaking. Yet I still felt a pervasive melancholy, a sense of something missing. The almond hedge is inside all of us, shutting out the unknown, and closing us off to a solution within our grasp. More than anywhere in South Africa, Cape Town has the resources at its disposal to right the wrongs of its past. So far, in this we had failed.

As we walked, Miriam hummed the words of a Bright Blue song, 'Weeping', which had become the informal anthem of the ECC in the 1980s. I sang along with a croaky voice, as I thought about the ultimate sadness of our cruel history, in which everyone had been losers. It seemed to sum up where we still are, as we walked back down the mountain to our imperfect, unformed, uncertain futures.

> *I knew a man who lived in fear:*
> *It was huge, it was angry, it was drawing near.*
> *Behind his house, a secret place,*
> *Was the shadow of the demon he could never face.*
> *He built a wall of steel and flame*
> *And men with guns, to keep it tame.*
> *Then, standing back, he made it plain*
> *That the nightmare would never, ever rise again –*
> *But the fear and the fire and the guns remain,*
> *It doesn't matter now,*
> *It's over anyhow.*
> *He tells the world that it's sleeping*
> *But as the night came round*
> *I heard its lonely sound:*
> *It wasn't roaring: it was weeping.*

Notes

1. The dead sea

1   Davis, R (2018) '#CapeWaterGate: In the end, what was Day Zero all about?' in Daily Maverick, 14 March, https://www.dailymaverick.co.za/article/2018-03-14-capewatergate-in-the-end-what-was-day-zero-all-about/ Accessed 25 June 2019.

2   Ramphele, L (2017) 'Even I use a bucket when taking a shower – Helen Zille' on CapeTalk 567AM, 18 February, http://www.capetalk.co.za/articles/245364/even-i-use-a-bucket-when-taking-a-shower-helen-zille Accessed 25 June 2019.

3   Merten, M (2018) 'Analysis: A drought of nature compounded by a drought in leadership' in Daily Maverick, 22 January, https://www.dailymaverick.co.za/article/2018-01-22-analysis-a-drought-of-nature-compounded-by-a-drought-in-leadership/ Accessed 25 June 2019.

4   HuffPost UK (2018) 'Cape Town past point of no return: Day Zero unavoidable – Zille', 22 January, https://www.huffingtonpost.co.za/2018/01/22/cape-town-past-point-of-no-return-day-zero-unavoidable-zille_a_23339682/ Accessed 25 June 2019.

5   The City's communications officer, Priya Reddy, confirmed that Resolve Communications had argued for the use of the Day Zero concept in order to frighten Capetonians into changing their attitudes towards the crisis.

6   Van der Merwe, M (2018) 'Water crisis: Curve balls and chaos at Cape Town council meeting reveal political games' in Daily Maverick, 19 January, https://www.dailymaverick.co.za/article/2018-01-19-water-crisis-curve-balls-and-chaos-at-cape-town-council-meeting-reveal-political-games/ Accessed 25 June 2019.

7   Davis, R (2018) '#CapeWaterGate: In the end, what was Day Zero all about?'

8   Van der Merwe, M (2018) 'De Lille announces new emergency water rations: 'We have reached a point of no return'' in Daily Maverick, 18 January, https://www.dailymaverick.co.za/article/2018-01-18-de-lille-announces-new-emergency-water-rations-we-have-reached-a-point-of-no-return/ Accessed 25 June 2019.

9 Norwood-Young, J (2018) 'Op-Ed: Don't let the City of Cape Town gaslight you – the water crisis is not your fault' in Daily Maverick, 23 January, https://www.dailymaverick.co.za/article/2018-01-23-op-ed-dont-let-the-city-of-cape-town-gaslight-you-the-water-crisis-is-not-your-fault/ Accessed 25 June 2019.

10 Zille, H (2018) 'From the inside: The countdown to Day Zero' in Daily Maverick, 22 January, https://www.dailymaverick.co.za/opinionista/2018-01-22-from-the-inside-the-countdown-to-day-zero/ Accessed 25 June 2019.

11 Ibid.

12 Merten, M (2018) 'Analysis: A drought of nature compounded by a drought in leadership'.

13 Davis, R (2018) '#CapeWatergate: DA hints Mayor De Lille to blame for water crisis mismanagement' in Daily Maverick, 16 January, https://www.dailymaverick.co.za/article/2018-01-16-capewatergate-da-hints-mayor-de-lille-to-blame-for-water-crisis-mismanagement/ Accessed 25 June 2019.

14 City Press (2016) 'Nomvula Mokonyane's Watergate', 10 July, https://city-press.news24.com/News/nomvulas-watergate-20160710 Accessed 27 June 2019.

15 Ibid.

16 Ibid.

17 Parliamentary Monitoring Group (2017) 'Contested audit findings 2016/17 by DWS: Auditor General briefing; BRRR', 2 November, https://pmg.org.za/committee-meeting/25407/ Accessed 28 July 2019.

18 Merten, M (2018) 'Leaving a department that has completely collapsed – the case against Nomvula Mokonyane' in Daily Maverick, 4 May, https://www.dailymaverick.co.za/article/2018-05-04-leaving-a-department-that-has-completely-collapsed-the-case-against-nomvula-mokonyane/ Accessed 25 June 2019.

19 South African Government News Agency (2009) 'R1.5bil Berg River Dam to supply 20% of Cape Town's water', 6 March, https://www.sanews.gov.za/south-africa/r15bil-berg-river-dam-supply-20-cape-towns-water Accessed 25 June 2019.

20 Western Cape Water Reconciliation Strategy (2009) 'Does Cape Town have enough water?', Newsletter, 5 March, http://www.dwaf.gov.za/Documents/Other/WMA/19/WCWRSNewsletterMarch09.pdf Accessed 25 June 2019.

21 Department of Water and Sanitation: Western Cape Water Supply System Augmentation Project (nd) 'Water is life, sanitation is dignity', http://www6.dwa.gov.za/WC/ Accessed 25 June 2019.

22 Norwood-Young, J (2018) 'Op-Ed: Don't let the City of Cape Town gaslight you – the water crisis is not your fault'.

23 Ibid.

24 Spaull, N (2018) 'Op-Ed: Cape Town, a city drowning in incompetence' in Daily Maverick, 22 January, https://www.dailymaverick.co.za/article/2018-01-22-op-ed-cape-town-a-city-drowning-in-incompetence/ Accessed 25 June 2019.

2. The black swan

1 The 'black swan' theory was conceived by risk analyst Nassim Taleb as a metaphor

to describe an event that comes as a surprise, has a major effect, and can somehow be rationalised with the benefit of hindsight. The expression was based on the ancient presumption that black swans did not exist, disproved when the first one was seen.

2 This experience was the subject of my previous book, How to Steal a City, published by Jonathan Ball Publishers in 2017.

3 The Reconstruction and Development Programme was a comprehensive development blueprint for transforming the economy and society, drawn up by the ANC and its tripartite alliance partners in 1993, and used as their platform for fighting and winning the first democratic elections in 1994.

4 Leon, T (2016) 'Why the election's biggest winner was Patricia de Lille' on Tony Leon website, 10 August, http://tonyleon.com/why-the-elections-biggest-winner-was-patricia-de-lille/ Accessed 25 June 2019.

5 Davis, R (2018) '#CapeWatergate: DA hints Mayor De Lille to blame for water crisis mismanagement' in Daily Maverick, 16 January, https://www.dailymaverick.co.za/article/2018-01-16-capewatergate-da-hints-mayor-de-lille-to-blame-for-water-crisis-mismanagement/ Accessed 25 June 2019.

6 Van Damme, P (2017) 'DA acts in the interest of a clean government that delivers for Cape Town' on DA website, 14 December, https://www.da.org.za/2017/12/da-acts-interest-clean-government-delivers-cape-town/ Accessed 21 August 2018.

7 Dougan, L (2018) 'Newsflash: I'm certainly not distracted, says Cape Town mayor De Lille amid water crisis' in Daily Maverick, 9 January, https://www.dailymaverick.co.za/article/2018-01-09-newsflash-im-certainly-not-distracted-says-cape-town-mayor-de-lille-amid-water-crisis/ Accessed 25 June 2019.

8 Davis, R (2018) '#CapeWatergate: DA hints Mayor De Lille to blame for water crisis mismanagement' in Daily Maverick, 16 January, https://www.dailymaverick.co.za/article/2018-01-16-capewatergate-da-hints-mayor-de-lille-to-blame-for-water-crisis-mismanagement/ Accessed 25 June 2019.

9 Ibid.

10 Ibid.

11 Davis, R (2018) '#CapeWatergate: Mayor Patricia de Lille fights back on water mismanagement claims' in Daily Maverick, 16 January, https://www.dailymaverick.co.za/article/2018-01-16-capewatergate-mayor-patricia-de-lille-fights-back-on-water-mismanagement-claims/ Accessed 25 June 2019.

12 Van der Merwe, M (2018) 'Water crisis: Curve balls and chaos at Cape Town council meeting reveal political games' in Daily Maverick, 19 January, https://www.dailymaverick.co.za/article/2018-01-19-water-crisis-curve-balls-and-chaos-at-cape-town-council-meeting-reveal-political-games/ Accessed 25 June 2019.

13 Ibid.

14 De Lille, P (2018) 'Water crisis: I wasn't consulted – Patricia de Lille' on PoliticsWeb website, https://www.politicsweb.co.za/comment/water-crisis-i-wasnt-consulted--patricia-de-lille Accessed 25 June 2019.

15 Van der Merwe, M (2018) 'News flash: Maimane steps in, prepares Cape Town for disaster measures' in Daily Maverick, 24 January, https://www.dailymaverick.co.za/

article/2018-01-24-news-flash-maimane-steps-in-prepares-cape-town-for-disaster-measures/ Accessed 25 June 2019.

16 Interview with James Selfe, MP, Cape Town, 2 July 2019.

3. A tale of two cities

1 Child, K (2018) 'Does Cape Town have something to hide, asks housing policy researcher' on TimesLive, 26 July, https://www.timeslive.co.za/news/south-africa/2018-07-26-does-cape-town-have-something-to-hide-asks-housing-policy-researcher/ Accessed 26 June 2019.

2 Personal communication with Pam Yako in August 2018.

3 Geach, C (2013) 'Race and space in Cape Town' on IOL website, 12 September, https://www.iol.co.za/news/south-africa/western-cape/race-and-space-in-cape-town-1576493 Accessed 26 June 2019.

4 Polgreen, L (2012) 'In a divided city, many blacks see echoes of white superiority' in The New York Times, 22 March, https://www.nytimes.com/2012/03/23/world/africa/in-cape-town-many-black-south-africans-feel-unwelcome.html Accessed 26 June 2019.

5 Geach, C (2013) 'Race and space in Cape Town'.

6 Trotter, H (2009) 'Trauma and memory: the impact of apartheid-era forced removals on coloured identity in Cape Town' in Burdened by Race: Coloured Identities in Southern Africa, UCT Press, Cape Town.

7 Ibid.

8 Ibid.

9 The Van Breda family started the Merino-wool industry in South Africa, and Michiel van Breda was the first mayor of Cape Town (1840–1844). The Cloetes were a powerful Cape family who owned Groot Constantia from 1778 to 1885, including the farm Hoop op Constantia on which I grew up.

10 Descendants of VOC slaves from Batavia, Sulawesi and the Malaysian peninsula.

11 Trotter, H (2009) 'Trauma and memory: the impact of apartheid-era forced removals on coloured identity in Cape Town'.

12 Ibid.

13 The Hottentots Holland mountain chain separates the Cape Peninsula from the hinterland. It was derisorily so named by the Dutch settlers, because when the Khoi enquired where they came from, the Dutch waved their hands towards the mountains, indicating the direction in which the Netherlands lay.

14 Watson, S (ed) (2009) A City Imagined. Penguin Global.

15 Frith, A (2011) Dot Map of South Africa, https://dotmap.adrianfrith.com/ Accessed 15 July 2019.

16 Reclaim the City website, http://reclaimthecity.org.za/ Accessed 26 June 2019.

4. Between a rock and a hard place

1 Interview with Catherine Stone, former director for spatial development in the City of

Cape Town, Cape Town, 26 June 2018.

2 Interview with Mark Noble, development manager for V&A Waterfront, Cape Town, 3 October 2018.

3 Interview with Japie Hugo, former executive director for economic, environment and spatial planning in the City of Cape Town, Cape Town, 16 July 2018.

4 Ibid.

5 Interview with Catherine Stone.

6 Interview with Japie Hugo.

7 Ibid.

8 Interview with Stephen Boshoff, former executive director for strategy and development in the City of Cape Town, Cape Town, 11 July 2018.

9 Interview with Jens Kuhn, former director for housing development in the City of Cape Town, Cape Town, 16 July 2018.

10 Ibid.

11 Ibid.

12 Interview with Seth Maqetuka, former executive director for human settlements in the City of Cape Town, Johannesburg, 17 July 2018.

13 Ibid.

14 Ibid.

15 Ibid.

16 Ibid.

17 Ibid.

18 Interview with a former official in the human settlements department in the City of Cape Town, 8 August 2018.

19 Interview with a former official in the City of Cape Town, 26 June 2018.

20 Interview with Shehaam Sims, former director of informal settlements in the human settlements department of the City of Cape Town, Oudtshoorn, 17 August 2018.

21 Ibid.

22 Interview with Frank Cumming, director of urban catalytic investments in the City of Cape Town, Cape Town, 10 July 2019.

23 Red Tape Reduction website, https://www.westerncape.gov.za/red-tape-reduction/ Accessed 26 June 2019.

24 The World Bank Doing Business website, https://www.doingbusiness.org/en/rankings Accessed 15 July 2019.

25 City of Cape Town (2017) Five-Year Integrated Development Plan, July 2017–June 2022, Executive Summary http://resource.capetown.gov.za/documentcentre/Documents/ City%20strategies,%20plans%20and%20frameworks/IDP%202017-2022%20 Executive%20Summary.pdf Accessed 26 June 2019.

26 Interview with Catherine Stone.

27 Ibid.

28 Ibid.

29 Interview with Mapule Moore, former official in the City of Cape Town, Cape Town, 10 September 2018.

30 Interview with Frank Cumming.
31 Interview with David Marais, property development official in the City of Cape Town, Cape Town, 10 July 2019.
32 Red Tape Reduction website.
33 Interview with Frank Cumming.
34 Interview with housing official in the City of Cape Town, Cape Town, 8 August 2018.
35 Interview with Mapule Moore.
36 Ibid.
37 Ibid.
38 Interview with Japie Hugo.
39 Interview with Seth Maqetuka.
40 Herron, B (2018) WCPDF: Affordable Accommodation Session – City of Cape Town's Housing Policy Shift, http://www.wcpdf.co.za/2018_conference/8.%20Brett%20Herron.pdf Accessed 27 June 2019.
41 City of Cape Town Integrated Annual Reports available at http://www.capetown.gov.za/document-centre/Document-overview/city-research-reports-and-review.
42 Email correspondence with Hugh Cole and Nomawethu Solwandle from the mayoral committee's office, 16 April 2019.
43 Interview with Deon van Zyl, chair of WCPDF, Cape Town, 5 September 2018.
44 Ibid.
45 World Bank Group (2018) Doing Business in South Africa 2018, World Bank, Washington DC, http://www.doingbusiness.org/content/dam/doingBusiness/media/Subnational-Reports/DB18_South-Africa.pdf Accessed 27 June 2019.
46 City of Cape Town (2018) Integrated annual report 2017/18.
47 Auditor-General South Africa (2018) Report of the Auditor-General to the Western Cape Provincial Parliament and the Council on the City of Cape Town.

5. Death by restructuring

1 De Lille, P and Kesson, C (2017) View from City Hall: Reflections on Governing Cape Town, Jonathan Ball Publishers, Johannesburg and Cape Town.
2 Ibid.
3 Interview with former City official, Cape Town, 9 July 2018.
4 Interview with former City official, Cape Town, 26 June 2018.
5 De Lille, P and Kesson, C (2017), View from City Hall: Reflections on Governing Cape Town.
6 Ibid.
7 Ibid.
8 Ibid.
9 Personal communication, Cape Town, 7 August 2018.
10 De Lille, P and Kesson, C (2017), View from City Hall: Reflections on Governing Cape Town.
11 Interview with former senior official in the City of Cape Town, Cape Town, 26 June 2018.

12 De Lille, P and Kesson, C (2017), View from City Hall: Reflections on Governing Cape Town.
13 Interview with an official in the City of Cape Town, Cape Town, 8 August 2018.
14 De Lille, P and Kesson, C (2017), View from City Hall: Reflections on Governing Cape Town.
15 Interview with Catherine Stone, former director for spatial development in the City of Cape Town, Cape Town, 26 June 2018.
16 De Lille, P and Kesson, C (2017), View from City Hall: Reflections on Governing Cape Town.
17 De Lille, P and Kesson, C (2017), View from City Hall: Reflections on Governing Cape Town.
18 Selfe, J, Kopane, P, Van der Walt, D, et al (2016) Report of the Federal Executive Task Team to examine the proposed City of Cape Town Mayco measured against the Organisational Development and Transformation Plan.
19 Interview with David Savage, City Support Programme, Cape Town, 9 July 2018.
20 Interview with Stephen Boshoff, former executive director for strategy and development in the City of Cape Town, Cape Town, 11 July 2018.
21 Interview with Frank Cumming, director of urban catalytic investments in the City of Cape Town, Cape Town, 10 July 2019.
22 Ibid.
23 Interview with Lungelo Mbandazayo, city manager in the City of Cape Town, Cape Town, 11 November 2018.
24 Interview with Andrew Boraine, former city manager of Cape Town, Cape Town, 8 July 2018.
25 Interview with Jens Kuhn, former director for housing development in the City of Cape Town, Cape Town, 16 July 2018.
26 Democratic Alliance Federal Executive (2017) Report of the Subcommittee Established to Enquire into the Tensions in the City of Cape Town, 10 December.
27 Ibid.
28 Interview with David Savage.
29 Head, T (2018) 'Cape Town dam levels: Water capacity increases yet again after rainfall' on The South African website, 11 June, https://www.thesouthafrican.com/news/cape-town-dam-levels-june-2-pc/ Accessed 30 July 2019.
30 Interview with David Savage.
31 Ibid.
32 Ibid.

6. Factory flaw

1 Interview with David Savage, City Support Programme, Cape Town, 9 July 2018.
2 Interview with Stephen Boshoff, former executive director for strategy and development in the City of Cape Town, Cape Town, 11 July 2018.
3 Ibid.

4 Interview with Lungelo Mbandazayo, city manager in the City of Cape Town, Cape Town, 11 November 2018.
5 Interview with Suzette Little, former mayoral committee member in the City of Cape Town, Cape Town, 17 May 2019.
6 Interview with Catherine Stone, former director for spatial development in the City of Cape Town, Cape Town, 26 June 2018.
7 Interview with Lungelo Mbandazayo.
8 Interview with Stephen Boshoff.
9 Johnson, V (2004) 'Public deception in Cape Town: Story of an insider witness' in Calland, R and Dehn, G (eds) Whistleblowing Around the World – Law, Culture and Practice, Open Democracy Advice Centre, Cape Town.
10 Ibid.
11 News24 archives (2001) 'Marais implicated in street row', 7 August, https://www.news24.com/xArchive/Archive/Marais-implicated-in-street-row-20010807 Accessed 27 June 2019.
12 Ibid.
13 Johnson, V (2004) 'Public deception in Cape Town: Story of an insider witness'.
14 Peter Marais went on to become Western Cape premier, a deal struck with his new ANC allies, but quickly got into trouble over allegations of sexual harassment, following which he resigned. In the 2019 elections the conservative right-wing Freedom Front Plus won one seat in the Western Cape Provincial Parliament – a seat Marais filled.

7. Where angels fear to tread

1 Cape Argus (2012) 'Beach loses blue flag status after Big Bay property development' on IOL website, 19 October, http://www.iolproperty.co.za/roller/news/entry/beach_loses_blue_flag_status Accessed 27 June 2019.
2 Ibid.
3 Personal communication with environmental expert, Cape Town, 12 March 2019.
4 Cape Argus (2012) 'Beach loses blue flag status after Big Bay property development'.
5 Yeld, J (2003) 'Nats hit by new funding scandal' on IOL website, 21 February, https://www.iol.co.za/news/politics/nats-hit-by-new-funding-scandal-101823 Accessed 24 July 2018.
6 Ibid.
7 Cape Argus (2012) 'Beach loses blue flag status after Big Bay property development'.
8 Personal communication, Cape Town, 12 March 2019.
9 The units were to be split as follows: 22–26% of the total for subsidised housing for households with an income of less than R3 500 per month, 25–30% for lower-gap housing for incomes less than R7 500, 26–34% upper-gap housing for incomes less than R15 000, and 18–24% semidetached and freestanding housing for incomes more than R15 000. See Council Secretariat (2012) 'Proposed Amendment of the Cape Town Spatial Development Framework for Remainder Portion 1 (Klipvalley) of Cape Farm 41, Remainder Cape Farm (Lange Rug) 36, Cape Farm (Lange Rug) 37, Cape Farm (Brakkekuyl) 38 and 39, Cape

Farm 1244, Cape Farm 1509, Cape Farm 80, Portion 1 of Cape Farm (Klein Zouterivier) 84 and Cape Farm 78, Known as Wescape (the Site)'. Council Memorandum C 44/12/12, City of Cape Town, Cape Town.

10 Interview with Gita Goven, chair of communiTgrow, Cape Town, 9 November 2018.

11 Furlong, A (2016) 'Wescape: Why build a new city for 800 000 people more than 40km away from Cape Town?' on Our Future Cities website, 14 June, http://futurecapetown. com/2016/06/wescape-thriving-new-city-or-failed-development-future-cape-town/#. W0c8RNIzaM- Accessed 28 June 2019.

12 Cape Times (2013) 'Cape Town planning officials slam property development, but politicians disagree' on IOL Property website, 28 March, http://www.iolproperty.co.za/ roller/news/entry/row_over_plan_to_house Accessed 28 June 2019.

13 Ibid.

14 Furlong, A (2016) 'Meet David Lee Pearson, the dodgy businessman behind Wescape' on GroundUp website, 24 August, https://www.groundup.org.za/article/meet-david-lee-pearson-dodgy-businessman-behind-wescape/ Accessed 28 June 2019.

15 Interview with Jens Kuhn, former director for housing development in the City of Cape Town, Cape Town, 16 July 2018.

16 Council Secretariat (2012) 'Proposed Amendment of the Cape Town Spatial Development Framework for Remainder Portion 1 (Klipvalley) of Cape Farm 41, Remainder Cape Farm (Lange Rug) 36, Cape Farm (Lange Rug) 37, Cape Farm (Brakkekuyl) 38 and 39, Cape Farm 1244, Cape Farm 1509, Cape Farm 80, Portion 1 of Cape Farm (Klein Zouterivier) 84 and Cape Farm 78, Known as Wescape (the Site)'. Council Memorandum C 44/12/12, City of Cape Town, Cape Town.

17 Ibid.

18 Ibid.

19 Property 360 (2013) 'Cape Town planning officials slam property development, but politicians disagree', 27 March, http://www.iolproperty.co.za/roller/news/entry/row_ over_plan_to_house Accessed 16 July 2019.

20 Gosling, M (2013) 'Row erupts over Wescape plan' in Cape Times, 27 March, https:// www.iol.co.za/capetimes/row-erupts-over-wescape-plan-1492597 Accessed 28 June 2019.

21 Furlong, A (2016) 'Meet David Lee Pearson, the dodgy businessman behind Wescape'.

22 Council Secretariat (2012) 'Minutes of a Special Meeting of the Executive Mayor and Members of the Mayoral Committee of the City of Cape Town', Minutes SMC 11/12, City of Cape Town, Cape Town.

23 Council Secretariat (2012.) 'Proposed Amendment of the Cape Town Spatial Development Framework for Remainder Portion 1 (Klipvalley) of Cape Farm 41, Remainder Cape Farm (Lange Rug) 36, Cape Farm (Lange Rug) 37, Cape Farm (Brakkekuyl) 38 and 39, Cape Farm 1244, Cape Farm 1509, Cape Farm 80, Portion 1 of Cape Farm (Klein Zouterivier) 84 and Cape Farm 78, Known as Wescape (the Site)'.

24 Council Secretariat (2012) 'Minutes of a Special Meeting of the Executive Mayor and Members of the Mayoral Committee of the City of Cape Town'.

25 Furlong, A (2016) 'Meet David Lee Pearson, the dodgy businessman behind Wescape'.

26 Ibid.

27 Interview with Japie Hugo, former executive director for economic, environment and spatial planning in the City of Cape Town, Cape Town, 16 July 2018.

28 Interview with Frank Cumming, director of urban catalytic investments in the City of Cape Town, Cape Town, 10 July 2019.

29 Furlong, A (2016) 'Eskom slams Province and City on Wescape' on GroundUp, 22 June, https://www.groundup.org.za/article/eskom-slams-western-cape-government-and-city-wescape-decision/ Accessed 30 July 2019.

30 CommuniTgrow Facebook page, https://www.facebook.com/communiTgrow/ Accessed 26 July 2018.

8. The promised land

1 Interview with Nazeer Sonday, PHA activist, Cape Town, 8 August 2018.

2 Ibid.

3 Personal communication, Cape Town, July 2018.

4 Anderson, V, Azari, S and Van Wyk, A (2009) 'Philippi Community Profile', South African Education and Environment Project, Cape Town, http://www.saep.org/media/docs/125810846813.pdf Accessed 16 July 2019.

5 Battersby-Lennard, J and Haysom, G (2012) Philippi Horticultural Area: A City Asset or Potential Development Node? Rooftops Canada Abri International and African Food Security Urban Network, Cape Town.

6 The PHA task team appointed by the City of Cape Town in 2009 found that agricultural production in the PHA was profitable, and that it contributed a major portion of Cape Town's vegetable needs, as well as providing employment and small-business opportunities for vulnerable groups. The report noted that the PHA was 'irreplaceable within 120km of Cape Town', and that strict adherence to agricultural zoning was needed to keep land prices in line with agricultural production values. See Recommendations of the Philippi Horticultural Area Task Team (2009) Report to Planning and Environment Portfolio Committee, City of Cape Town, Cape Town, http://gctca.org.za/wp-content/uploads/2013/07/RECOMMENDATIONS-OF-PHILIPPI-HORTICULTURAL-AREA-TASK-TEAM.pdf Accessed 16 July 2019. All areas then deemed to be viable and productive agricultural areas needed to be retained for agriculture.

7 Anderson, V, Azari, S and Van Wyk, A (2009) 'Philippi Community Profile'.

8 Battersby-Lennard, J and Haysom, G (2012) Philippi Horticultural Area: A City Asset or Potential Development Node?

9 Van der Merwe, M and Swart, H (2017) 'Cape of storms to come' in Daily Maverick, https://features.dailymaverick.co.za/cape-of-storms-to-come/cape-of-storms-to-come-part-2---chapter-1.html Accessed 29 June 2019.

10 Cameron, B (2012) 'Rockland saga lifts veil on conflicts of interest' on IOL Personal Finance, 2 September, https://www.iol.co.za/personal-finance/columnists/bruce-cameron/rockland-saga-lifts-veil-on-conflicts-of-interest-1373837 Accessed 16 July 2019.

11 Bredell was then minister of the provincial Department of Environmental and Development Planning.

12 Van der Merwe, M and Swart, H (2017) 'Cape of storms to come'.
13 Kriel, PD (2014) 'In the Ex Parte Application of: Executive Officer of the Financial Services Board Applicant in Re the Collective Investment Scheme and Financial Services Business of Rockland Asset Management And Consulting (Pty) Ltd (Registration No. 2002/017672/07) and Rockland Targeted Development Investment Fund (Registration No. IT4321/2004) and the Business of Rockland Property Investment Fund (Registration No. IT4320/2004): Progress Report July 2014'. Report to High Court, case no. 15844/2012, Western Cape High Court, Cape Town.
14 Ibid.
15 Neille, D, Van der Merwe, M and Dougan, L (2017) 'Cape of storms to come' in Daily Maverick, https://features.dailymaverick.co.za/cape-of-storms-to-come/cape-of-storms-to-come-part-1.html Accessed 10 July 2019.
16 Personal communication with lawyer acting for pension funds, Johannesburg, 23 October 2018.
17 Van der Merwe, M and Swart, H (2017) 'Cape of storms to come'.
18 MSP website, https://www.msp.property/profile/ Accessed 23 July 2018.
19 Interview with Susanna Coleman, PHA campaigner, Cape Town, 8 August 2018.
20 Uvest Property (2013) Letter to executive mayor re 'Prospective City & Private Sector Co-Operation Agreement: Schaapkraal Development Opportunity, Philippi', 29 May.
21 The comments were attributed to Johan du Plessis, lawyer for Oakland City, and revealed in the correspondence between the developers and the City obtained as part of the review application.
22 Hugo, J (2012) 'Proposed Amendment of the Cape Town Spatial Development Framework Applicable to Land Units 539; 541-545; 554-558; 572; 574; 575; 578; 605-607; 609-617; 622; 626; 628; 630; 632; 634; 662; 664; 1932 and 1933, Philippi, Schaapkraal (in Terms of the Municipal Systems Act No 32 of 2000 and the Land Use Planning Ordinance, 15 of 1985).' Report to Economic, Environment and Spatial Planning Portfolio Committee, City of Cape Town, Cape Town.
23 On 28 May 2012 the CTSDF was approved and for the first time an urban edge was delineated around the PHA. The CTSDF was approved by council as a component plan of the IDP, and it was also approved by the Western Cape province as a section 4(6) Structure Plan in terms of the Land Use Planning Ordinance.
24 Hugo, J (2012) 'Proposed Amendment of the Cape Town Spatial Development Framework Applicable to Land Units 539; 541-545; 554-558; 572; 574; 575; 578; 605-607; 609-617; 622; 626; 628; 630; 632; 634; 662; 664; 1932 and 1933, Philippi, Schaapkraal (in Terms of the Municipal Systems Act No 32 of 2000 and the Land Use Planning Ordinance, 15 of 1985).'
25 Council Secretariat (2012) 'Minutes of a Special Meeting of the Executive Mayor and Members of the Mayoral Committee of the City of Cape Town', Minutes SMC 11/12, City of Cape Town, Cape Town.
26 Interview with Japie Hugo, former executive director for economic, environment and spatial planning in the City of Cape Town, Cape Town, 16 July 2018.
27 Council Secretariat (2013) 'Matters Receiving Attention List' of the Mayoral Committee

(list updated on 8 July 2013) in 'Minutes Of A Meeting Of The Executive Mayor And Members Of The Mayoral Committee Of The City Of Cape Town', 16 July, City of Cape Town, Cape Town.

28 Summary meeting notes re 'Private Sector Human Settlement Initiative' emailed to participants on 19 June 2013.

29 Email dated 20 June 2013 sent by director: programmes and special projects in the mayor's office (Afzal Brey) copying Uvest letter of 29 May 2013 to the executive director of the economic, environment and spatial planning directorate (Japie Hugo), who forwarded it to Catherine Stone and Kendall Kaveney noting that 'this is one of four projects the Mayor wants us to work on'.

30 Interview with Japie Hugo.

31 Ibid.

32 Email dated 8 July 2013 from the director of SPU (Craig Kesson) to the acting executive director of the economic, environment and spatial planning directorate (Kendall Kaveney) confirming that the mayor had issued an instruction to the economic, environment and spatial planning portfolio committee chair to review the Uvest application based on an agreement with the premier at an intergovernmental committee meeting.

33 Email dated 10 July 2013 from the director of SPU (Craig Kesson) to the acting executive director of the economic, environment and spatial planning directorate (Kendall Kaveney).

34 Interview with Catherine Stone, former director for spatial development in the City of Cape Town, Cape Town, 26 June 2018.

35 Kaveney, KA (2013) 'Recommendation from Executive Mayor: 16 July 2013. MC 60/07/13 Review of the Decision Taken in November 2012 Regarding the Cape Town Spatial Development Framework'. Report to Council C 80/07/13. City of Cape Town, Cape Town.

36 Ibid.

37 Council Secretariat (2013) 'Minutes Of The Meeting Of The Council Of The City Of Cape Town' held on 31 July, City of Cape Town, Cape Town.

38 Interview with Japie Hugo.

39 Interview with Jens Kuhn, former director for housing development in the City of Cape Town, Cape Town, 16 July 2018.

40 Ibid.

41 Van der Merwe, M and Swart, H (2017) 'Cape of storms to come'.

42 Ibid.

43 Habitat Council and Another v Provincial Minister of Local Government, Environmental Affairs and Development Planning, Western Cape and Others, [2013] ZAWCHC 112, which set aside the provincial appeal authority over planning decisions.

44 Interview with Catherine Stone, former director for spatial development in the City of Cape Town, Cape Town, 25 July 2018.

45 Van der Merwe, M and Swart, H (2017) 'Cape of storms to come'.

46 Part 1 Delegation 12(1) of the Systems of Delegation (Version 6 dated 29 October 2014) gives the mayor the power 'to decide on any application where Spatial Planning and Land

Use Management portfolio committee recommends refusal'.

47 City of Cape Town (2014) Food System and Food Security Study for the City of Cape Town, unpublished study by University of Cape Town, Cape Town.

48 Council Secretariat (2015) 'Minutes Of The Adjourned Meeting Of The Council Of The City Of Cape Town', 25 March, Item C 11/03/15, City of Cape Town, Cape Town.

49 Council Secretariat (2015) 'Minutes Of A Meeting Of The Executive Mayor And Members Of The Mayoral Committee Of The City Of Cape Town', 20 January 2015, City of Cape Town, Cape Town.

50 Spatial Planning and Land Management Act, No 16 of 2013.

51 On 1 July 2016 the municipal planning tribunal was set up, consisting of officials in the full-time service of the municipality and non-officials with 'knowledge and experience of spatial planning, land-use management and land development or the law related thereto'. See Daniels, D (2016) 'The Municipal Planning Tribunal in the City of Cape Town', http://www.wcpdf.co.za/2016_conference/DavidDaniels.pdf Accessed 16 July 2019.

52 Isaacs, L (2018) 'PHA land rezoning application refused as larger battle looms' in Cape Times, 27 June, https://www.iol.co.za/capetimes/news/pha-land-rezoning-application-refused-as-larger-battle-looms-15708379 Accessed 17 July 2019.

53 Van der Merwe, M and Swart, H (2017) 'Cape of storms to come'.

54 Personal communication with Nazeer Sonday, Cape Town, 18 June 2019.

9. Between the devil and the deep blue sea

1 Sachs, A (2018) 'Op-Ed: First it was Oudekraal – now the City of Cape Town wants to sell off Maiden's Cove' in Daily Maverick, 9 July, https://www.dailymaverick.co.za/article/2018-07-09-first-it-was-oudekraal-now-the-city-of-cape-town-wants-to-sell-off-maidens-cove/ Accessed 29 June 2109.

2 Albie Sachs in meeting with members of Maiden's Cove for All, Cape Town, 3 October 2018.

3 ibid

4 McKune, C (2015) 'De Lille and the contentious Clifton Scenic Reserve megaproject' in Mail & Guardian, 10 July, https://mg.co.za/article/2015-07-09-de-lille-and-the-contentious-clifton-scenic-reserve-megaproject Accessed 29 June 2019.

5 Ibid.

6 Ibid.

7 Ibid.

8 De Lille, P (2015) 'Letters to the editor: July 17 to 23 2015' in Mail & Guardian, 17 July, https://mg.co.za/article/2015-07-17-letters-to-the-editor-july-17-to-23-2015/ Accessed 20 June 2019.

9 Dolley, C (2018) 'Factors fuelling fight over Cape Town's controversial R1bn prime land tender' in Mail & Guardian, 24 May, https://mg.co.za/article/2018-05-24-factors-fuelling-fight-over-cape-towns-controversial-r1bn-prime-land-tender Accessed 29 June 2019.

10 Chambers, D (2018) 'Maiden's Cove will remain untouched by developers' in Sunday Times, 28 October, https://www.timeslive.co.za/sunday-times/

news/2018-10-28-maidens-cove-will-remain-untouched-by-developers/ Accessed 29 June 2019.

11 Albie Sachs in meeting with members of Maiden's Cove for All.

12 Ibid.

13 Webber Wentzel attorneys (2015) 'Sale of Immovable Property Agreement between Paardevlei Properties Proprietary Limited Registration Number: 19S9/Ll07165/07 ('Seller') and The City of Cape Town duly represented by the Acting executive Director Human Settlements ('Purchaser')', signed on 3 June.

14 Show Me Helderberg website (2015) 'City of Cape Town buys Paardevlei land for housing crisis', 1 July, https://showme.co.za/helderberg/property/city-of-cape-town-buys-paardevlei-land-for-housing-crisis/ Accessed 29 June 2019; and Williams, M (2014) 'Mini-city's high speed hook up' on IOL website, https://www.iol.co.za/business-report/technology/mini-citys-high-speed-hook-up-1738667 Accessed 11 July 2019.

15 Personal communication with human-settlements official, Cape Town, 9 July 2018.

16 Interview with Mapule Moore, former TDA official, Cape Town, 10 September 2018.

17 Interview with Melissa Whitehead, executive director in charge of TDA, Cape Town, 26 August 2018.

18 Interview with Mapule Moore.

19 Interview with Japie Hugo, former executive director for economic, environment and spatial planning in the City of Cape Town, Cape Town, 14 May 2019.

20 Interview with Mapule Moore.

21 Municipal financial years in South Africa run from 1 July until 30 June the following year. The 2014/15 financial year ended on 30 June 2015.

22 Interview with Melissa Whitehead.

23 Announced at the Greater Tygerberg Partnership conference in 2018, https://gtp.org.za/gtp-conference/gtp-conference2018/ Accessed 17 July 2019.

24 Interview with Mapule Moore.

25 Ibid.

26 Interview with town planner involved with Two Rivers Urban Park, Cape Town, 6 August 2018.

27 GroundUp (2018) 'Foreshore development was one of the reasons for De Lille fallout' in Daily Maverick, 26 February, https://www.dailymaverick.co.za/article/2018-02-26-groundup-foreshore-development-was-one-of-the-reasons-for-de-lille-fallout/ Accessed 29 June 2019.

28 Socioeconomic Profile, City of Cape Town (2017) Western Cape Government, https://www.westerncape.gov.za/assets/departments/treasury/Documents/Socio-economic-profiles/2017/city_of_cape_town_2017_socio-economic_profile_sep-lg_-_26_january_2018.pdf

29 Interview with Andrew Boraine, former city manager in the City of Cape Town, Cape Town, 8 July 2018.

30 Interview with Catherine Stone, former director for spatial development in the City of Cape Town, Cape Town, 26 June 2018.

10. How to steal a civic

1 In March 2013 the City of Cape Town adopted a new integrated zoning scheme which established for the first time a single and common zoning scheme for the entire metropolitan area, replacing the 27 zoning schemes that had until then been applicable in various parts of the metropole.

2 Most of Observatory is zoned General Residential 2 with a maximum building height of 15 metres, while properties along Main Road, Lower Main Road and Station Road are zoned General Business 1 with the same building height. There are pockets of land behind the arterial roads and jutting into the residential area that are zoned General Residential 2 and 3, with building heights of 20 and 24 metres, respectively – and it is these portions that have caused the greatest consternation among residents.

3 Minutes of the Observatory Civic Association Annual General Meeting held at the Observatory Community Centre on 31 October 2017.

4 Meeting with OCA large-developments subcommittee in Cape Town on 3 October 2018. See also Roeland, M (2017) 'Developers accused of hijacking Observatory civic association' on News24, 29 November, https://www.news24.com/SouthAfrica/News/developers-accused-of-hijacking-observatory-civic-association-20171129 Accessed 30 June 2019.

5 Leslie London at meeting with OCA large-developments subcommittee in Cape Town on 3 October 2018.

6 Ibid.

7 Observatory Civic Association (2017) Minutes of Special General Meeting held on 28 November 2017 in Observatory Community Hall, Cape Town.

8 Seekings, J (2011) 'The changing faces of urban civic organisation' in Transformation (75), http://transformationjournal.org.za/wp-content/uploads/2017/04/T75_Part16.pdf Accessed 29 June 2019.

9 The forerunner of Bokcra, the Schotche Kloof Civic Association, was banned in the 1980s, and Bokag was formed in its place. The civic organisation was unbanned, together with other organisations, in 1990.

10 Van Voore, R (2018) Report: Investigation into Allegations Involving the Executive Mayor Alderman Patricia de Lille, Bowman Gilfillan, Cape Town.

11 Interview with Seehaam Samaai and Razeen Diedericks, Cape Town, 12 March 2019.

12 Minutes of meeting of BKYM in Cape Town on 10 June 2018.

13 Kamaldien, Y (2018) 'Defiant Bo-Kaap youth movement gets legal backing' on IOL website, 16 November, https://www.iol.co.za/capeargus/news/defiant-bo-kaap-youth-movement-gets-legal-backing-18142650 Accessed 17 July 2019; and Van Emden, J (2019) In The High Court Of South Africa (Western Cape Division, Cape Town) in the matter between SJJMC Property (Pty) Ltd t/a Blok Urban Living (Pty) Ltd (registration number 2011/123016/07) and Bo-Kaap Neighbourhood Watch and various other parties: Replying affidavit, 5 February.

14 Pather, R (2019) 'Bo-Kaap "fights off capture" in Mail & Guardian, 15 February, https://mg.co.za/article/2019-02-15-00-bo-kaap-fights-off-capture Accessed 17 July 2019.

15 Norton Rose Fulbright (2018) 'Collaboration to Find a Solution Agreement between SJJMC (Pty) Ltd t/a Blok Urban Living and Bo-Kaap Youth Movement', signed on 27 July.

16 Interview with Seehaam Samaai and Razeen Diedericks.
17 Minute of meeting between Blok Urban Living (Pty) Ltd (Jacques van Embden), Prime Projects (Russell Baker), Bo Kaap Youth (Mujahid Hartley), Norton Rose Fulbright (Muneeb Gambeno, Lauren Fine, Claire Kotze) in Cape Town on 23 July 2018.
18 Interview with Seehaam Samaai and Razeen Diedericks.
19 Van Emden, J (2019) In The High Court Of South Africa (Western Cape Division, Cape Town) in the matter between SJJMC Property (Pty) Ltd t/a Blok Urban Living (Pty) Ltd (registration number 2011/123016/07) and Bo-Kaap Neighbourhood Watch and various other parties: Replying affidavit, 5 February.
20 Ibid.
21 Pretorius, K (2019) 'Association raises concern over Bo-Kaap zoning' in Weekend Argus, 19 February, https://www.iol.co.za/news/south-africa/western-cape/association-raises-concern-over-bo-kaap-zoning-19348883 Accessed 30 June 2019.
22 Payne, S (2019) 'Cape Town city council votes in favour of Bo-Kaap's heritage protection' in Daily Maverick, 29 March, https://www.dailymaverick.co.za/article/2019-03-29-cape-town-city-council-votes-in-favour-of-bo-kaaps-heritage-protection/ Accessed 30 June 2019.
23 Interview with Seehaam Samaai and Razeen Diedericks.
24 Personal communication with Janey Bell, former vice-chair of SFB, 26 April 2019.
25 Clark, C (2018) 'Developers accused of 'capturing' Sea Point ratepayers association' in GroundUp, 15 February, https://www.groundup.org.za/article/developers-accused-capturing-sea-point-ratepayers-association/ Accessed 30 June 2019.
26 Ibid.
27 Ibid.
28 Ibid.
29 Pather, R (2018) 'Developer behind Bromwell Street evictions believes he is creating opportunities' in Mail & Guardian, 2 February, https://mg.co.za/article/2017-02-02-developer-behind-bromwell-street-evictions-believes-he-is-creating-opportunities Accessed 17 July 2019.
30 Personal communication with Janey Bell, former vice-chair of SFB, Cape Town, 3 October 2018.
31 Interview with Gavin Silber, Cape Town, 7 August 2018.
32 Personal communication with Janey Bell, 26 April 2019.
33 Clark, C (2018) 'Developers accused of 'capturing' Sea Point ratepayers association'.
34 Albie Sachs at meeting with members of Maiden's Cove for All, Cape Town, 3 October 2018.
35 Herman, E and Chomsky, N (2002) Manufacturing Consent: The Political Economy of the Mass Media, Penguin Random House.
36 South African History Online (2016) 'Conflict among civic organisations', https://www.sahistory.org.za/article/conflict-among-civic-organisations Accessed 30 June 2019.
37 Ibid.

11. The riddle of the sphinx

1 Interview with Deon van Zyl, chair of WCPDF, Cape Town, 5 September 2018.

2 Confidential personal communication, Cape Town, 3 October 2018.

3 Confidential personal communication, Cape Town, 5 September 2018.

4 Interview with Barbara Southwood, former city planner in the City of Cape Town, Cape Town, 14 March 2019.

5 BusinessTech (2018) 'These are the best and worst municipalities in South Africa', 30 September, https://businesstech.co.za/news/government/274161/these-are-the-best-and-worst-municipalities-in-south-africa/ Accessed 30 June 2019.

6 Corruption Watch (2018) It's Time To Act, Vol 2, Issue 2, https://www.corruptionwatch.org.za/wp-content/uploads/2018/08/Corruption-Watch-ACT-Report-2018-eBook-OUT-Agent-Orange-Design-07082018.pdf Accessed 17 July 2019.

7 Jenkins, T and London, L (2019) 'Political donations: the silence of the developers' on GroundUp, 6 May, https://www.groundup.org.za/article/political-donations-silence-developers/ Accessed 30 June 2019.

8 See for instance Feigenblatt, H, Tonn, J, Moses, M and Rumpsa, S (2014) 'The Money, Politics and Transparency Campaign Financing Indicators: Assessing Regulation and Practice in 54 Countries across the World in 2014', research findings in Money, Politics and Transparency. Global Integrity, Washington, DC.

9 On 21 June 2018, in the Constitutional Court matter between MVC and the Minister of Justice and Correctional Services, the court declared that information on political parties' private donations is essential for the effective exercise of the right to vote.

10 Clarke, S (2018) 'Open Letter To President Cyril Ramaphosa' on My Vote Counts website, 10 August, https://www.myvotecounts.org.za/2018/08/open-letter-to-president-cyril-ramaphosa/ Accessed 17 July 2019.

11 Interview with Janine Ogle, national coordinator of My Vote Counts, August 2018, Cape Town.

12 Interview with Grant Pascoe, former member of the mayoral committee in the City of Cape Town, Cape Town, 16 July 2018.

13 Van der Westhuizen, T (2002) 'Harksen donation sparks debate' in News24 archives, 10 April, https://www.news24.com/xArchive/Archive/Harksen-donation-sparks-debate-20020410 Accessed 30 July 2019.

14 Webb, B (2006) 'DA admits to Kebble donation' on IOL website, 21 August, https://www.iol.co.za/news/politics/da-admits-to-kebble-donation-290211 Accessed 30 July 2019.

15 Email communication with James Selfe, 18 July 2019.

16 Interview with Grant Pascoe.

17 Ibid.

18 Ibid.

19 Ibid.

20 Email communication with James Selfe.

21 Interview with Grant Pascoe.

22 Email communication with James Selfe.

23 Interview with Grant Pascoe.

24 Email communication with James Selfe.

25 Ibid.

26 Interview with Grant Pascoe.

27 Ibid.

28 De Lille's golf club in Rondebosch carried pictures of the 2015 event http://photosbymich.co.za/2015/09/mayors-golf-day-2015-rondebosch-golf-club/; the ongoing sponsorship was extensively advertised by Sun International; see for instance Sun International website (2017) 'GrandWest Helps Raise R620 000 For Mayoral Special Fund', 11 September, https://www.suninternational.com/golf/news/grandwest-mayoral-golf-day-rondebosch-golf-course-cape-town/ Accessed 17 July 2019.

29 McKune, C (2015) 'De Lille and the contentious Clifton Scenic Reserve megaproject' in Mail & Guardian, 10 July, https://mg.co.za/article/2015-07-09-de-lille-and-the-contentious-clifton-scenic-reserve-megaproject Accessed 10 July 2019.

30 Interview with Helen Zille, then premier of Western Cape, Cape Town, 1 November 2018.

31 Zille, H (2016) Not Without a Fight: The Autobiography, Penguin Random House, Cape Town.

32 Ibid.

33 Ibid.

34 Interview with Grant Pascoe.

35 Address by Brett Herron to Cape Town Press Club, Cape Town, 26 February 2019.

36 Interview with Brett Herron, former mayoral committee member in the City of Cape Town, Cape Town, 8 November 2018.

37 Herron, B (2018) 'Statement by the City's mayoral committee member for transport and urban development, Councillor Brett Herron' on ScribD website, https://www.scribd.com/document/392129787/Brett-Herron-Resignation#from_embed Accessed 1 July 2019.

38 Address by Brett Herron to Cape Town Press Club, Cape Town.

39 Interview with James Selfe, MP, Cape Town, 2 July 2019.

40 Interview with Brett Herron.

12. The gilded calf

1 September, L (2016) 'State capture: Premier Helen Zille's "from Red Tape to Red Carpet" for private developers' on Facebook, 18 March, https://www.facebook.com/notes/lester-september/state-capture-premier-helen-zilles-from-red-tape-to-red-carpet-for-private-devel/1527384437565458/ Accessed 1 July 2019.

2 Western Cape Property Development Forum website, https://www.wcpdf.co.za/ Accessed 1 July 2019.

3 Progressive Business Forum website, http://www.pbf.org.za/ Accessed 1 July 2019.

4 September, L (2016) 'State capture: Premier Helen Zille's "from Red Tape to Red Carpet" for private developers'.

5 Interview with Susanna Coleman, PHA campaigner, Cape Town, 8 August 2018.
6 Interview with Deon van Zyl, chair of WCPDF, Cape Town, 5 September 2018.
7 Ibid.
8 Ibid.
9 Ibid.
10 Ibid.
11 Ibid.
12 Mahlaka, R (2019) 'FSCA clears Resilient companies of insider trading' on Moneyweb website, https://www.moneyweb.co.za/in-depth/investigations/fsca-clears-resilient-companies-of-insider-trading-allegations/ Accessed 1 July 2019.
13 Ibid.
14 Rose, R (2019) 'How sweet turned sour for Tongaat Hulett' in Financial Mail, 11 July, https://www.businesslive.co.za/fm/features/cover-story/2019-07-11-how-sweet-turned-sour-for-tongaat-hulett/ Accessed 17 July 2019.
15 McKune, C, AmaBhungane and Thompson, W (2018) 'Steinhoff's secret history and the dirty world of Markus Jooste' in Financial Mail, 1 November, https://www.businesslive.co.za/fm/features/cover-story/2018-11-01-steinhoffs-secret-history-and-the-dirty-world-of-markus-jooste/ Accessed 1 July 2018.
16 Ibid.
17 Ibid.
18 Ibid.
19 Interview with John Coetzee, Uvest head of development projects, Cape Town, 3 October 2018.
20 Ibid.
21 Ibid.
22 Van der Merwe, M and Swart, H (2017) 'Cape of storms to come' in Daily Maverick, https://features.dailymaverick.co.za/cape-of-storms-to-come/cape-of-storms-to-come-part-2---chapter-1.html Accessed 1 July 2019.
23 Joubert, P (2014) 'Who is Walter Hennig?' in Sunday Times, 29 June, https://www.pressreader.com/ Accessed 1 July 2019.
24 Department of Justice Office of Public Affairs (2017) 'Gabonese-French dual citizen sentenced to 24 months imprisonment for bribing African officials' on the United States Department of Justice website, https://www.justice.gov/opa/pr/gabonese-french-dual-citizen-sentenced-24-months-imprisonment-bribing-african-officials Accessed 1 July 2019.
25 Stevenson, A (2016) 'Och-Ziff to pay over $400 million in bribery settlement' in The New York Times, 29 September, https://www.nytimes.com/2016/09/30/business/dealbook/och-ziff-bribery-settlement.html Accessed 1 July 2019.
26 Company searches conducted on MSP, Uvest, Palladino and Mvelaphanda subsidiaries; see also Van der Merwe, M and Swart, H (2017) 'Cape of storms to come'.
27 Joubert, P (2014) 'The story Hennig and partners don't want you to read' in Sunday Times, 29 June, https://www.timeslive.co.za/sunday-times/lifestyle/2014-06-29-the-story-hennig-and-partners-dont-want-you-to-read/ Accessed 1 July 2019.

28 Personal communication with Pearlie Joubert, Cape Town, 27 March 2019.
29 Interview with Marianne Thamm, Cape Town, 16 November 2018.
30 Confidential personal communication, Cape Town, March 2019.
31 Confidential personal communication, Cape Town, 3 October 2018.
32 Yeld, J (2003) 'Nats hit by new funding scandal' on IOL website, 21 February, https://
   www.iol.co.za/news/politics/nats-hit-by-new-funding-scandal-101823 Accessed 24 July
   2018.

13. The road forks

1 I have reconstructed the events in the caucus based on Ra'eesa Pather's excellent
   description as well as interviews with Suzette Little, JP Smith and Ian Neilson.
2 Pather, R (2018) 'Evidence in the De Lille dossier' in Mail & Guardian, 10 August, https://
   mg.co.za/article/2018-08-10-00-evidence-in-the-de-lille-dossier Accessed 11 July 2019.
3 Democratic Alliance Federal Executive (2017) Report of the Subcommittee Established to
   Enquire into the Tensions in the City of Cape Town, 10 December.
4 Ibid.
5 Ibid.
6 Ibid.
7 Ibid.
8 Zille, H (2016) Not Without a Fight: The Autobiography, Penguin Random House, Cape
   Town.
9 Election results from http://www.elections.org.za/content/Elections/
   National-and-provincial-elections-results/
10 Zille, H (2016) Not Without a Fight: The Autobiography.
11 Ibid.
12 Ibid.
13 Interview with Ian Neilson, deputy mayor of Cape Town, Cape Town, 9 November 2018;
   and interview with Belinda Walker, former member of the mayoral committee in the City
   of Cape Town, Cape Town, 14 March 2019.
14 Zille, H (2016) Not Without a Fight: The Autobiography.
15 Interview with Belinda Walker, former member of the mayoral committee in the City of
   Cape Town, Cape Town, 14 March 2019.
16 Interview with Brett Herron, former mayoral committee member in the City of Cape
   Town, Cape Town, 8 November 2018.
17 Interview with Seth Maqetuka, former executive director for human settlements in the
   City of Cape Town, Johannesburg, 17 July 2018.
18 Interview with Helen Zille, then premier of Western Cape, Cape Town, 1 November 2018.
19 Interview with Brett Herron.
20 City of Cape Town Integrated Annual Reports, 2013/14, 2014/15, 2015/16, 2016/17 and
   2017/18.
21 Interview with City of Cape Town official in regulatory planning division, Cape Town,
   7 August 2018.

22 City of Cape Town (2017) Five-Year Integrated Development Plan, July 2017–June 2022, Executive Summary, http://resource.capetown.gov.za/documentcentre/Documents/City%20strategies,%20plans%20and%20frameworks/IDP%202017-2022%20Executive%20Summary.pdf Accessed 26 June 2019.
23 Interview with Seth Maqetuka.
24 City of Cape Town (2017) Five-Year Integrated Development Plan, July 2017–June 2022, Executive Summary.
25 National Treasury (2019) City of Cape Town – 2018/19 mid-year budget and performance assessment.
26 Interview with Shehaam Sims, former director of informal settlements in the human-settlements department of the City of Cape Town, Oudtshoorn, 17 August 2018.
27 Ibid.
28 Interview with Belinda Walker.
29 Ibid.
30 Interview with Suzette Little, former mayoral committee member in the City of Cape Town, Cape Town, 17 May 2019.
31 Ibid.
32 Ibid.
33 Petersen, T (2018) 'From De Lille's bodyguard to chief whip – Shaun August on why he gave it up' on News24, 4 November, https://www.news24.com/SouthAfrica/News/from-de-lilles-bodyguard-to-chief-whip-shaun-august-on-why-he-gave-it-up-20181102 Accessed 1 July 2019.
34 Interview with James Selfe, MP and chair of the DA federal executive, Cape Town, 2 July 2019.
35 Interview with Shehaam Sims.
36 ibid.
37 Ibid.
38 Interview with Ian Neilson, deputy mayor of Cape Town, Cape Town, 9 November 2018.
39 Interview with Andrew Boraine, former city manager in the City of Cape Town, Cape Town, 8 July 2018.
40 Ibid.
41 Interview with Belinda Walker.
42 Ibid.
43 Interview with Shehaam Sims.
44 Ibid.

14. Walking on broken glass

1 Interview with Ian Neilson, deputy mayor of Cape Town, Cape Town, 9 November 2018.
2 Interview with Belinda Walker, former member of the mayoral committee in the City of Cape Town, Cape Town, 14 March 2019.
3 Interview with Ian Neilson.
4 Interview with JP Smith, member of the mayoral committee in the City of Cape Town,

Cape Town, 14 March 2019.

5 Interview with senior City official, Cape Town, 9 November 2018.

6 Interview with Belinda Walker.

7 Interview with Ian Neilson.

8 Interview with Belinda Walker.

9 Interview with Ian Neilson.

10 Interview with Belinda Walker.

11 Democratic Alliance Federal Executive (2017) Report of the Subcommittee Established to Enquire into the Tensions in the City of Cape Town, 10 December.

12 Ibid.

13 Ibid.

14 Ibid.

15 Interview with JP Smith.

16 Democratic Alliance Federal Executive (2017) Report of the Subcommittee Established to Enquire into the Tensions in the City of Cape Town.

17 Evans, J (2017) 'De Lille shakes up Cape Town mayoral committee' in News24, 16 January, https://www.news24.com/SouthAfrica/News/de-lille-shakes-up-cape-town-mayoral-committee-20170116 Accessed 1 July 2019.

18 News24 (2017) 'De Lille resigns as DA Western Cape leader', 30 January, https://www.news24.com/SouthAfrica/News/de-lille-resigns-as-da-western-cape-leader-20170130 Accessed 1 July 2019.

19 Interview with James Selfe, MP and chair of the DA federal executive, Cape Town, 2 July 2019.

20 Interview with Ian Neilson.

21 Interview with JP Smith.

22 Democratic Alliance Federal Executive (2017) Report of the Subcommittee Established to Enquire into the Tensions in the City of Cape Town.

23 Ibid.

24 Ibid.

25 Ibid.

26 Personal communication with Xolani Sotashe, leader of opposition in Council, Cape Town, 8 August 2018.

27 Dolley, C (2018) 'De Lille's controversial Cape Town investigating unit 'shut down' could be reversed' on News24, 15 January, https://www.news24.com/SouthAfrica/News/de-lilles-controversial-cape-town-investigating-unit-shut-down-could-be-reversed-20180115 Accessed 27 July 2019.

28 Smith, JP (2017) 'Complaint: Conduct of Patricia de Lille', 12 July, submitted to DA federal executive.

29 Dolly, C (2018) 'Nkohla's credibility in black communities an asset to the DA – De Lille' on News24, 30 January, https://www.news24.com/SouthAfrica/News/nkohlas-credibility-in-black-communities-an-asset-to-the-da-de-lille-20180130 Accessed on 11 July 2019.

30 Interview with JP Smith.

31 Interview with Brett Herron, former mayoral committee member in the City of Cape Town, Cape Town, 8 November 2018.
32 Interview with City of Cape Town official, Cape Town, 8 August 2018.
33 Personal communication with Frank Cumming, Cape Town, 10 July 2018.
34 Ibid.
35 Interview with Suzette Little, former mayoral committee member in the City of Cape Town, Cape Town, 17 May 2019.
36 Democratic Alliance Federal Executive (2017) Report of the Subcommittee Established to Enquire into the Tensions in the City of Cape Town.
37 Special leave is additional to annual leave and sick leave. Employees can be granted special leave for a range of circumstances, such as studies, bereavement or other personal circumstances. Councillors don't actually get leave, but council does go into recess for periods, so the use of the term by the DA in this context is misleading.
38 News24 (2017) 'De Lille, Smith suspension an embarrassment – analyst', 4 October, https://www.news24.com/Analysis/de-lille-smith-suspension-an-embarrassment-analyst-20171004 Accessed 2 July 2019.
39 Interview with John Steenhuisen, MP, Cape Town, 1 October 2018.
40 Ibid.
41 Ibid.
42 Ibid.
43 Interview with Brett Herron.

15. Things fall apart

1 Confidential personal communication, Cape Town, 9 July 2018. (Subjectivity is lessened by evaluating proposals against clear criteria which can be measured and scored.)
2 De Lille, P and Kesson, C (2017) View from City Hall: Reflections on Governing Cape Town, Jonathan Ball Publishers, Johannesburg and Cape Town.
3 Olver, C (2017) How to Steal a City, Jonathan Ball Publishers, Cape Town and Johannesburg.
4 Affidavit made by Craig John Kesson at Cape Town on 9 November 2017, under the provisions of the Protected Disclosures Act, No 26 of 2000.
5 Ibid.
6 The substance of the allegations had been previously raised with the city manager and reported to accounting firm Moore Stephens, which summarised the allegations in its own report on the tender dated 10 August 2017; see Bowman Gilfillan Report: 'Investigation into allegations involving the Executive Mayor Alderman Patricia de Lille', Cape Town, 16 October 2018.
7 Bowman Gilfillan Report: 'Investigation into allegations involving the Executive Mayor Alderman Patricia de Lille', Cape Town, 16 October 2018.
8 Affidavit made by Craig John Kesson at Cape Town on 9 November 2017, under the provisions of the Protected Disclosures Act, No 26 of 2000.
9 Interview with Brett Herron, former mayoral committee member in the City of Cape

Town, Cape Town, 8 November 2018.

10 Moore Stevens report as quoted in Bowman Gilfillan Report: 'Investigation into allegations involving the Executive Mayor Alderman Patricia de Lille', Cape Town, 16 October 2018.

11 GroundUp (2018) 'Proposed Foreshore development compared to apartheid', 27 February, https://www.dailymaverick.co.za/article/2018-02-27-groundup-proposed-foreshore-development-compared-to-apartheid/ Accessed 2 July 2019.

12 Ibid.

13 Ibid.

14 Affidavit made by Craig John Kesson at Cape Town on 9 November 2017, under the provisions of the Protected Disclosures Act, No 26 of 2000.

15 Dolley, C (2018) 'City of Cape Town's Foreshore tender 'made potential corruption easy' – deputy mayor' on News24, 23 July, https://www.news24.com/SouthAfrica/News/city-of-cape-towns-foreshore-tender-made-potential-corruption-easy-deputy-mayor-20180723 Accessed 2 July 2019.

16 Affidavit made by Craig John Kesson at Cape Town on 9 November 2017, under the provisions of the Protected Disclosures Act, No 26 of 2000.

17 Ibid.

18 Ibid.

19 Ibid.

20 Ibid.

21 Ibid.

22 Dolley, C (2017) 'It's criminal, not whistleblowing – De Lille hits back at executive director's claims' on News24, 29 November, https://www.news24.com/SouthAfrica/News/its-criminal-not-whistleblowing-de-lille-hits-back-at-executive-directors-claims-20171129 Accessed 2 July 2019.

23 Affidavit made by Craig John Kesson at Cape Town on 9 November 2017, under the provisions of the Protected Disclosures Act, No 26 of 2000.

24 The report also called for disciplinary action against the transport officials involved, and two transport officials were subsequently dismissed, but Melissa Whitehead, who was in charge of the department, was ultimately responsible. See affidavit made by Craig John Kesson at Cape Town on 9 November 2017, under the provisions of the Protected Disclosures Act, No 26 of 2000.

25 Affidavit made by Craig John Kesson at Cape Town on 9 November 2017, under the provisions of the Protected Disclosures Act, No 26 of 2000.

26 Ibid.

27 Ibid.

28 Interview with external expert, Cape Town, 9 July 2018.

29 Ibid.

30 Ibid.

31 Affidavit made by Craig John Kesson at Cape Town on 9 November 2017, under the provisions of the Protected Disclosures Act, No 26 of 2000.

32 Ibid.

33 Dolley, C (2017) 'It's criminal, not whistleblowing – De Lille hits back at executive director's claims'.

34 Dolley, C (2017) 'More info leaks and unauthorised investigation claims rock City of Cape Town' on News24, 22 November, https://www.news24.com/SouthAfrica/News/more-info-leaks-and-unauthorised-investigation-claims-rock-city-of-cape-town-20171122 Accessed 2 July 2019.

35 Democratic Alliance Federal Executive (2017) Report of the Subcommittee Established to Enquire into the Tensions in the City of Cape Town, 10 December.

36 Dolley, C (2017) 'Claims are a malicious attack on my integrity – De Lille' on News24, 23 November, https://www.news24.com/SouthAfrica/News/claims-are-a-malicious-attack-on-my-integrity-de-lille-20171123 Accessed 2 July 2019.

37 Democratic Alliance Federal Executive (2017) Report of the Subcommittee Established to Enquire into the Tensions in the City of Cape Town.

38 Ibid.

39 Ibid.

40 Ibid.

41 Ibid.

42 Interview with Brett Herron, former mayoral committee member in the City of Cape Town, Cape Town, 8 November 2018; and interview with Suzette Little, former mayoral committee member in the City of Cape Town, Cape Town, 17 May 2019.

43 Interview with James Selfe, MP and chair of the DA federal executive, Cape Town, 2 July 2019.

44 Van der Merwe, M (2017) 'Explainer: The DA vs De Lille, and her fight-back plans to remain mayor of Cape Town' in Daily Maverick, 20 December, https://www.dailymaverick.co.za/article/2017-12-20-explainer-the-da-vs-de-lille-and-her-fight-back-plans-to-remain-mayor-of-cape-town/ Accessed 2 July 2019.

45 Dentlinger, L (2018) 'First on EWN: Explosive allegations of corruption, cover-ups within City of CT' on Eyewitness News, 5 January, https://ewn.co.za/2018/01/05/first-on-ewn-explosive-allegations-of-corruption-cover-ups-within-city-of-ct Accessed 22 August 2018.

46 In late 2016 Gerhard Ras had received a very generous redundancy payout; see Mtyala, Q (2016) 'Hush-hush millions for council executives' in Cape Times, 24 August, https://www.iol.co.za/capetimes/hush-hush-millions-for-council-executives-2060713 Accessed 18 July 2019.

47 Dentlinger, L (2018) 'Council orders investigation into claims of corruption cover-ups by De Lille' on Eyewitness News, 5 January, https://ewn.co.za/2018/01/05/council-orders-investigation-into-claims-of-corruption-cover-ups-by-de-lille Accessed 22 August 2018.

48 Interviews with various city officials and former city officials, Cape Town, July–November 2018.

49 De Lille, P (2018) 'Statement by the City's Executive Mayor, Patricia de Lille', City of Cape Town, Cape Town, 19 January, http://resource.capetown.gov.za/documentcentre/Documents/Speeches%20and%20statements/19%20January%2018-%20special%20council%20meeting.pdf Accessed 27 July 2019.

50 Confidential personal communication, Cape Town, 9 July 2018.

51 Ibid.

52 Van der Merwe, M (2018) 'DA vs Cape Town mayor: Quo Vadis, Patricia de Lille? in Daily Maverick, 4 February, https://www.dailymaverick.co.za/article/2018-02-04-da-vs-cape-town-mayor-quo-vadis-patricia-de-lille/ Accessed 2 July 2019.

53 News24 (2018) 'De Lille's bid to have secret ballot at the discretion of City Speaker, court rules', 14 February, https://www.news24.com/SouthAfrica/News/breaking-de-lilles-bid-to-have-secret-ballot-at-the-discretion-of-city-speaker-court-hears-20180214 Accessed 2 July 2019.

54 Interview with Suzette Little, former mayoral committee member in the City of Cape Town, Cape Town, 17 May 2019.

55 Chabalala, J (2018) 'City of Cape Town announces qualifying bidder for freeway precinct project' on News24, 12 February, https://www.news24.com/SouthAfrica/News/city-of-cape-town-announces-qualifying-bidder-for-freeway-precinct-project-20180212 Accessed 2 July 2019.

56 GroundUp (2018) 'Foreshore development violates Cape Town's transport policy, say experts' in Daily Maverick, 22 February, https://www.dailymaverick.co.za/article/2018-02-22-groundup-foreshore-development-violates-cape-towns-transport-policy-say-experts/ Accessed 2 July 2019.

57 Ibid.

58 De Klerk, A (2018) 'DA adopts recall clause' on Times Live, 8 April, https://www.timeslive.co.za/politics/2018-04-08-da-adopts-recall-clause/ Accessed 27 July 2019.

59 Interview with Melissa Whitehead, executive director in charge of TDA, Cape Town, 26 August 2018; and interview with Stephen Lukey, former manager of Foreshore Land Transaction Agreement, Cape Town, 13 June 2019.

60 Confidential personal communication via email, 15 July 2019.

61 Confidential notes from meeting with executive mayor on 6 April 2017, 'Subject: CTICC Marshalling Yard', attended by De Lille (chair), Herron, Ebrahim, CTICC CEO Ellingson and others.

62 702 (2018) 'Listen: Did De Lille dig her own grave in this interview with Eusebius?', 8 May, http://www.702.co.za/articles/302660/listen-did-de-lille-dig-her-own-grave-with-this-interview-with-eusebius Accessed 2 July 2019.

63 Evans, J (2018) 'De Lille still calls herself "the mayor" in court challenge' on News24, 8 May, https://www.news24.com/SouthAfrica/News/de-lille-still-calls-herself-the-mayor-in-court-challenge-20180508 Accessed 2 July 2019.

64 Interview with James Selfe.

65 Pather, R (2018) 'De Lille resigns as Cape Town mayor effective October 31' in Mail & Guardian, 5 August, https://mg.co.za/article/2018-08-05-de-lille-resigns-as-cape-town-mayor-effective-october-31 Accessed 2 July 2019.

66 Merten, M (2018) 'Maimane/de Lille 'mutual agreement' enables DA to focus on 2019 elections' in Daily Maverick, 6 August, https://www.dailymaverick.co.za/article/2018-08-06-maimane-de-lille-mutual-agreement-enables-da-to-focus-on-2019-elections/ Accessed 11 July 2019.

67 GroundUp (2018) 'De Lille requests investigation into Foreshore property sale', 30 September, https://www.groundup.org.za/article/de-lille-requests-investigation-foreshore-property-sale/ Accessed 2 July 2019.

68 Brandt, K (2019) 'Good party calls for a probe on the sale of land in Cape Town' on Eyewitness News, 7 July, https://ewn.co.za/2019/07/07/good-party-calls-for-a-probe-on-the-sale-of-land-in-cape-town Accessed 30 July 2019.

69 Deklerk, A, Mokone T and Shoba, S (2018) 'Patricia de Lille has (another) last laugh' in Sunday Times, 28 October, https://www.timeslive.co.za/sunday-times/news/2018-10-28-patricia-de-lille-has-another-last-laugh/ Accessed 2 July 2019.

70 Payne, S (2018) 'Defiant De Lille resigns – but is not going quietly' in Daily Maverick, 31 October, https://www.dailymaverick.co.za/article/2018-10-31-defiant-de-lille-resigns-but-is-not-going-quietly/ Accessed 3 July 2019.

71 Kamaldien, Y (2018) '#DeLille triumphs again as DA abandons Steenhuisen report' on IOL website, 16 November, https://www.iol.co.za/capeargus/news/delille-triumphs-again-as-da-abandons-steenhuisen-report-18142170 Accessed 2 July 2019.

72 Chambers, D (2018) 'Patricia de Lille saga vents record blast of hot air in Cape of Storms' in Business Day, 25 October, https://www.businesslive.co.za/bd/politics/2018-10-25-patricia-de-lille-saga-vents-record-blast-of-hot-air-at-last-gasp-in-cape-of-storms/ Accessed 2 July 2019.

16. The almond hedge

1 Pijoos, I (2018) 'We're all to blame for power cuts, says Eskom chairman Mabuza' in Sunday Times, 6 December, https://www.timeslive.co.za/news/south-africa/2018-12-06-were-all-to-blame-for-power-cuts-says-eskom-chairman-mabuza/ Accessed 18 July 2019.

2 Rabie, J (2018) 'City of Cape Town betrayed farmers by surrendering Day Zero predictions' on News24, 13 March, https://www.news24.com/Columnists/GuestColumn/city-of-cape-town-betrayed-farmers-by-surrendering-day-zero-predictions-20180313 Accessed 2 July 2019.

3 Dougan, L (2018) 'Day Zero is called off for now, but restrictions retained' in Daily Maverick, 28 June, https://www.dailymaverick.co.za/article/2018-06-28-day-zero-is-called-off-for-now-but-restrictions-retained/ Accessed 2 July 2019.

4 Interview with Jens Kuhn, former director for housing development in the City of Cape Town, Cape Town, 16 July 2018.

5 Evans, J (2018) 'City of Cape Town cancels Foreshore Freeway Precinct project' on News24, 18 July, https://www.news24.com/SouthAfrica/News/city-of-cape-town-cancels-foreshore-freeway-precinct-project-20180718 Accessed 2 July 2019.

6 Van Voore, R (2018) Report: Investigation into Allegations Involving the Executive Mayor Alderman Patricia de Lille, Bowman Gilfillan, Cape Town.

7 Evans, J (2018) 'City of Cape Town cancels Foreshore Freeway Precinct project'.

8 Cape Argus (2018) 'No further development for Philippi Horticultural Area, council says', 25 April, https://www.iol.co.za/capeargus/news/no-further-development-for-philippi-horticultural-area-council-says-14645816 Accessed 2 July 2019.

9 De Lille, P (2019) 'What really went wrong in the City of Cape Town' in Daily Maverick, 12 April, https://www.dailymaverick.co.za/opinionista/2019-04-12-what-really-went-wrong-in-the-city-of-cape-town/ Accessed 2 July 2019.

10 City of Cape Town (2018) Inclusionary Housing: Concept document, http://www.wcpdf.co.za/wp-content/uploads/2018/10/City-of-Cape-Town-Draft-Inclusionary-Housing-Concept-Note_20180928.pdf Accessed 3 July 2019.

11 Cogger, J and Rossouw, J for GroundUp (2018) 'Affordable housing: City of Cape Town and developers at crossroads' on Daily Maverick, 11 September, https://www.dailymaverick.co.za/article/2018-09-11-affordable-housing-city-of-cape-town-and-developers-at-crossroads/ Accessed 3 July 2019.

12 De Klerk, A, Mokone, T and Shoba, S (2018) 'Patricia de Lille has (another) last laugh' in Sunday Times, 28 October, https://www.timeslive.co.za/sunday-times/news/2018-10-28-patricia-de-lille-has-another-last-laugh/ Accessed 30 July 2019.

13 Isaacs, L (2018) 'Brett Herron resigns from DA, Cape Town City Council' on Eyewitness News, 1 November, https://ewn.co.za/2018/11/01/brett-herron-resigns-from-da Accessed 1 July 2019.

14 Primedia Broadcasting (2018) 'Brett Herron Resignation', 1 November, https://www.scribd.com/document/392129787/Brett-Herron-Resignation#from_embed Accessed 3 July 2019.

15 Cloete, N (2018) 'DA a waste of time' on IOL website, 17 November, https://www.iol.co.za/weekend-argus/news/da-a-waste-of-time-says-herron-18157703 Accessed 18 July 2019.

16 Personal communication with Helen Zille, Cape Town, 1 November 2018.

17 De Lille, P (2019) 'What really went wrong in the City of Cape Town'.

18 Ibid.

19 2019 National and Provincial Elections Results dashboard, https://www.elections.org.za/NPEDashboard/app/dashboard.html Accessed 3 July 2019.

20 Ibid.

21 Kiewit, L (2019). 'How Auntie Patty became Minister De Lille' in Mail & Guardian, 30 May, https://mg.co.za/article/2019-05-30-how-auntie-patty-became-minister-de-lille Accessed 1 July 2019.

22 ibid.

23 Ibid.

24 Ibid.

25 Interview with Lungelo Mbandazayo, city manager in the City of Cape Town, Cape Town, 11 November 2018.

26 Ibid.

27 Ibid.

28 Ibid.

29 Interview with Aslam Cassiem, DA ward councillor, Cape Town, 24 June 2019.

30 Worden, N (ed) (2012) Cape Town Between East and West: Social Identities in a Dutch Colonial Town, Jacana Media, Johannesburg.

31 'Cape Town the Segregated City' on South African History Online, https://www.sahistory.org.za/article/cape-town-segregated-city Accessed 3 July 2019.

A note on city governance

1 'House Divided' speech (1858) on Abraham Lincoln Online website, http://www. abrahamlincolnonline.org/lincoln/speeches/house.htm Accessed 1 July 2019.
2 Statistics South Africa (2019) 'Selected building statistics of the private sector as reported by local government institutions (preliminary)'. Statistical release, Pretoria.
3 Property Sector Charter Council (2018) '2016/17 State of Transformation Report for the South African Property Sector' at https://www.saibpp.co.za/wp-content/ uploads/2018/11/2018-State-of-Transformation-Report-for-the-Property-Sector.pdf Accessed 26 July 2019.
4 Some municipalities have a multi-party executive committee system instead of an executive mayor, which functions on a collective decision-making basis. The provincial minister for Local Government has the power to decide whether a municipality is run according to an executive-committee or an executive-mayor system.
5 The current portfolios on the Cape Town mayoral committee are finance; community services and health; corporate services; economic opportunities and asset management; energy and climate change; human settlements; safety and security; spatial planning and environment; transport; urban management; and water and waste.
6 Auditor-General South Africa (2018) Consolidated General Report on the Local Government Audit Outcomes: MFMA 2016-17. Auditor-General of South Africa, Pretoria, http://www.agsa.co.za/Portals/0/Reports/MFMA/201617/GR/MFMA2016-17_FullReport.pdf Accessed 15 July 2019.
7 Olver, C (2017) How to Steal a City, Jonathan Ball Publishers, Cape Town and Johannesburg.
8 'House Divided' speech (1858) on Abraham Lincoln Online website.

A note on city governance

~~~

In his famous 'House Divided' speech[1] in 1858 while campaigning to be a US senator, Abraham Lincoln anticipated the dark clouds of civil war that gathered in the USA as northern Union and southern Confederate states split over the issue of abolition of slavery. When that war became reality, it took the lives of 620 000 soldiers and devastated the nation so deeply that the scars endure to this day.

While the casualties of the political crisis in Cape Town are measured in careers, not lives, a similar form of demonic possession seemed to take hold of the City administration in its longest and driest summer. For a two-year period, as the citizens of Cape Town wondered whether they would be able to continue living in a city without water, the ruling Democratic Alliance (DA) engaged in a vicious internal factional contest that devastated the City administration, paralysed its response to the water crisis, and eventually hurt the DA at the polls.

And Lincoln's words resonate in other ways too. His assertion that 'this government cannot endure, permanently half slave and half free', challenged his young country to finally decide the issue of slavery once and for all. While Cape Town abolished slavery nearly 180 years ago, unresolved

279

racial and social divisions still cleave our society and inform our politics. This is the context in which a near-cataclysmic drought took Cape Town to the brink.

South Africa is semi-arid, and its climate varies from bone-dry desert in the northwest to subtropical and wet in the east. The City of Cape Town sits on a peninsula in the southwest corner of the country, jutting out into the cold Atlantic Ocean, with a wide expanse of sandy flats connecting it to the mainland. Its location makes its climate unique: unlike the rest of the country, Cape Town has a Mediterranean climate, with wet winters and hot, dry summers. The winter rains, driven by cold fronts from the South Atlantic, usually lash the peninsula between May and August.

Cape Town is a thirsty city – its four million residents consume the equivalent of 2 000 swimming pools of water a day – fed by a complex network of dams, pipelines and tunnels known as the Western Cape Water Supply System. Very little of Cape Town's water is sourced within the city boundaries.

The six main dams – Theewaterskloof, Wemmershoek, upper and lower Steenbras, Voëlvlei and Berg River – are all located in the Cape fold mountains to the north and east of Cape Town. Management of the dams and infrastructure is split between the national Department of Water and Sanitation and the City of Cape Town – a recipe for conflict when things go wrong.

The water level in the storage dams is replenished by the winter rains falling in the mountains of the Cape Fold Belt. The climate does go through dry periods, which run in approximately 20-year cycles, but judging from the rainfall patterns over the last century, it seems there's a steadily drier trend, most likely due to climate change caused by human behaviour.

Cape Town had very low winter rainfall in the late 1920s and early 1930s, and a prolonged dry spell in the 1970s and 1980s. The onset of the 2014 drought appears to be part of another cyclical dry spell, and even though there were good rains in 2018, it may still have some years to run. While the city itself experienced drought, its real severity was in the water-catchment areas, where it has been the worst on record – the kind of drought expected only once every 300 years.

The challenge of responding to the drought was complicated by the way government is structured in South Africa. We have a quasi-federal three-tier system of government, in which national, provincial and local government have to work together to perform functions and deliver services.

As one of South Africa's eight designated metropolitan areas, Cape Town is governed by a single-tier metropolitan authority – a massive unicity, with 27 000 employees and an annual budget of about R50 billion.

South Africa's widely acclaimed, indeed progressive, constitution puts local government in charge of utility services such as water, sanitation, refuse collection, electricity reticulation and municipal roads. Local government is also given powers over local planning, land management, community facilities and public health.

Provincial and national government are responsible for functions such as housing, social services, curative healthcare and education, even though they end up delegating some aspects of these services to municipalities with the necessary capacity.

In responding to the drought, the national Department of Water and Sanitation was responsible for water resources – the big dams and inter-basin transfers that keep large cities going – while the Cape Town metro was responsible for potable water-supply systems. (Provincial government was responsible only for disaster management and some water-services provision through their housing programmes, which limited what they could do to help.) The precise delineation of these two areas was controversial, with the City and national government accusing each other of not playing their part.

The division of powers and functions between spheres of government is important in other ways. Property deals and interests feature prominently in the story of Cape Town, and this is because, more than in any other sphere of government, local government has a profound impact on property values – it allocates development rights to property, it provides bulk infrastructure such as water, sewerage and electricity mains or road networks, and it controls the development of public open space and surrounding property.

Municipalities allocate development rights through a number of steps – for instance, they delineate where development can take place, determine what kind of development is permitted (residential, agricultural, industrial, commercial or mixed use), specify building heights and restrictions, and approve building plans. Each of these steps progressively lifts the value of the land being developed. As an indication of the wealth created by this process, the monetary value of building plans approved in the larger municipalities (which constitutes only one of the steps in the land-enablement process) was R111,4 billion in 2018, the bulk of it residential, but some R24,3 billion of it for commercial, retail and industrial purposes.[2] This feeds into the growth of the property market as a whole, which was valued at R5,8 trillion in 2015, an increase of R1 trillion from a baseline study done four years previously.[3]

Most of the actors in Cape Town's political drama are functionaries within the municipality, and it's useful to give some context to this. As with all other municipalities, Cape Town is governed by a council, of which half are directly elected ward councillors representing particular constituencies (wards being geopolitical subdivisions of municipalities used for electoral purposes), and half are proportional-representation councillors, chosen according to the number of votes each political party gets in an election.

The legislative and executive power of the municipality vests in the council, but it's impossible to run a city by committee – Cape Town has 231 councillors, a very large number to make any decision. For this reason, the executive (decision-making) power of the council is delegated to a political head – the executive mayor.[4] Council elects the mayor from among the councillors, and council can remove the mayor through a vote of no confidence (something that's particularly pertinent for Cape Town, where various attempts were made to remove the mayor during the course of 2017 and 2018).

The mayor in turn appoints a mayoral committee (a bit like the national cabinet of ministers), and each of the ten members of the mayoral committee is put in charge of a particular portfolio.[5]

It is council that ultimately decides on which powers it wishes to delegate to the mayor or other committees, and council can take back those delegations or assign them to other functionaries. As the drama in Cape Town unfolded, the delegation of decision-making power came to play a big role in the political crisis.

The administration of the City is headed by a city manager, who is in charge of running the affairs of the city, and is ultimately accountable for its financial management. City managers are appointed by council, and are meant to be non-political. In practice they end up playing a very difficult 'bridging' role between the politicians and the administration. They account directly to the mayor and mayoral committee, but lines of accountability are quite complicated, because each of the city manager's heads of department (referred to as executive directors) also account to their respective mayoral-committee member in charge of their portfolio. This results in multiple lines of accountability, with political instructions being given directly to department heads, in addition to the instructions given to a city manager by the mayor and mayoral committee. Some city managers complain that they end up accounting to multiple bosses, and that every councillor in the city thinks that they can give them instructions.

Three features about South African local government make it unique. These are the highly fractured and unequal legacy of apartheid, the extent of community involvement in protesting against and then transforming local government through locally negotiated transitional arrangements, and the extent of subsequent legislative and fiscal commitment to a decentralised local-government system.

The precocious mobilisation of political forces before the institutions of local government had properly solidified in 2000 was necessary to defeat apartheid, but it resulted in widespread political involvement in administrative matters such as procurement and appointments, and fuelled the emergence of patronage-based politics.

Metropolitan municipalities (metros) have fared comparatively better than smaller municipalities. They're better resourced – for instance, Cape Town is able to spend about R12 000 per person each year, compared to some of the smallest municipalities which can afford only R400 per person. Metros also have a much higher proportion of technically qualified and educated staff. But their size and capacity don't shield them from patronage and corruption; in fact, the scale of their budgets – they have a combined expenditure of nearly R200 billion, some 55% of all local-government spending – means that they attract corrupt businessmen and politicians.[6]

In my studies of different cities I found that all political parties seem to use power to advantage themselves, their supporters and their funders to varying degrees. But there's an important difference between governing regimes some take a short-term view of the future, and create value for a narrow group of interests based on what they can extract immediately, while others take a longer-term view, reconciling competing interests in the City and creating value for a broader group of stakeholders. But in my experience, all regimes, whether extractive or growth-oriented, seek to control the processes of allocating development rights, and they deliberately 'repurpose' local-government administrations in order to enable this. Repurposing entails appointing the 'right' people (who can be relied on to swing decisions in a particular direction) into key positions, and creating an environment in which the consequent distribution of benefits seems like the natural order of things. In other words, repurposing has the effect of entrenching a particular distribution of rights (which may be extractive or value enhancing).

Local-government politics and the exercise of power are essentially about how value (what I refer to as 'rents') is appropriated and distributed – this is the politics of rent-seeking. Cape Town occupies one, better-governed, pole of this spectrum, while my last book, *How to Steal a City*,[7] described what could be considered as the other, 'state capture', pole.

Cape Town may sound like the best place to be on this spectrum, but, as I discovered through the course of my research, it's not necessarily a happy place. Rents are highly centralised, the city is socially divided, the politics is fractious, and the City administration is authoritarian and governed by fear. Understanding why this is so, in such a well-resourced, largely corruption-free administration, is the subject of this book.

Some of the key actors involved in the drama refused to speak to me. Patricia de Lille did return my call after months of trying to get hold of her, but she was in the middle of an election campaign and the conversation didn't go anywhere. Craig Kesson refused to meet with me. I've had to use their publicly recorded utterances to give them voices within this narrative, but the story is surely poorer for the absence of their direct testimony.

And, given the knowledge limitations of what we're writing about – the intimate nature of political power and the trade-offs that power brokers make, the hidden world of party financing and the deals politicians strike to keep themselves in power, and the morbid nature of battles for political power and ideology – in places there is simply not sufficient evidence available to support satisfactory conclusions. For this reason, at times I've had to draw inferences based on scanty evidence, and I have no doubt that in places I've got things wrong. These are my own opinions and I present them as such.

The story that unfolds in these pages – my own interpretation of what has taken place – is disturbing and full of drama, a drama that affected every Capetonian in some way. For the people caught up in it, on both sides of the divide, it was deeply traumatic. For many of my interviewees, especially those who chose to go on the record, it wasn't an easy process. There are consequences of disclosure, not least because many of the actors described here, both politicians and administrators, remain in government, and are vulnerable. Because of the risk informants face, in some instances I've concealed their identity or altered their characters in certain ways to obscure who they are. These instances have been carefully limited, and I hope do not detract from the conclusions that can be drawn.

As a student and one-time government practitioner, I've more and more come to realise that real power lies in our knowledge and understanding. I hope that this story contributes in some small measure to understanding what went down in Cape Town in the last few years of the De Lille administration.

As Lincoln stated when he invoked the metaphor of the house divided, 'If we could first know where we are, and whither we are tending, we could then better judge what to do, and how to do it.'[8]

Political timeline of the Western Cape province and Cape Town metro

Year	Western Cape	Cape Town
1994	First democratic national and provincial elections. NP wins Western Cape with 53% of vote.	Cape Town run by 27 separate municipalities inherited from apartheid era.
1996		6 transitional local councils formed in Cape Town coordinated by a metropolitan-wide authority.
1999	NNP maintains control of Western Cape in alliance with DA.	
2000		Single Cape Town metropolitan municipality established. DA (newly amalgamated with NNP) wins majority; Pieter Marais appointed as mayor.
2001		Pieter Marais removed as mayor by DA, and NNP/DA alliance falls apart.
2002		Constitution amended to allow floor-crossing in municipal councils. NNP-aligned councillors defect to ANC, which takes control of council; Nomaindia Mfeketo appointed mayor.
2004	ANC takes control of Western Cape in alliance with NNP; Ebrahim Rassool appointed premier.	
2006		DA wins 43% of seats in Cape Town council, and assembles a coalition with smaller parties to hold a narrow majority; Helen Zille elected mayor.

2007		Patricia de Lille's ID joins DA-led coalition, strengthening the DA's majority in Cape Town.
2009	DA wins narrow majority (51,5%); Helen Zille appointed premier.	Dan Plato replaces Zille as mayor of Cape Town.
2010	Zille and De Lille finalise agreement to merge ID with DA.	
2011		DA wins outright majority (61%); Patricia de Lille appointed mayor.
2014	DA strengthens control of Western Cape with 59% of vote.	
2016		DA wins two-thirds majority; De Lille appointed mayor for second term.
2018		De Lille resigns as mayor after acrimonious breakup with DA. Dan Plato appointed mayor in her place.
2019	National and provincial elections show loss of DA support (to 55% in Western Cape). De Lille appointed minister for Public Works and Infrastructure in national cabinet.	

Glossary of terms used in City administration

caucus – internal meeting of representatives of a political party, usually in relation to an elected legislative body such as parliament or municipal council

city council – a body of elected political representatives which holds both legislative and executive power over the running of a municipality

City Hall – the symbolic seat of power in a municipality

city manager – the administrative head and accounting officer of a municipality

councillor – a representative of a ward and/or political party on the council

delivery department – a municipal department responsible for infrastructure services or housing

director – a senior manager in a municipality, reporting to an executive director

executive council (province) – the political decision-making body (cabinet) of provincial government

executive director – head of department within a municipality, reporting to the city manager

executive mayor – the political head of a municipality who wields executive powers (as opposed to a ceremonial mayor)

DA federal congress – the DA's highest decision-making body, which meets every three years, and elects national office bearers

DA federal council – a big body (well over 100 people) consisting of elected office bearers, provincial and regional leaders and delegations from legislatures; it meets at least three times a year, and is the highest decision-making body between federal congresses

DA federal executive – consists of elected office bearers and provincial leaders, and manages operational day-to-day affairs of the party

human-settlements department – a department in national, provincial or local government responsible for housing delivery

integrated development plan – a statutory five-year plan for the comprehensive development of a municipal area and the coordination of municipal functions

line departments – departments within a municipality responsible for specific functional areas (as opposed to transversal departments which perform cross-cutting support functions)

mayor – the political head of a municipality

mayoral committee – a political executive structure which advises the executive mayor

portfolio committee – a committee of council or parliament which exercises oversight over a particular functional area

Strategic Policy Unit – the policy coordination unit that was set up within the office of Cape Town's mayor

subcouncil – a subcommittee of council overseeing an administrative subdivision of the municipality

Transport and Urban Development Authority – a mega-department in Cape Town formed through the amalgamation of transport, planning and human-settlements functions

urban edge – a device used by urban planners to fix the limits of urban development and prevent urban sprawl

Acknowledgements

This book is a product of many people's efforts, but most importantly the 60 plus interviewees who endured the mercurial and at times alarming instincts of the author. Their patience in talking me through the issues, which I sometimes struggled to grasp first time round, was admirable. In the end I was able to engage with people inside and outside government at many levels – politicians, senior officials, technocrats, academic researchers, community activists and private developers. I remain deeply indebted to all of them for their insights and forbearance.

The principle of informed consent, the foundation of research ethics, only goes so far – when I told participants that I was researching 'the political economy of rent-seeking in South African local government', they were clearly at a vast disadvantage in not being familiar with the obscure jargon. The most alarming moment for any interviewee is when, having been lulled into a conversation about a painful past by an outwardly charming researcher, you realise that the probing questions and line of investigation are not just taking you back to the trauma of the moment but involving you in a bigger enquiry whose ultimate purpose you aren't sure about. I only hope that I have done right by everyone who so kindly put up with my digging, by reflecting their views in a balanced way that does justice to their story.

Many of the people I interviewed remain caught up in a still-dysfunctional system, and their disclosures and frank views make them vulnerable. Their bravery in coming forward needs to be applauded. Some participants have justifiably insisted on remaining anonymous, and where I've used material from these interviews, I've tried to disguise the source in various ways. This has involved small but necessary deceptions, for which I apologise. Hopefully the story still shines through undiluted.

The remarkable feature of the Cape Town drama is the rich body of literature and journalism available on the subject. Many of the elements of the story have been brought into the public domain by journalists working for the *Daily Maverick*, the *Mail & Guardian*, *News24* and the Independent Group. Their insights and analyses have enabled me to weave together a tapestry of city politics, and produce what I hope builds on their efforts with a coherent and compelling story.

The unprecedented Cape Town water crisis was followed in fine detail by *Daily Maverick* journalists such as Rebecca Davis, Marianne Merten, Marelise van der Merwe, Nic Spaull and Jason Norwood-Young, who produced some of the best analyses we have on the subject. They were able to truly channel the angst of the people of Cape Town as they navigated a profound social and political crisis. The chapters on the water crisis in Cape Town use their work extensively.

The DA's internal factional battles and the subsequent fallout with De Lille were minutely documented in a series of articles that captured the intense drama of the moment. I'm deeply indebted to Ra'eesa Pather and Lester Kiewit from the *Mail & Guardian*, Jenni Evans and Caryn Dolley from *News24*, Marelise van der Merwe, Marianne Merten and Suné Payne of the *Daily Maverick*, and Lindsay Dentlinger from Eyewitness News.

Property deals have also been carefully unravelled through a rich tradition of investigative journalism in Cape Town, starting with John Yeld and his coverage of the Big Bay scandal in the early 2000s. Two journalists in particular have opened up the sleazy underbelly of the Cape Town mafia and their property deals – Marianne Thamm through her writing on the protection rackets in Cape Town's underworld, and Pearlie Joubert with her coverage of Walter Hennig, Mark Lifman and Mark Willcox and the Shimmy Beach Club.

Ashleigh Furlong produced an excellent analysis of the Wescape saga, including his revelations about the developer behind it. This was complemented by Melanie Gosling's relentless reporting for IOL, and Rob McGaffin, who unpacked the underlying economics (or lack thereof) of the development.

The developments in the Philippi Horticultural Area were beautifully described in a series of in-depth articles by Marelise van der Merwe, Heidi Swart, Diana Neille and Leila Dougan. Lisa Isaacs writing for the *Cape Times* produced a series of articles on the various regulatory decisions and legal challenges, and Bruce Cameron on IOL documented the financial transactions behind Oakland City.

There have also been many insightful studies into the economic, social and cultural importance of the PHA. I've drawn in particular on the 2009 community profile produced by Valerie Anderson, Sepideh Azari and Anya van Wyk, and a land use assessment of the PHA done by Jane Battersby-Lennard and Gareth Haysom in 2012.

I'm also indebted to Craig McKune for his excellent coverage of the Maiden's Cove saga, as well as Caryn Dolley and Kevin Davie who produced some excellent writing for the *Mail & Guardian*. Davie produced a delightful description of Mark Willcox which has allowed me to present aspects of his complex character.

Cape Town journalists have also closely followed the capture of civic organisations. The battle of the Bo-Kaap residents against developers and the manipulation of their civic structures was covered by Ra'eesa Pather and Yazeed Kamaldien for the *Mail & Guardian* and Suné Payne for the *Daily Maverick*. Christopher Clark for *GroundUp* did an excellent piece on the Sea Point, Fresnaye and Bantry Bay Residents' and Ratepayers' Association.

GroundUp has also followed developments on the Foreshore with an eagle eye. I'm particularly grateful to Jonty Cogger, Jared Rossouw and Daneel Knoetze for their various articles. The spectacular unravelling of the Foreshore Freeway project was also documented by Jeanette Chabalala and Jenni Evans writing for both *News24* and the *Daily Maverick*.

A number of books on Cape Town provided valuable background material on the city and its social origins. Nigel Worden edited a 2012 collection of research into early Cape Town, while Henry Trotter produced a chilling chapter on forced removals in Cape Town as part of a 2009 publication. Before his untimely demise the poet Stephen Watson gifted us with an evocative collection of vignettes on Cape Town.

I found the poetic description of much of Cape Town's history in 'Cape Town: the Segregated City' in South African History Online to be particularly helpful. There's an excellent series of articles and books by Jeremy Seekings on the civic movement and community struggles. And Victoria Johnson provided a brilliant whistleblower account of city administration under Pieter Marais.

Political works that were invaluable sources for this book include Helen Zille's autobiography, a frank account of her period in power in the City and the province. A former journalist, Zille has also produced some great articles on her politics and the Cape Town water crisis. Patricia de Lille and Craig Kesson, meanwhile, gifted us with their strategic view of the world, before their spectacular falling out, in a 2017 book. And Craig Kesson's whistleblower affidavit itself reads like a gripping tale of political interference and mismanagement. I've used it extensively in capturing the final moments of the Cape Town fallout.

The DA's own internal reports are also good reading. The so-called Steenhuisen report, produced by a subcommittee set up by the DA's federal executive under the leadership of John Steenhuisen, provides valuable insights into the factional split in Cape Town and its genesis.

Academic colleagues at the Wits Institute for Social and Economic Research and the Public Affairs Research Institute participated with me in various discussions, including a reading group on patronage politics and the state, and shared their insights into theories about rent-seeking and state capture. Many of their ideas are woven into the analytical parts of the book. I'm particularly indebted to my patient and deeply thoughtful PhD supervisor, Keith Breckenridge.

Writing a book is a profoundly selfish business. Some authors seem to be able to do it with aplomb, but I'm increasingly unable to do it without cutting myself off from the world for an extended period. Home duties fall by the wayside, dishes gather in the sink, friends are ignored and deaths in the family pass unnoticed, while the endless vicissitudes on the road to publication bore even my closest friends. In producing this book I have a huge debt to repay to my ever-trusting and supportive partner Jeremy, as well as to my family and friends who encouraged me along the way. I also owe a big thankyou to my dear friend Miriam and her delightful daughters, who put me up in Cape Town, encouraged me in my research and listened patiently to the endless stories. Kedibone became a high-school sleuth and helped me scan and sort reams of documents.

I wouldn't have been able to produce this book without an enormous amount of editorial support – first, from my longstanding writing mentor and editor Caroline Lambert, who guided me through each stage of producing the book. She's much more than just an editor, and has essentially collaborated with me in the production of the book, and channelled my wild and rambling scribbling into a body of work that was fit for publication. And second, from the team at Jonathan Ball Publishers, led by Jeremy

Boraine. It's rare to find in a publisher someone who immediately gets the grand idea behind a book and is prepared to marshal the support an author needs in getting to the finish line. Jonathan Ball's editor Tracey Hawthorne massively tightened up the text, pointed me to areas needing work and patiently insisted on cross-referencing every detail, while JG Theron from Werksmans Attorneys has done a meticulous legal review and steered me away from unsustainable claims and unjustifiable libel.

I'm also indebted to many friends who've read and commented on sections of the book, including Pam Yako, Andrew Boraine, Michael Evans and Anthea Stevens. Despite all their helpful suggestions and comments, what appears in these pages is my own interpretation of what took place, which at times may be wide of the mark.

Last, I'd like to thank the members of the band Bright Blue for giving me permission to use the words of 'Weeping'. It was the song that captured the bittersweet times of the 1980s civil war, and became an anthem that we used extensively to mobilise against conscription into the apartheid army. Thank you, Bright Blue, for gifting us with this poetic piece.

Index

heads of department (executive
directors) 283–284
Hennig, Walter 169–170
Heritage Western Cape 105, 135, 234
Herron, Brett
  bus-chassis payments 210–211
  De Lille and 180–181, 192–193, 216
  Good party 225, 241, 243
  Kesson and 72
  mayoral committee 191, 194
  property-development projects 103,
    115, 157–158, 161, 207–208,
    220–221, 222
  resignation of 239–240
  signage bylaw 198
homelands 99
'House Divided' speech 279, 286
housing
  delivery of 46–52, 56, 58–59, 67, 122,
    182–183, 234–236, 244
  Foreshore 207, 221
  Good party 241
  Monwabisi 54
  Oakland City 102
  Paardevlei 117–118
  Salt River 157–158, 223, 234, 239
  SFB 140–141
  Woodstock 157–158, 223
Housing Development Agency 103
Hout Bay 48–49
How to Steal a City 26, 285
Hugo, Japie 44–46, 57, 90, 93–95,
  105–106, 108, 118, 121, 168
human-settlements department 57,
  66–68, 182, 245

ID *see* Independent Democrats
IDP *see* integrated development plan
Imizamo Yethu informal settlement 48–49
Independent Democrats (ID) 16–17, 157,
  177–181, 183–186, 199–200, 237–238
infill development 90–91, 120

infrastructure 6, 9–10, 59, 212, 280
integrated development plan (IDP) 53,
  69, 182
internet portal for building and land-use
  applications 126

Jacobson, Isa 141
Jacoby, Kevin 75–76, 208, 209, 210
Jenkins, Tauriq 128–129
Johannesburg 10, 15
John (retired Capetonian) 86–87
Johnson, Victoria 84
Jonga Entabeni 89
Jooste, Markus 166
Joubert, Pearlie 170

K2015298271 115
Kaiser, Gisela 76
Kaveney, Kendall 106–108
Kebble, Brett 150, 154
Kempen, Suzanne 139
Kesson, Craig
  affidavit by 211–213, 215
  background of 24–27, 62
  bus rapid-transit system 205–206
  De Lille and 62, 202, 205, 209–215
  investigations into allegations
    against 214–215, 218
  probity division 209–211
  property-development projects 105–
    108, 110, 207–209
  restructuring 52, 62–70, 72, 232
  signage bylaw 198
  View from City Hall 61–64, 75, 204
  water crisis 76, 212
Khayelitsha 168
Khoi people 1–2, 31–32, 120, 132, 248
Kieser, Ben 84–85
King, Malcolm 166
Koeberg nuclear-power station 91–92,
  94, 95
Krotoa (Eva) 31–32